KT-437-878

Dreams of Hope

**The remarkable memoir of an Irish woman's life,
from the tenements of Dublin to
Luton and Australia**

LILY O'CONNOR

BRANDON

A Brandon original paperback

First published in Britain and Ireland in 2006 by
Brandon
an imprint of Mount Eagle Publications
Dingle, Co. Kerry, Ireland and
Unit 3, Olympia Trading Estate, Coburg Road, London N22 6TZ, England

Copyright © Lily O'Connor 2006

The author has asserted her moral rights.

2   4   6   8   10   9   7   5   3   1

ISBN 0 86322 358 3

This book is sold subject to the condition that it shall not, by way of trade
or otherwise, be lent, resold, hired out or otherwise circulated without the
publisher's prior consent in any form of binding or cover other than that in
which it is published and without a similar condition being imposed on the
subsequent purchaser.

Cover design: Anú Design
Cover photograph: *Time & Life*/Getty Images
Typesetting by Red Barn Publishing, Skeagh, Skibbereen
Printed in the UK

SOUTH LANARKSHIRE LIBRARIES	
C60049512$	
CAW	487154
920.OCON	£9.99
HA	

RECEIVED

1 1 DEC 2006

C60049512 $

I⠀⠀O'Connor was born in Dublin's inner city ⠀⠀ements and on her marriage emigrated with her ⠀sband to Luton in England, and later to Geelong in Australia. Her first book, *Can Lily O'Shea Come Out to Play?* was published in 2000 and reprinted in 2001. She lives in Victoria, Australia.

20. 02. 12

CONTENTS

Part One: Dublin

The Ladies' Choice	11
Paddy Wouldn't Play for Buttons	16
The Girl Must Be the Strong One and Say *No*	19
Irish Textiles Social Club	23
I Was Glad It Was Flash	27
The Wedding Breakfast	30
We Won't Tell Eileen	36
Married Life and the Child of Prague	43
That's What Mammy Always Said	47
Mrs O'Connor Was Right	50
It Was a Woman's Business in the Rotunda	55
Dublin, You Let Your Men Go	62
The Postman Cycled Right By	65
I Can't Keep Two Homes Goin'	68
If She Dies, Missus, Can I Have Her Rockin' Horse?	72
Just a Fella I Met at the Canal	76
A Moneylender is Our Only Hope	79
I'll Be Back	82

Part Two: From Luton to Torquay and Back Again

Sit Down, I've Somet'in' to Tell Ya	89
Lily in Luton	94

Four Healthy Children, a Wringer and a
Brand-New Fridge   98
Homesick   101
The Moneylender's Son   105
Stop the Bus, Paddy Wants to Wee-Wee   107
I Didn't Need Much Encouragement   111
Living by the Sea   114
Paddy the Magician   118
Paddy the Photographer   120
T'ink of Torquay as a Holiday   122
Get Rid of Dat Pram   125
It's Up to Your Own Conscience   129
The Luton Labour Club   133
Back Home to Dublin   137
Don't Be Mindin' Dese Awl Wans   141
Things Happen in Threes   145
Mrs O'Connor Dies   149
Me Braincells Are Dying   154
Little Canada Holiday Camp   157
Back to Vauxhall for Browny   162
A Gentleman's Agreement   165
How in the Name a' God Could I Take Them There?   169
I've Always Wanted to See America   173
Thank God for Stockwood Park   177
Down the Sink with Johnnie Walker   180
From Land's End to God Knows Where   185
Come to Sunny Australia   189
The Guesthouse   192

Part Three: Geelong, Australia

What Have We Come To?	199
Only Mad Dogs and Immigrants	203
Paddy Should Be Here	209
She'll Be Right	213
Now for the Garden	216
Do We Have to Do What Everyone Else Does?	221
Now for the Schools	225
They Wanted Me as Well	230
Johnnie Walker's Me Only Friend	232
Dat's What I Love about the Yanks	235
I Bought Ya Dat Lovely White Cat, Didn't I?	241
Dey're Bold Little Boys Again	243
Love from Your Dream Boat	246
The Maggies	248
Hard to Kill a Bad Thing	251
That's It, Paddy O'Connor	255
The Full Circle	258
Good on Ya, Dad	261
The Birthday Dinner	267
He Wouldn't Go Without Saying Goodbye	271
What's for Dinner, Mum?	274
Are We Not to Go On?	278
Acknowledgements	282

For Paddy

"I know how men in exile feed on dreams of hope." Aeschylus, *Agamemnon*

PART ONE

Dublin

THE LADIES' CHOICE

I WATCHED HIM. He led the floor with the best dancers, the girls who knew his every step. Down the hall they'd glide, fishtailing as one. I took everything in: his friendly eyes, the well-pressed navy blue suit, the snow-white shirt and the short brown hair pushed forward into a quiff. And he was the right height.

But I knew he'd never ask me up. My only hope was the ladies' choice.

Tonight I was confident. I had my lucky red dress on, with lipstick to match. And my brown hair curled up right for a change. I waited all night patiently. The drums rolled and the MC reached for his mike: 'Ladies, it's your choice. Please take your partner for the next dance.'

Down the hall of Dublin's Elite Ballroom I hurried and tapped his shoulder. 'Would you like to dance?'

His pale blue eyes smiled. 'I'm Paddy O'Connor,' he said, leading me on to the floor.

'Haven't seen you here before,' I said, as he twirled me around corners.

'I usually dance in the Irene. What's yer name?'

'Lily O'Shea.'

He returned the ladies' choice and every other dance that night.

'Would ya like to come to the pictures tomorra' night?' he said, walking me to the cloakroom.

'Can you get tickets?'

'I'll get dem black market after mass in the mornin',' he said. 'Dere's always fellas outside the Carlton sellin' dem.'

I woke up Sunday morning thinking about Paddy. He lived in the city. I lived in Cabra West. He worked in Irish Textiles making ladies' jumpers. I worked in the Abbey Clothing Factory making men's trousers. I couldn't wait for the evening to see him.

But, as the day wore on, I began to worry. He could have had any girl in the hall, the city girls, the good dancers who were attractive and sure of themselves. Why would he turn up to me?

I didn't go.

Bridie, my pal, heard all about Paddy in work on Monday.

'Ya're awful, Lily,' she said, flying along on her sewing machine. 'He could've been waitin'.'

She put a bit of doubt in me. By the end of the week, I thought Saturday night would never come.

On with the lucky red dress and into the Elite Ballroom with Bridie I rushed. There was no sign of Paddy.

'Get your coat, Bridie. He'll be in the Irene.'

Sure enough, there he was, on the floor, swinging around with the best dancers. As he quickstepped by, his eyes caught mine and he smiled.

He'll ask me up, I thought, feeling relieved. Interval came and interval went. Bridie met a fella and left. I inched closer to the band, letting on to be enjoying myself. The night rolled on and the last dance was announced. The band struck up, but no sign of Paddy.

Goodnight, Sweetheart,
Till we meet tomorrow.
Goodnight, Sweetheart,
Sleep will banish sorrow.

Turning to go for my coat, I felt a tap on my shoulder. There he was. Without a word, he took my arm and led me on to the floor.

'Why did ya not turn up last week?' he said. 'I waited for over an hour in the freezin' cold sleet.'

'I didn't t'ink you'd come.'

Silence for the rest of the dance. The lights went up, and the girls rushed off to the cloakroom.

'Well, how about tomorra'?' he said.

'I'll be there,' I said, running for my coat.

All day Sunday, I skipped up and down the stairs getting ready to go out. No worries this time, I knew he'd turn up. By six o'clock, it was lashing rain. Up with the red umbrella and down for the 22 bus I dashed. I stood waiting outside Findlater's shop in O'Connell Street, watching other couples meet. Seven o'clock came and seven o'clock went. Paddy was nowhere to be seen.

'Home already?' Mammy said, opening the hall door.

'He left me standin' in the rain,' I said, shaking out my umbrella.

'He got his own back,' she said. 'You let him down last week.'

I was raging with him all week, but I kept thinking about what Mammy had said. I'd let him down the previous week. By Saturday I'd forgiven him. It was back to the Irene for me.

As usual, he was leading the floor, having a great time. I jumped up with the first fella who asked me to dance. Whenever I passed Paddy on the floor, I laughed and tricked around with my partner, making sure Paddy saw me.

The dance finished. Paddy appeared and gripped my hand for the slow waltz. 'Sorry for not turnin' up last week.'

I said nothing.

'I saw ya waitin'',' he said, smiling. 'I was on the opposite side of the street.'

'You saw me waitin' for you?' I said, stopping.

He grabbed me and swung me around. 'Ya let me down. I wanted ya to know what it felt like.'

The dance finished. I pushed my way to the cloakroom. He hurried after me. 'Will ya come to the pictures tomorra'? I promise ya I'll be dere.'

I looked away.

'Here. Take me wallet. I'll meet ya outside the Carlton,' he said, marching off.

Sitting on the bus going home, I peeped into his wallet. A photo fell out. It was Paddy in a sports jacket with a white opened-neck shirt, his face serious and clean-shaven. His eyes held me; soft and sincere they were.

Mammy saw the photo Sunday morning. 'I like him,' she said. 'He'll be there waiting for you this time.'

She was right. All smiles he was, leading me into the Carlton. We took our coats off and sat down. He handed me a box of Cadbury's. I was worried. The last fella who bought me chocolates had made me turn Catholic, then left me because I wasn't holy enough for him.

'I used to be a Protestant,' I said.

'Why did ya turn?'

'Because I was engaged to a Catholic boy. He insisted I become a convert.'

'Dat would have been hard on yer mother, Lily. I'm a Catholic, bit it wouldn't have made any difference to me.'

I knew then Paddy was for me.

The evening flew by. He walked me to my bus stop. The 22 pulled in. The conductor banged the bell. *Ding-ding*. I jumped on and held on to the rail.

'See ya next Saturday, same time outside Findlater's shop, den we'll go on to the Carlton,' he called after me.

I sat back in the bus happy. When a fella asks you to the pictures of a Saturday night instead of going to a dance, it means he's serious about you.

From then on, it was the pictures Saturday nights for Paddy and me, and a walk in the Botanical Gardens Sunday afternoons.

Everything was going great in my life until something awful happened: Mammy was diagnosed with TB. I blamed Daddy. He'd left Mammy for another woman, had more children and lived on the same road as us. Mammy, terribly ashamed, neglected herself. She stayed in, took to her bed and died.

I bought a black jumper for Mammy's funeral, dyed my brown skirt black and sewed a black star on to the sleeve of my beige coat. It was 1952, a cold October morning. Paddy came into the Protestant church with me.

'I'll see ya next Saturday,' he said, leaving me home.

'I can't go to the pictures. I have to be in mournin' for months.'

'But ya still have to eat,' he said, giving me a hug. 'We'll go to the Maple Leaf in O'Connell Street.'

There were only the three of us at home now – Sylvia, Johnny and me. Sylvia, the youngest, a slim happy girl, was forever tidying and polishing our few sticks of furniture. We had the shiniest brass letter box on Drumcliffe Road. Johnny, a tall dark-haired teenager, loved tricking around. He had a quick easy smile like my father, but was soft and sincere like Mammy.

I lived for Saturday nights to see Paddy. As my bus crawled into O'Connell Street, I'd see him outside Findlater's shop waiting for me. Then into the Maple Leaf we'd hurry and order egg and chips, bread and butter, and a big pot of tea. After an hour of chatting about our week at work, he'd stab his cigarette out and pay the bill. Linking arms, we'd saunter up and down O'Connell Street, looking in shop windows.

This went on for weeks. I was happy just being with him, but Paddy wanted more.

'I'm fed up walkin' around,' he said one Saturday night, steering me into Caffola's.

This was the first time I was ever in Caffola's. You only went into Caffola's with a partner. Their tiny cups of delicious cream coffee were not cheap. And you didn't stay long. It was popular with couples after the pictures and would soon fill up.

'C'mon, I'll take ya home,' Paddy said, when a couple squeezed in on our table.

We ran for my bus, jumped on, climbed up the stairs and sat down. He held my hand. 'Can I come in for a cup a' tea?' he whispered.

I sat wondering what to do. What would the neighbours think? Mammy was only dead, and here was I bringing in a fella. The neighbours could take up a petition and have us all evicted. I'd seen it happen when I was little.

We walked silently up Drumcliffe Road towards our house.

'I won't stay long,' he said, squeezing my hand in his Crombie coat pocket.

'I'd rather you didn't come in.'

'I'm not kissin' ya goodbye at the corner any more. It's freezin'.'

'Just for a minute then.'

'I have to catch the last bus anyway.'

He opened the gate. I glanced at our front window. 'The light's out,' I whispered, reaching for my key. 'Sylvia's in bed.'

But she wasn't. She was curled up in front of the fire on Mammy's big old armchair, the only armchair we had. We sat each side of her on kitchen chairs, chatting about the pictures we'd like to see. Paddy kept glancing at Sylvia, hoping she'd make a move and go to bed. She didn't. She kept poking the fire. He hung around for an hour waiting and missed the last bus back to the city. I loaned him my bike.

'I'll bring yer bike back tomorra',' he said, when I closed the gate after him.

In bed that night, I worried. Paddy was a city fella, used to going out. First he gave up dancing for me, now he'd given up the pictures. He'd get sick of me.

PADDY WOULDN'T PLAY FOR BUTTONS

IT WAS SUNDAY afternoon. We'd had our dinner and cleared the table. I put the remains of the corned beef safely away in the cold oven for tea and opened the windows to let the cabbage smell out.

The letter box tapped. It was Paddy with my bike. 'Grab yer umbrella. We'll go for a walk,' he said, slipping off his bicycle clips.

'I can't. I promised to play ludo.'

'Are ya not sick a' stayin' in?'

A face peeped over my shoulder. It was Johnny. 'Why don't ya play, Paddy? Make up the foursome. It's a bit a' gas.'

Johnny was all geared up for the game. He dragged the table closer to the fire. 'We're ready, Sylvia,' he shouted up the stairs.

Sylvia skipped down the stairs, humming, face all made up, looking like a film star. Paddy wolf-whistled her as he wheeled in my bike.

'Are you playin', Paddy? Good,' she said, smiling. 'We won't let Johnny win today.'

We sat around the table choosing our men. I emptied out our tobacco tin full of buttons. 'Here's your buttons, Paddy,' I said, placing a pile beside him.

'Buttons?' he said. 'What for?'

'We play for buttons,' I said, sorting out glass ones for myself.

'I'm not playin' for buttons,' he said, pushing them away. 'For God's sake, Lily, let's play for ha'pennies at least.'

The buttons were gathered up slowly and put back in the tin. Johnny smiled and went through his pockets, slipping a few ha'pennies to Sylvia.

'Here's some for you, Lily,' Paddy said, sliding a few across the table.

I pushed them back. 'It's all right. I have me own,' I said, reaching for my bag.

Johnny handed Paddy the dice and Mammy's green swan egg cup. 'Here, you start,' he said.

Paddy shook the egg cup, threw a six and put his red man out.

Three throws later and my little green man was still waiting to start.

'Home,' Paddy laughed, scooping all our ha'pennies up.

'I t'ought ya hadn't played ludo before,' Johnny said, leaning back in his chair, tapping his cigarette into the grate.

Our letter box rattled. We all looked at the door.

'I'll go,' Johnny said, pushing his chair back.

'I won't have to work this week,' Paddy joked, tapping his winnings.

Sylvia and I said nothing as we put another ha'penny out. Johnny peeped back round the door. 'It's a gypsy boy,' he whispered. 'It's lashin' rain. He's in his bare feet. Wants t'know if ya want t'buy a statue, a cracked Jesus.'

'Bring him in,' Paddy said.

Sylvia glanced at me. I looked up at Johnny.

'Bring him in,' he said again.

A small boy slipped in, holding a statue, his hair dripping wet, his bare feet blue with the cold.

'Sit here by the fire,' Paddy said, squeezing in a chair for him. 'Get a bit a' heat.'

The boy's face lit up.

'What's yer name?' Johnny asked.

'Sean,' he said, standing the statue under the table beside him. He wiped his dirty nose with the sleeve of his jersey, sat down and watched Sylvia and me from under his eyes.

Paddy smiled at him and handed him our egg cup with the dice. 'Ya can play my game. It's yer turn.' He pointed to our few ha'pennies. 'Ya might win all their money.'

The steamy smell of damp wool drifted over to us as the boy's jersey dried against his skin. He spat into the egg cup for luck, shook it and threw the dice.

Sylvia gave me a look that said *That's Mammy's good egg cup he spat into.*

Sean struggled to count the numbers on the board.

'I'll move yer man for ya,' Paddy said, winking at Johnny. 'Dere ya are, yer game.'

For the rest of the afternoon, Sean had us all in stiches, jumping up and down, winning game after game. 'Home! Home! I'm home!' he shouted, counting his winnings and stuffing them into his pocket.

He cleaned us out. Our ha'pennies disappeared.

Johnny stood up and gave the fire a good poking to bring it back to life, then emptied the coal bucket onto it. The boy made a move to go.

'Stay for tea, Sean,' Paddy said.

Sylvia and I slipped into the scullery to make tea. She cut up a loaf of bread and buttered it while I sliced up the leftover meat. Two plates of thick corned-beef sandwiches were put on the table. I struggled in with Mammy's old dented teapot stewing away and put it down by the fire.

Paddy poured Sean out a cup, then sugared and milked it for him.

'Here, take a sandwich?' Johnny said, holding the plate.

'Don't take the top piece,' Paddy laughed. 'Lily always puts the stale piece on top.'

'It's not stale,' I said. 'It's the cat's skin, the first slice of the loaf.'

'I like the cat's skin,' Sean said, taking the smooth brown sandwich. 'An' I love corned beef.'

Johnny sprang up to pull the curtains and switch on the light.

'Jaysus, it's dark,' Sean said, jumping up. 'I'll be murdered.' He sped to the door, forgetting to hide the hole in the backside of his trousers.

'Don't forget your statue, Sean,' I said, as I hurried after him.

The rain had stopped, and the street lamps were on. Without another word, Sean took off into the damp dark night, our ha'pennies jingling in his pocket.

Paddy appeared beside me, slipping on his Crombie. 'I'm off, love. I don't want to miss the last bus again.'

We walked to the gate.

'I'm glad ya let dat boy in,' he said, hugging me.

'If it hadn't been for you, we'd have never let him in.'

'Lily, dat boy could've been me. My father died when I was his age. Me mudder had a gang of us to rear. The backside was out of my trousers. I'd be ashamed of me life when the girls saw me bare bum.'

An icy wind blew up. Paddy buttoned up his overcoat and ran for the 22.

The Girl Must Be the Strong One and Say *No*

'C'MON UPSTAIRS FOR a few minutes,' Paddy whispered, taking my hand.

'Oh no, Paddy. Sylvia or Johnny might come back.'

It was Saturday afternoon. We were in the house on our own, sitting in Mammy's big armchair, kissing.

'C'mon, let's go upstairs,' he pleaded. 'We're never on our own.'

He eased me up out of the chair, checked the back door, then led me upstairs to the front bedroom.

'It's too bright,' I whispered, looking at him untying his shoelaces.

'Pull the curtains den.'

I dragged the curtains across, then darted back. 'Oh God, Paddy. You know our neighbour opposite, Mrs O'Neill?'

'What about her?'

'She's sittin' in front of her parlour window. She saw you come in an' now she knows you're up here with me in the bedroom.'

'Ah t'hell wit' her. Ya worry too much.'

'Did you lock the back door?'

'Ya know I did.'

Paddy grabbed my hand and pulled me down onto the bed. I held back.

'What's wrong?' he said.

'Nuttin'.'

But there was something. I could hear the voices of the older women at work warning me. *The girl must be the strong one and say no. The men can't help it.*

He climbed under my blanket. 'Are ya gettin' in?' he said.

'No,' I whispered, unzipping my skirt and folding it over a chair.

'Yer wastin' time, Lily,' he said, holding back the blanket. 'C'mon.'

I slipped in beside him. 'You'll be careful, won't you?'

'I will. We'll just lie close together.'

'Don't go too far.'

'I won't. I promise ya.'

The hall door slammed shut.

'Who's dat?'

'Jesus, it must be Johnny. Sylvia's no key.'

We lay there listening. A record went on. A song echoed up through the floorboards.

I'm through with love,
I'll never fall again.
I'm through with love,
I'll never fall again.

'Oh God, it's Johnny,' I said, fixing my bra. 'He's broken off with his girlfriend again.'

We jumped out of bed. Paddy grabbed up his shoes while I quickly zipped up my skirt. 'What'll I say?'

'Don't worry, I'll t'ink of somet'in'.'

We traipsed downstairs, straightening our clothes. Johnny was sitting at the table, his head in his hands. Paddy pulled his cigarettes out of his jacket and offered him one.

'I was fixin' the curtains for Lily,' he said. 'The wire had stretched; her curtain was saggin'.'

Johnny nodded and took the cigarette from Paddy.

I glanced over at the record player. 'Have you fallen out with your girlfriend again?' I said, smiling.

'No, I felt like playin' it,' he said, knocking it off.

Paddy tapped his ash in the grate. I smoothed my black skirt with my hand. No one was saying anything. I picked up Granny's pink seashell from the mantelpiece and showed it to Paddy. 'Do you want to hear the tide comin' in?' I said, holding it up to his ear.

He pushed my hand away. 'No, I don't want to hear the tide comin' in.'

Johnny laughed and pointed to my hair.

'What's wrong with it?' I said.

'It's all tossed.'

Paddy threw his butt in the grate and reached for his jacket. 'I'm goin'.'

I followed him to the door. 'Why are you leavin' so early?'

'I want to see Awl Jack, a friend of mine. Me mudder's given me a few bob to pay him for lookin' after me da's grave. He wouldn't take it from her. He's shy wit' the women.'

'Are ya playin' ludo tomorra', Paddy?' Johnny called out.

'Ask Lily.'

I closed the hall door and came back in.

'What's wrong wit' youse two?' Johnny said.

I snatched the comb from my bag and looked in the mirror above the mantelpiece.

'I know one t'ing,' I said, combing my hair. 'I'm gettin' out of black. I don't care what the neighbours say. Mammy wouldn't want me to be stayin' in all the time. She'd want me to be out enjoyin' meself.'

Sunday morning, the curtains in my bedroom were dragged back tight. The weak yellow sun was doing its best to shine. Out came the pale pink twinset that Paddy had bought me for Christmas. I skipped down the stairs, filled the black iron kettle, plonked it on the cooker and waited for it to warm. Humming away, I gave myself a good wash in the basin with Lifebuoy soap. Back upstairs, I dressed, powdered my face, pencilled my eyebrows and put on a bit of lipstick. I found the scissors and unpicked the black star on my beige coat.

Outside, the neighbours in their best Sunday coats and hats were rushing to catch the ten o'clock mass in Cabra West's little chapel. I slipped out the gate. Then I saw him. My father. I couldn't mistake that straight army-stride of his. There he was, arm in arm with the other woman, heading to mass. *What a hypocrite*, I thought. *He never went to church with us or Mammy.* I took off in the opposite direction for mass in Aughrim Street.

Paddy's face lit up when I opened the hall door to him that afternoon. 'Ya look great, glad yer out a' black. Let's go upstairs again,' he said, laughing.

'Now, Paddy, don't start. We're goin' out.'

Linking arms, we dawdled down to the Botanical Gardens in Glasnevin and sauntered through the big iron gates.

'Did you see Awl Jack?' I asked him.

'I didn't leave him till all hours. I love listenin' to his travels. He's been all over the world, Australia, everywhere.' He put his hand into his jacket pocket and pulled out a snap. 'He gave me this last night. It was taken in Australia, when he was a stockman on a cattle station.'

I looked at the snap of Awl Jack. He was a short, fit-looking man, cracking a whip, a big belt holding up his loose baggy trousers, a large hat shading him from the sun.

'Is he not married?' I said, handing it back.

'Jack? Jack loves his freedom.'

I steered Paddy playfully towards a narrow pathway lined with trees covered in pale pink blossoms. Feeling alive again, I caressed their straight smooth trunks flowing with sap. The breeze caught the petals and sprinkled them down on us.

'Why don't we get married?' Paddy said, turning towards me.

I kicked some of the petals. 'You just want to have a party.'

He stopped. 'What d'ya t'ink I am, Lily? Marry ya just for a party?'

I slipped my freezing cold hand into his overcoat pocket for warmth. 'Let's go into the hothouses to get a bit a' heat,' I said, looking around for them.

'I've somet'in' else to tell ya,' Paddy said, squeezing my hand in his pocket. 'I'm startin' up a social club in Irish Textiles. I'll make a few extra bob.'

'That's great.'

'I'm not waitin' years to marry ya.'

Irish Textiles Social Club

'C'MON, GRAB A wing, I want to show ya this room,' Paddy said, when I met him in the city one Saturday evening.

We turned the corner into Parnell Street. Two men were boxing in the middle of the path, their hands clenched as they punched each other. We stepped over their good jackets lying on the ground.

'Let's have a look?' I said, stopping.

Paddy took hold of my arm and whisked me on. 'I live in the city, Lily. Ya never stop to look at fights. Ya keep goin'. I could get dragged into it.'

We dodged in and out of couples, past the dusty windows of pubs. I dropped my fur glove and quickly threw the other one down. Paddy stopped and stared at me. 'Why did ya throw the other glove down?' he asked, picking them up.

'So I won't have a disappointment,' I laughed.

'You an' yer superstitions.'

He rushed me across the road and stopped outside a small tenement house.

'This is it,' he said. 'I've got the front parlour.'

I nearly died. I was born and reared in a tenement house and hated them. And this was the worst one I ever saw. There wasn't a pick of paint left on the hall door with the scratches. A heavy black iron knocker was all that remained of its well-to-do past. Paddy pushed the door open, but I held back. I hadn't forgotten the smell of urine and baby sick in these dark tenement halls and you never knew who'd be sleeping behind the door.

'Hold on to me,' he said.

We tiptoed through the hall, me hanging out of his sleeve, looking for the right door. A stench of pee sailed up from the floorboards. He fumbled with the key in the lock. A baby wailed above, a mother shouted. At last the door gave in and we stumbled into a large room. The evening sun showed up the dirt on the long, filthy windows.

'It's only a few bob a week,' Paddy said. 'Look, isn't it great?'

I stared around and shivered. It could have been the tenement room I grew up in.

The walls were peeling with the remains of three different wall-papers.

'Are you goin' to clean it?'

'Lily, I've cleaned it up.' He pointed to a tin bucket. 'I borrowed me mudder's scrubbin' brush an' floorcloth, an' gave the floor a good scrubbin' wit' Lifebuoy soap an' Jeyes Fluid.'

I went over to the window and gazed out at people passing. 'It's good it's in the city. Very handy.'

He pointed to the fireplace. 'Look at the lovely old-fashioned mantelpiece, Lily,' he said, running his hand along a dusty shelf dotted with cigarette burns and circled with tumbler stains.

A gas globe hung each side.

'Do the lights work?'

'Dey do now. I pinched the globes from an empty room at the top.'

Although I couldn't picture people dancing here, Paddy had no trouble. He waltzed me around the room, laughing. 'I'm gettin' a record player on HP an' a few of the latest records dey can dance to.'

'Have you told them at work?'

He pulled out a piece of paper from his pocket. 'I'm puttin' this up on the board in Irish Textiles Monday.'

Irish Textiles Social Club
Starts next Saturday
In Parnell Street opposite the Green Pub.
Admittance. One shilling.
8.00pm to midnight
Paddy O'Connor.

Having locked the room up well, we hurried down to the Maple Leaf and enjoyed our tea of chips and eggs, and bread and butter. Paddy talked non-stop about his new club, the records he was buying and borrowing. Then it was home for me. 'Come straight to the club next week,' he said, seeing me to the bus stop.

I was a piece worker in the Abbey Clothing. The more trousers I made, the more money I earned. My machine ran like mad that week to make a few extra bob to buy something new to wear on

Saturday. I loved Friday afternoons in work, when we got paid and finished early to clean and oil our machines. The girls would be in a great mood, singing away, looking forward to the weekend. I joined in with them as they sang 'The Tennessee Waltz' at the top of their voices.

First thing Saturday morning, I was on the 22 bus into the city to spend my few bob in Cassidy's, my favourite fashion shop. Then it was back to do my washing and ironing. By the time I'd painted my nails and plucked my eyebrows, it was time to go out. All dressed up in my new pale blue jumper, I hurried up for the 22.

I jumped off the bus at Parnell Street and walked straight down to his club. There he was setting up the new record player on an old orange box a dealer had given him. A bundle of records lay beside him. I bent down and picked one up. 'Oh, great, you've got "The Tennessee Waltz".'

'I won't be able to dance wit' ya, Lily. I have to put on the records.'

By eight o'clock, the room was packed with fellas and girls and thick cigarette smoke, just like a real dance hall. Overcoats were stacked in a corner on a bockety old chair Paddy had found in the cellar. A sweeping brush and a small tin shovel were thrown behind it.

We all stood waiting for the dance to begin.

'Grab yer partners for a quickstep,' Paddy sang out. 'This will warm youse up.'

The shy fellas, who couldn't dance, stabbed out their cigarettes, tipped the girl next to them and shuffled onto the floor, smiling.

These shy fellas wouldn't have been so quick to ask a girl up in one of the large dance halls around the city. They'd be too afraid to walk down the long floor and risk rejection in front of everybody.

'In the Mood' went on full blast. A fella tipped me and I found myself being swung around.

Paddy didn't mind who I danced with. He knew I was his.

'Put a slow waltz on,' I whispered to him in between dances.

The records were played over and over. After an hour, we knew all the words by heart.

Halfway through the night, a skinny little fella, draped in a dirty dustcoat down to his ankles, slithered in without paying. Paddy jumped up and stood in front of him. 'What d'ya want?'

'I came in t'give youse a song.'

'One song, den leave,' Paddy said, turning off the record player.

The little fella stood in the middle of the room. We gathered around, watching him. With his eyes closed, he sang in a strong tenor voice, 'Maaaar-thaaa, rambling rose of the wildwood.'

The fellas beamed and went silent. 'Good man yerself,' they said, clapping him.

The singer needed no encouragement and belted out 'Martha' again.

The girls, who wanted to dance, were annoyed. 'Lily, will ya tell Paddy t'get rid of dat awl gurrier,' they said.

Paddy laughed. 'He's a great voice. He's goin' now; he's harmless,' he said, lighting up a cigarette.

All the fellas slipped out for a quick pint, then returned warmed up, raring to go. On went the 'Blue Tango' and 'Jealousy'. With a bit of drink in them, they were in great form, striding up and down the room with the girls, all fancying themselves as Valentino.

At the end of the night, when they were all gone, Paddy emptied his box and counted the money. He swept up the cigarette butts and ash, then spread his Crombie on the floor. The door was locked and the lights were switched off. The light from the lamp outside filtered through the windows, casting creepy shadows on the walls.

'Ya looked great dancin' in yer bit a' blue,' he whispered, pulling me down onto his coat. 'I've been dyin' to hold ya all night.'

'We'll miss the last bus if we don't hurry.'

'T'hell wit' the bus. We'll get a taxi.'

'God, Paddy, yer hands are awful cold.'

The club filled up every week. Thanks to Paddy, couples met and planned to marry. By the end of the year, he'd made a few extra bob and passed his club onto the next ambitious fellow.

I Was Glad It Was Flash

'LILY, GET UP, get up! It's half-past eight,' Nora shouted through our letter box.

You'd never believe it. It was my wedding day, 29 December, and I'd slept in.

Buttoning up my flannelette nightie, I dived out of bed and into the cold damp air of winter. Down the stairs I ran and let my bridesmaid in. Nora tore upstairs to dress. I sped into the scullery and shoved on the kettle. After a quick wash, I followed her up.

My wedding dress was laid out on my bed. I was so lucky; Paddy's sister, Eileen, a Royalette, the image of Bette Davis, had had it made up by the Theatre Royal dressmakers for me.

'It's real Elizabethan, isn't it, with its high collar,' Nora said, clipping my peaked satin headdress on. 'Has Paddy seen it yet?'

'Eileen said not to let him see it. It'd bring bad luck.'

'Hurry, Lily. Your car's here,' she said, peeping out the window.

I pencilled my eyebrows, powdered my face and put on my lipstick.

The car beeped again. We traipsed downstairs. Johnny was pinning on his white carnation, Sylvia was fixing her hat. Annie, my married sister from Donnybrook, was meeting us at the church.

'Hope our dresses don't crease,' Nora said. 'Dere's an awful mist outside.'

Johnny banged the hall door shut behind us and jumped in beside the driver of a big black shiny car. No matter how poor you were, no Dublin wedding was complete without those two big black shiny cars, one for the bride and her family, and one for the groom and his. It was the only time you'd ever be in one, except when you died. Soon we were on our way to the Church of the Most Precious Blood, the new chapel in Cabra West.

'Where's yer father? Isn't he givin' ya away?' the driver asked, turning around.

'He gave us away a long time ago,' I said.

The driver pushed his bottom lip out and nodded.

'I'm givin' her away. I can't wait,' Johnny laughed.

'The groom's here,' the driver said, as he drew up beside the other black shiny car.

Paddy had come up from his home in Gardiner Street with his mother and three brothers, Mikie, Frank and Chris.

Our driver slid out of his seat and opened the door for us. He stood gazing up at the huge chapel. 'Is dis the new chapel?' he said, blessing himself. 'Ya must be the first bride t'get married in dis chapel.'

I lifted my dress and hurried up the stone steps into the church. Down the long aisle I walked with Johnny to an intermezzo from *Cavalleria Rusticana.* I chose this music. They were for ever playing it on the radio in work, and I loved it. Eileen arranged for the Theatre Royal's organist to play it. Paddy sat up straight in his new navy blue suit, a white carnation in his lapel. His hair was cut short, oiled and pushed forward into a perfect quiff. His blue eyes beamed when I glanced at him. His best man, Liam, sat smiling beside him.

Flash Kavanagh celebrated our mass. This thin little priest was very popular because he said mass in fifteen minutes. His twelve o'clock mass every Sunday would be packed with men. You could see them standing outside the church on the steps, heads bowed, knees bent, thumping their chests.

I was glad it was Flash. I'd had no breakfast and didn't want to faint.

Paddy held my hand tightly as we stood on the bottom step outside the chapel posing for photos. The group photo outside the chapel was just as important as the cars. The rows of high steps leading up to the chapel doors were made for big Catholic families. The guests could stand on different levels behind the bride and groom, proudly displaying their white carnations. I married into the large O'Connor family. All Paddy's brothers and sisters, along with their partners, were there on the steps, except Sammy, who lived in England, and Lizzie, the eldest, who lived around the corner from me on Killalla Road. She was down in Gardiner Street in Mrs O'Connor's flat, busily preparing our wedding breakfast.

Eileen stood proudly in her sleek mink coat, close to her husband, Mick. Her sister, Phil, in her brown beaver coat and high heels, called to her Mike to stand in beside her. Even Paddy's

Uncle Pa, who Mrs O'Connor had been black out with, was up on the steps with them all.

Mrs O'Connor, a proud no-nonsense woman, stood beaming in her blue Sunday coat and small felt hat beside Paddy. 'Where's Awl Jack?' she said, looking around.

'He wouldn't come, Mud. But he gave me a five-shillin' piece for Lily.'

I could hear the laughter behind me, everyone chatting away, all talking at the same time. The photographer was in front, his camera set up, anxious to take a picture.

'Will youse all stop talkin' an' look at the camera?' he yelled.

'Ah get on wit' ya,' Mrs O'Connor called back to him.

'All in together now,' he said. 'A big smile.'

Local children, swinging nearby on the chapel's railings, thought he was talking to them. They ran up and squeezed into the photo as well.

THE WEDDING BREAKFAST

'JAYSUS, WE CAN'T take dem all,' the drivers complained, as Paddy lined everyone up next to the two lovely black cars.

But the drivers were good and squeezed in as many as they could. The rest of our guests followed down on the 22 bus.

The two big cars weaved in and out of the busy traffic in Parnell Street. Flimsy orange papers and boxes littered the kerbs near the dealers. Women, cabbages hanging out of their shopping bags, stopped and stared. Others hurried on, tightening their headscarves against the heavy mist that was falling. Our driver turned into lower Gardiner Street and pulled in at number five.

Up the stairs we trailed to Mrs O'Connor's flat, my Elizabethan wedding dress sweeping each step behind me.

The kitchen looked huge. Paddy had removed the furniture to make room for a long table.

'Where did you get the snow-white tablecloth?' I said, trying to take everything in.

'Dey're our sheets,' he said. 'A weddin' present from me Uncle Pa.'

Our three-tiered wedding cake took pride of place on the table. White satin ribbons streamed down from the ceiling and were tacked to each tier. Eileen had been busy that morning. A whole seasoned ham sat on a plate beside it.

Paddy squeezed my hand. 'D'ya smell the ham, Lily?' he said. 'Mikie bought it for us. He even had it sliced.'

Mikie, Paddy's older brother, the good-looking bachelor, had a steady job in the Hammond Lane Foundry. We all thought he was well off.

Lizzie, a big down-to-earth Dublin mother, was flat out cutting up fresh loaves. Leaving the bread, she hurried over and grabbed me. 'Sorry I couldn't get t'yer weddin', Lily. My John was dere for both of us.' She gave me a big hug and kiss then went back to finish cutting up the last of the bread.

'Glad to see Lizzie has her teeth in,' Paddy whispered.

Mrs O'Connor slipped off her coat and hat, put her prayer

book away and bustled around her kitchen. 'Ya must be freezin' in dat dress, Lily, an' famished wit' no breakfast,' she said, poking life into her range. 'Sit dere beside the fire.'

Nora, Sylvia and Johnny sat nearby on kitchen chairs up against the wall. Paddy stood beside me, rubbing his hands.

'Look how t'in he's gone wit' the worryin' over dis weddin',' Mrs O'Connor said, pointing to him. 'He's like a matchstick. Ya could put him in a matchbox.'

She saw me glance up at her mantelpiece. A brand-new statue of a boy with a crown on his head was perched on it. He looked like a little king.

'Dat's yer Child of Prague, Lily,' she said. 'No Catholic home should be wit'out one.'

A cup of tea was handed to me. 'Here, dat'll warm ya up,' Lizzie said, getting one for the others.

Before I had time to wrap my hands around the cup, I could hear the rest of the guests tramping up the stairs, laughing.

'Put yer coats in dere on the beds,' Lizzie called out, pointing to a back room.

Annie, my sister, sauntered in, her dark hair turned under in a page-boy style, her tailor-made skirt showing off her slim figure. Her Paddy couldn't come. He was in Crooksling Sanatorium recovering from an operation.

'I wish he was here to see you, Lily,' she said, feeling my dress.

Paddy ran over and hugged her. 'Sit dere, Annie,' he said, fetching her a chair.

They all poured in. Mrs O'Connor's kitchen was bursting at the seams. The girls sat down on the kitchen chairs while the fellas stood around, smoking cigars and joking.

'Here y'are,' Mikie said, handing out bottles of Guinness and glasses.

Soon glasses were clinking and big pots of tea were brewing. Plates of bread and butter and thick slices of ham were passed around.

A neighbour, carrying her baby under her shawl, crept in to wish me good luck. She nudged me aside with her eyes. 'Paddy's good t'his mammy,' she said quietly. 'An' if he's good t'his mammy, he'll be good t'his wife.'

Mrs O'Connor handed her a cup of tea. 'She's the first bride t'come out of dat new Catholic Church in Cabra West,' she boasted.

I didn't know for definite I was, but it sounded good, so I went along with it.

'Have ya only the two sisters an' brother?' the neighbour asked, sipping her tea.

'I have a big brother in Australia an' a big sister in England. They're married. But I haven't heard from them since Mammy died.'

'An' ya won't either,' she said. 'The mammy holds the family together. When she goes, dey go. Ya'll never hear from dem again.'

Lizzie handed me her mother's big carving knife, worn down to the shape of a scythe. 'Cut the cake, Lily,' she said.

Everyone went quiet. Paddy guided my hand with the knife as we sliced the bottom tier.

'I don't feel married,' I said.

The women fell over the place with the laughing.

'Wait till yer married ten years like me,' Eileen said, nodding towards her Mick.

'Ya'll feel married den all right,' Mick said, grinning at Paddy.

'C'mon, Paddy, up dere an' dance wit' the bride,' Phil called out.

Paddy waltzed me around the kitchen, singing, 'Oh how we danced on the night we were wed.'

Everyone joined in. The drink was taking effect.

'A bit a' quiet, please,' Phil said. 'My Mike's goin' t'give us "Mammee".'

Phil's Mike, a tall thin man, dressed immaculately, wiped the Guinness from his mouth and set his glass down.

'A bit of action, Mike. Go on,' Phil called out.

Mike swaggered over to Mrs O'Connor, bent down and spread his arms out in front of her. His well-oiled hair, parted in the middle, shone with the brilliantine. Out he burst with:

Mammee! Mammee!
The sun shines east.
The sun shines west.
I know where the sun shines best.
Mammee.

He plonked back down on a chair, laughing; he couldn't remember another word. His big hand reached out for his drink on the table.

Next it was Eileen, the Royalette. She knocked back her Scotch, stood up straight in her high heels and kicked up one leg after the other in perfect timing to our clapping, just like she did on the stage.

Phil, an ex-Royalette, not to be outdone, sprang up and joined her for a few high kicks as well.

After a big clap from the men, Paddy and Mikie shuffled up and down the room behind each other, hands on shoulders, singing 'Underneath the Arches'.

The Guinness flowed. The O'Connors were in a great mood, singing away.

'One voice only,' Phil shouted.

Frank, another brother, the living image of Frankie Lane, stood up, stretched out his arms and sang 'Jezebel'.

'C'mon, Kit, yer next,' Eileen called over to Chris, the baby of the family. 'Givus "Are Ya Dere, Mor-ee-ar-itee".'

Chris had us all in stitches, marching up and down the room, taking off a Dublin policeman. Mrs O'Connor sat there, smiling proudly, drinking tea and watching all her sons perform.

Lizzie's husband, Awl John, sat down beside me. Like many Dublin fathers, he became Awl John when Young John was born.

'It's yer day, Lily, ya have t'sing,' he said, his big face smiling.

Not giving myself time to think, I jumped up. My heart thumped like mad as I sang 'Your Cheating Heart'.

Awl John whistled as I finished the song with a little wiggle of my bum. 'Dat's yer party piece from now on,' he laughed.

The drink ran out. The men made a collection and slipped down the stairs for another dozen. Paddy went with them. The women sat chatting, drinking cups of tea and eating chunks of wedding cake. Lizzie put her coat on and gathered up the loose lumps of hard icing left lying around the plate. 'I'm takin' these home for me gang,' she said, stuffing them into her handbag. 'Dey'll love dem. An' listen, Lily, don't go cuttin' yer top tier. Ya keep dat for the christenin'.'

Keeping the top tier was never questioned. A baby was sure to arrive nine months later.

Eileen nudged me as she was clearing the table. 'Paddy's mad about ya, Lily. He t'ought today would never come.' She stopped and looked over at Annie, who had gone quiet. 'How's yer Paddy, Annie?' she said sympathetically. 'When will he be home, God help him?'

'I'm goin' out to see him now,' Annie said, reaching for her handbag.

Paddy walked in with the men, carrying bottles. 'Where's Annie off to?' he said, seeing her with her hat and coat on.

'Out to Crooksling to see Paddy.'

'C'mon, we'll go wit' her.'

I slipped into my going-away clothes, a bottle-green corduroy dress and a pale-green figured coat, then on went my white hat and high heels. The Crooksling bus dropped us close to the sanatorium. The crisp mountain air was refreshing after Mrs O'Connor's smoky kitchen.

Annie's Paddy, a Limerick man, was sitting up in bed, chatting his head off to the other men in the ward. We all thought he was the mortal image of James Mason with his lovely black wavy hair. His face lit up when he saw us.

'Ah, be Gad, if it isn't me new brother-in-law,' he said. 'Fancy youse coming out here to see me on yer wedding day.'

Paddy gripped his hands warmly. 'God, ya look great, Paddy. Ya'll be out in no time.'

Annie sat down on the chair beside his bed. 'The weddin' was lovely, Paddy,' she said. 'Everyone was askin' after you. Show him your five-shillin' piece, Lily.'

'With gold and silver I thee wed,' he said, examining it.

I admired the jewellery boxes he was making out of old Christmas cards and clear X-ray film. Every red stich was perfect. Paddy was a tailor. I looked around the ward. The men were all sitting up busily sewing their boxes.

'Here, this one's for you, sister-in-law,' he said, handing me one in the shape of a pirate's treasure chest.

'We'll wait at the bus stop for ya, Annie,' Paddy said, taking my arm.

It wasn't long before Annie came charging down the hill towards us. She was in a great mood. Her Paddy was coming home soon.

Back in Gardiner Street, we tiptoed up Mrs O'Connor's stairs and into her flat.

'Will ya look who's back?' Eileen's Mick said, grinning, when we walked in the door. 'The newly-weds. Imagine a bride leavin' her own weddin'.'

'How is he, Annie?' Eileen said, tapping her cigarette.

'Ya should've seen his face when he saw us,' Paddy said. 'It lit up.'

'He'll recover now,' Mrs O'Connor said. 'T'see a bride on her weddin' day brings good luck.'

Annie's face beamed. She took off her coat and hat, then sat down beside Nora. They laughed and chatted away. I slipped my coat off and found a chair beside them.

'What time does the boat leave, Paddy?' Eileen said.

'Six o'clock.'

'Well, youse better make a move. Have ya got Maisie's address? Tell her I was askin' for her. She's lookin' forward t'meetin' ya.'

Eileen was very good. She'd organised everything, even our honeymoon.

WE WON'T TELL EILEEN

DOWN IN THE street, waiting for the taxi, Paddy held my hand, warming it. Nora and Annie joked around, shuffling their feet and rubbing their arms for a bit of heat in the damp evening air.

The taxi skidded up beside us, and the driver jumped out. 'C'mon,' he said, 'if youse want t'catch dat boat.' He grabbed our case and packed it into his boot.

'I'll put yer bouquet on Mammy's grave in the mornin', Lily,' Annie said, kissing us goodbye.

Nora, laughing away, emptied her box of confetti over our heads. Paddy and I brushed ourselves down and jumped into the back of the taxi, giggling.

'Where are youse off to on yer funnymoon?' the driver said, as he drove us down to the boat.

'We're stayin' in London, Drury Lane,' Paddy said.

'Drury Lane! G'way. Where all the t'eatres are? D'ya know someone livin' dere?'

'Me sister does. We're stayin' wit' friends of hers.'

It was pitch dark when he dropped us off at the North Wall. The boat was docked and people were scrambling up the ramp.

'Oh God, it's the *Maud*,' Paddy said.

We all dreaded the *Princess Maud*. It was well-known for rolling about on the Irish Sea, no matter what the weather. A real boneshaker, everyone said. But we were on our honeymoon and had each other. A seaman reached out a hand and guided us across the wobbly ramp onto the boat.

'It'll be nice and warm inside,' Paddy said, pushing open a door.

The tiny lounge was crammed with men fighting their way to the bar. We made our way through the smoky haze, looking for a seat. There wasn't one to be seen. Men had settled down with their drinks, keeping an eye on their battered old cases and wet paper parcels of corned beef.

'Paddy, how come it's so packed?'

'Dey're goin' back to dere jobs over in England. Dey've been at home with dere families for the Christmas.'

The boat moved off. I held on to his arm. 'C'mon outside on deck,' he said, picking up our case.

We held on to the boat's rail for dear life as we inched our way towards a wooden bench looking out to sea. Our case sat safely beside us as Paddy spread his Crombie over our laps and we tucked it in each side.

'Have ya still got yer period?'

'It's me last day,' I whispered.

'I've waited so long,' he said, touching my leg. 'Another night won't matter.'

The sea pounded against the side of the boat, sending up sprays of salty water. I tried my best not to look at the men gripping the rail and heaving over the side. Others struggled by, balancing trays of steaming-hot cups of tea.

'Would ya like a cup a' tea,' Paddy said, pulling back the Crombie.

The *Maud* docked in Holyhead after hours of rocking on the Irish Sea. The train was waiting beside the boat to take us to London. At last we could sit back and snuggle up into a warm comfortable seat for the long night trip through Wales and England. We were weary when it finally pulled into Euston Station, but London's icy-cold air soon woke us up.

'We'll get a taxi,' Paddy said, grabbing the case.

The black London taxi clattered through the city to Drury Lane. The driver dumped our case on the path, took our money and drove away. Paddy pointed to a row of high narrow houses squashed together. 'It's one of those,' he said.

We found the number and knocked for ages.

'God, that wind'd go through you,' I whispered, my teeth chattering.

He put the case down and banged off the door. 'It'll be lovely an' warm inside.'

The door opened. A small stout woman, drying her hands on her apron, peeped out. 'What d'ya want?' she said in a flat Dublin accent.

'Are you Maisie? I'm Paddy O'Connor. Me sister Eileen told me ya were expectin' us.'

'Eileen O'Connor? Ah Sweet Jesus, I forgot all about youse.

Youse are on yer honeymoon. C'mon upstairs to the kitchen. Lar's gone t'work.'

We followed Maisie up steep narrow stairs to a warm cluttered kitchen with an old armchair. The chair's seat was sunken in the middle as if someone had just struggled up out of it. A cupboard was next to the fire. I recognised the Child of Prague standing on it. Holy pictures hung around the kitchen. Maisie bent down and gave the fire a good poking.

Paddy took out his wallet. 'I'd like to fix up wit' ya,' he said. 'How much will I give ya?'

'Not at all. Not at all. I'd be insulted.'

'Are ya sure?' he said, taking out two pounds.

'I'll take it t'please ya,' she said, stuffing the notes into her apron pocket.

Paddy unstrapped our case and opened it. He rummaged inside and took out a white paper parcel. 'Here ya are,' he said. 'This is from Eileen.'

Maisie unwrapped the parcel and stared at a bunch of pale fat sausages. She dug her nose into them. 'Hafners. God love her. Me tongue has been hangin' out for a Hafner. C'mon, I'll take youse up t'yer room. Get yerselves settled. Den come down for a cup a' tea an' a bit a' fry.'

We were led up dark stairs to a tiny room with a sloping roof. It had barely enough space for its narrow sagging bed. A large picture of the Sacred Heart hung on the wall behind it. An icy gale rattled a window in the ceiling above. Paddy glanced at a small gas-ringed fire in a corner. Maisie saw him. 'Dat doesn't work. It's broke,' she said, turning to go.

We lay on the bed, shivering, the Crombie on top of us. Soon the smell of sausages floated up.

'C'mon, love,' Paddy said. 'Let's go down. I'm dyin' for a decent cup a' tea.'

'Sit down dere,' Maisie said, brushing old newspapers off chairs. She put two small plates of black and white pudding with fried bread in front of us.

'Tell me, Paddy,' she said. 'How's Eileen? I haven't seen her for ages. Is she still dancin'? Is she still livin' in Inchicore? How's yer mammy? How's Phil? How many's at home now?'

Paddy couldn't get a word in edgeways. But it didn't seem to matter. Maisie just kept talking.

He gave me the eye to get my coat. 'T'anks, Maisie,' he said, slipping his jacket on. 'We're goin' out to stretch our legs an' get a breath of fresh air.'

We rambled around the narrow streets nearby, dodging people huddled under big heavy overcoats, collars up. The sun struggled to shine. London shop windows were full of souvenirs for Queen Elizabeth's Coronation year. Paddy held my arm as we skipped down the steps to the Underground. He was great at following the maps, hurrying me on and off trains. In and out of tunnels we zoomed. The hours flew by.

'Let's go back, Paddy,' I said. 'I'm jaded tired. Me feet are blistered with these new shoes.'

We were knocking for ages before Maisie opened it.

'I've made a bit a' stew,' she said. 'Youse must be perished.'

'It's cold enough for snow,' Paddy said, following her up the stairs.

We sat in her warm kitchen while she cut up bread to dip in the stew. We heard a knock at her hall door. 'Dat'll be Lar,' Maisie said, disappearing down the stairs. After a few whispers, she traipsed back up, carrying a black overcoat. 'He won't be long. He's gone for a wash.'

Minutes later, in walked a short, proud-looking man, patting his face on an old striped towel. 'Did youse have a good crossin'?' he said.

'We came over on the *Maud*,' Paddy said.

'Dat awl rust bucket still floatin'?'

Lar was a man's man. He had nothing to say to me. Throwing his towel to his wife, he dropped down into his armchair. His body moulded perfectly into it. Maisie handed him a hot bowl of thick meaty stew and a spoon. After he'd finished, he burped, stood up, grabbed his coat and nudged Paddy. 'C'mon, we're goin' for a pint.'

'I won't be long,' Paddy said, hurrying down the stairs after him.

Before I knew where I was, he was gone and I was left with Maisie. She tidied the table silently, then collapsed in Lar's chair. She picked up his paper, squinted her eyes and began to read.

'What pub did they go to?' I said, fuming.

'Just round the corner. Lar's local.'

Without another word, I was up the stairs to our room. On went the lipstick. On went the new coat. And down the steep stairs I stomped.

'I'm goin' out,' I said, passing the kitchen.

Maisie dropped the paper and sprung up. 'Oh no, yer not. A girl doesn't go walkin' around London on her own at night. Dis is not Dublin, ya know.'

I carried on down to the hall door, pulled it open and slipped outside.

The cold night air bit into my face. I walked down the lane towards a main street, making sure to count the black iron lamp-posts as I went. There were pubs on every corner. Warm clouds of smoke, the smell of drink and roars of laughter hit me each time I peeped into their cosy bars. A fella was waiting in one of the doorways, shuffling his feet, blowing into his hands. 'Can I help ya, luv? Fancy a drink?'

'I'm waitin' on me husband. He's just behind me,' I said. 'Oh there he is.'

I tore back up Drury Lane and banged off Maisie's door. Heavy footsteps thumped down her stairs. Her face lit up when she saw me. She pulled me inside. 'C'mon, I'll make ya a nice hot cup a' tea,' she said. 'Lar has work tomorra'. Dey won't be long.'

An hour later, there were loud voices on the stairs. A flushed-faced Paddy waltzed into the kitchen and gave me a big hug. Then it was up to the icebox.

'Sorry for goin' out, love,' he said. 'It's a Dublin t'ing to do. Lar wouldn't take no for an answer.'

'I went out too,' I said, delighted with myself.

'Ya went out on yer own? Ya shouldn't have done dat.'

'Well, you went out,' I said, shivering.

He bent down to the gas fire, fiddled with its knob, turning it on and off.

'What are you doin'?' I said.

'See if I can get this fire goin'.'

'No, don't. For God's sake, Paddy, don't,' I said, watching him as he crawled under the bed.

'It's not broken,' he whispered. 'The gas is turned off at the tap on the wall.'

While he was under the bed, I quickly undid my stockings from my suspender belt and slipped them off. Then I unbuttoned my dress and changed into my new satin nightdress.

He crept out from under the bed and fumbled around with the fire. The tiny gas ring glowed red and the room thawed out.

I slipped into bed. 'The sheets are icy,' I said.

He folded his trousers on the case. 'Move over an' let me in. I'll soon warm ya up.'

We squeezed up in this little bed, lying close. Soon the springs were creaking and whining, making a terrible noise.

'They'll hear us,' I said.

'Let dem. We're married, aren't we? It might bring back a few memories.'

Paddy was sitting on the side of the bed, fully dressed, smiling down at me when I woke the next morning. 'C'mon, love. I want to show ya the sights of London.'

He dragged me down to Oxford Street to see the Christmas lights, then it was up to Trafalgar Square. He gave me a quick history lesson on Nelson, but I wasn't a bit interested in Nelson and his battle. It was the Lyons' tea rooms that held my interest. I couldn't pass one. I'd steer him in out of the cold. We'd sit chatting over a pot of tea and a little lemon-iced cake.

Then it was back to Drury Lane. Thank God Paddy had worked out the fire. We collapsed on the bed and missed out on the New Year celebrations.

Early next morning, we heard Lar and Maisie rushing around. 'It's New Year's Day, Paddy,' Lar shouted up. 'It's a holy day of obligation. Ya better hurry. The chapel's a few minutes' walk away.'

I curled up against Paddy.

'We better get up,' he said.

'Put the fire on for a minute. It's freezin'.'

'Lily, we'll be late.'

And late we were. The church was packed. The only seats left were up the front. Paddy and I scurried up the aisle to them. A Dublin priest, up in the pulpit, was giving out hell. 'It's the New Year,' he shouted, his face all red. 'Start it right. Don't miss mass.

Be in time. Give yer children a good example. London is full of temptations.'

Coming back from communion, Paddy gripped my arm near a side doorway.

'Quick. Out here,' he whispered, pushing the door open.

We lingered over a pot of tea in Lyons', then sauntered back to Drury Lane. Lar opened the door. Up into the kitchen Paddy and I tripped, giggling all the way. Silence greeted us. Maisie had a face on her. 'Youse were very late for mass,' she said, banging the kettle down on the fire.

'An' we saw youse rush out after communion,' Lar said, picking up his paper. 'Youse didn't even wait for the blessin'.'

Paddy glanced at me. 'I have to make a call,' he said, taking my arm. He hurried me down the stairs.

'We're goin' to Bedford. I'll ring Sammy. Three days in Dreary Lane wit' these two is enough,' he whispered. 'We won't tell Eileen.'

It was dark when the train pulled into Bedford. Sammy, a tall, good-looking man with Paddy's nose, welcomed us with open arms. His English wife, Audrey, hugged us warmly. 'You must be freezing, Lily,' she said, rubbing my hands. 'I have a good fire for you.'

Over supper, Paddy chatted away to Sammy, filling him in on all the family news. I sat with Audrey in front of the fire, sipping my tea, my shoes off, my feet lovely and warm.

Sammy showed us upstairs to a bright cosy bedroom and put down our case.

'We can't take yer room,' Paddy said, looking at the comfy double bed.

'Youse are on yer honeymoon,' he said, smiling.

Where they slept, we didn't know. We could only guess they'd squeezed in with their children. And we didn't know ourselves getting breakfast in bed every morning.

The rest of our honeymoon was spent in a dreamy haze, strolling by the River Ouse, feeding the swans. In the evenings, we played cards with Sammy and Audrey's children. We were down to our last few bob. Somehow Audrey knew. On the morning we were leaving, there was a pound note on our breakfast tray.

MARRIED LIFE AND THE CHILD OF PRAGUE

'I'M OFF TO live in the Wild West,' Paddy said, hugging his mother.

It was our first day back from our honeymoon. We had come down to collect our wedding presents. Mrs O'Connor wasn't too pleased that we were going to live in Mammy's house in Cabra West.

'Youse'd be better off on yer own,' she said. 'Even if it's only a cellar.'

'I don't want to live in a cellar,' I said. 'An' I promised Mammy that I'd stay on in the house with the others when I married.'

She put down her prayer book. 'An' what do dey t'ink? Do dey not mind?'

'Sylvia is pleased,' I said, fiddling with my rings. 'We're doin' up the house an' paying off a lovely new dining-room suite with a cocktail sideboard to match. An' Johnny doesn't care. He's mostly at sea with me father.'

Paddy gathered up our cups and rinsed them out, then began packing our presents.

His mother stood up, opened her range door and poked it hard, sending sparks flying.

'Ya'll need t'change the name of yer house from O'Shea to O'Connor,' she said firmly. 'Go down to the Corporation an' change it.'

'I don't need to.'

'Youse won't be dere long, if ya don't. It's in yer father's name. He can claim it.'

'But the house was Mammy's. Daddy's never lived in it.'

She slammed her range door and straightened up. 'Lily, when the mother dies, the house goes to the father, whether he lives dere or not.'

Paddy saw me upset. 'Her father has his own house, Mud,' he said. 'He lives wit' another woman.'

'Dat doesn't matter, Paddy. I've seen it happen all too often. He only needs t'have one row wit' her an' he'll move in to the house an' t'row the lot of youse out.'

I changed the subject. Opening up the lid of our new canteen of cutlery, I took out one of the knives. 'Aren't the bone handles lovely?' I said. 'Liam gave them to us.'

'The best man always gives cutlery, Lily,' Mrs O'Connor said, not looking at it.

Paddy picked up his wedding present from Irish Textiles, a delicate brass clock with three little colourful angels swinging beneath it. A glass dome, as big as a bell, protected it from the dust. I gathered up my farewell presents from the girls in work, my first electric iron and a shiny chrome butter dish. A girl was expected to leave work when she married, to look after her husband and the home.

We made a move to go. 'Don't forget yer Child of Prague, Lily,' Mrs O'Connor said, taking it down from her mantelpiece.

I was hoping she'd forget *that*. Who was the Child of Prague? Having once been a Protestant, I didn't know. I wasn't used to statues.

We struggled on and off the 22 bus, carrying the Child of Prague and all our presents. Most of our presents were for the bed. The bed was important. Awl John had made the bed. Lizzie had French-polished the headboard till it shone like a mirror. The two of them carried it around one night. It looked great. My pals gave me white sheets. Eight pairs I had now.

Paddy untied the string of a brown paper parcel. Two thick white woollen blankets fell out.

'Aunt Rosie always gives blankets,' he said, proudly.

I was delighted with them. The only blankets I had were Mammy's coarse grey ones, the ones Daddy had brought home from the boats years ago.

I took the Child of Prague from Paddy. 'Let's put it on top of the wardrobe,' I said. 'Out of harm's way. It won't get broken up there.'

Down in the kitchen, we counted out our life's savings, the eleven pounds the Abbey Clothing Factory had paid me off with.

We bussed it back into the city and bought two green fireside chairs, a china cabinet and a black astrakhan rug to put in front of the fire.

Clerys delivered our furniture the very next morning. Paddy

wasted no time in upending our old armchair and carrying it out to the garden on his back.

'Where are you goin' with Mammy's good armchair?' I said, running after him.

'I'm makin' a bonfire out of it. I've slept in the bugger. It's sunken an' full of hoppers. Dey've eaten me alive.'

I watched him from the scullery window. There he was, smoking away as Mammy's armchair smouldered and crackled. Tiny sparks drifted up into the damp wintry air.

That night, we sat on our new comfy chairs with our feet up on Mammy's black iron fender, drinking cups of tea and chatting. But not for long. Paddy had work the next day.

He loved his job in Irish Textiles. He'd be the first up every morning. I'd get a cup of tea in bed, see him out the door and watch him cycle like mad down Drumcliffe Road into the city.

Then I'd get stuck into my jobs. First, I'd rake out the fire and empty the ashes, making sure to keep back the cinders. With the washing done, I'd hurry down to the city for his Hafner sausages, then into Archers for his black and white pudding. On the way home, I'd stop off at the shops to buy bread and a bundle of sticks to get the fire going again. Before I knew where I was, it'd be getting dark, and Paddy would be speeding up the road home for his dinner.

He couldn't wait for the weekends to get started on the house. It wasn't long before every corner of Mammy's house was either painted or papered. It didn't know itself getting all this attention. The house began to smile again.

Hearing a lot of banging outside one afternoon, I wandered out to see what Paddy was up to.

'I made ya a lovely new coal-hole,' he said, lighting up.

Although the shed was hanging on its ear and made from odd bits of old wood nailed together, I was over the moon with it. No more would that coalman have to traipse through our kitchen in his scruffy old boots and empty his sacks under the stairs. He could now use the side entrance to Paddy's new coal-hole. And we could now hang our coats up under the stairs in our lovely new cloakroom.

'Get yer coat on, love,' Paddy said, cleaning up. 'We'll go down an' put a deposit on dat cream and green kitchen cabinet ya have yer eye on in Parnell Street.'

'God, HP is great all the same,' I said, as the 22 bus rumbled home. 'We'd have nuttin' only for it.'

That's What Mammy Always Said

ONE NIGHT, I decided to cook Paddy something special. My clean apron was wrapped around my good skirt. While the potatoes and turnip were boiling away, I put a spoonful of dripping into Mammy's big iron frying pan. Humming away, I took the floppy lump of liver out of the cold oven and made sure to cut all the gristly bits out. Soon it was spitting and spluttering on the pan. I popped a tin of beans into a pot of water and placed it on the stove.

The hall door opened and closed. It was Paddy, wheeling my bike in from work.

'Stay in the kitchen,' I called out. 'I'm makin' you somet'in' nice.'

I opened up Liam's cutlery and nearly died – two knives were crossed in the box, the sure sign of a row. That's what Mammy always said. I quickly undid them and set the table.

Everything was going great. The liver sizzled away on the pan. The tin of beans rattled like mad in the boiling water.

Bang! The beans hit the ceiling.

'Jesus, what the hell was dat?' Paddy said, flying into the scullery.

'The tin must have burst,' I said, staring at it.

'Did ya not punch a hole in the top of the tin?'

'I didn't know you had to do that,' I said, wiping the beans up.

'Lily, ya have to puncture the lid of a tin before ya put it in boilin' water.'

'Go back an' sit down. Dinner won't be long.'

I scooped up the brown liver onto the plates, then poured the hot smoky fat from the pan over the potatoes and turnip, just like Mammy always did.

'Dinner's ready,' I sang out to Sylvia.

A plate of bread and butter was put on the table, and the three of us sat down.

'What's dat?' Paddy said. 'Where's me sausages?'

'I got you liver for a change.'

'I don't like liver.'

'Liver is good for you. It puts blood in you. That's what Mammy always said.'

'I don't care what yer Mammy always said. I hate it.'

Sylvia looked over at me. 'I like it,' she said.

'It's even raw,' he said, pointing to blood on his plate. He shoved his dinner away. 'Don't ever give me liver again.' He picked up his bread and buttered it. 'Did ya never do any cookin' for yer mammy?'

'Mammy always said we'd be doin' it time enough.'

'Well me mudder made us all do our bit. We all knew how to cook.'

I said nothing.

'I'll fry meself an egg,' he said, getting up.

Sylvia and I ate the rest of our dinner in silence. Paddy hurried in with a fried egg on top of two pieces of crispy fried bread. I collected the plates and slunk into the scullery to make a fresh pot of tea.

Soon I was back with Mammy's old teapot stewing away. Paddy still had a face on him. I tried to cheer him up. A joke my father used to play on me came to mind.

'What's that over there, Paddy?' I said, holding my spoon in my cup of scalding black tea.

'Where?' he said, turning around.

Whipping my spoon out of my cup, I pressed it down on the back of his hand.

He nearly jumped out of his skin. 'Jesus, what the hell are ya doin'?'

'I was only jokin'.'

'Ya call dat a joke?' he said, blowing on the back of his hand.

'Daddy always used to do that to me.'

'I don't care what yer daddy used to do. Don't *ever* do dat to me again.'

Sylvia began clearing the table. I ran upstairs and slammed our bedroom door. The Child of Prague came flying down from the wardrobe. I nearly had a fit. The head broke off. I hid the two pieces under my clothes in the bottom of the wardrobe, then fell onto the bed crying.

Paddy came up after me. He sat on the bed and tried to make up. I moved away.

'I'm sorry, love,' he said, 'but I hate liver. An' I'm not very fond of hot spoons on the back of me hand either. I t'ink yer tryin' to kill me.'

'I hate it when you talk to me like that in front of Sylvia.'

'Just buy me Hafners in future an' I'll be happy.'

He lay back on the bed, his hands linked behind his head. 'Where's me Child of Prague gone?' he said, gazing up at the wardrobe.

Mrs O'Connor Was Right

'I'VE COME UP t'see all the jobs me son's done,' Mrs O'Connor said, when I opened the hall door one Sunday afternoon.

Paddy charged out from behind me. 'Come in, Mud,' he said, giving her a big kiss. 'Ya got the bus all right den?'

'Course I got the bus all right. What d'ya t'ink I am?'

She walked around the kitchen, inspecting every little corner. 'He's done a good job, Lily,' she said. 'It looks lovely.'

Paddy marched his mother into the scullery and ran his hands down the fresh cream wallpaper above the stove. 'I had no trouble strippin' the old paper off this wall, I can tell ya,' he said, smiling at me. 'Lily had it up wit' brass tacks.'

'Well, I didn't know how to make paste,' I said. 'No one ever showed me.'

'Don't be mindin' him, Lily. He can talk. When he papered my kitchen, he put the first strip up crooked. Then the whole lot had t'follow. An' what about poor Lizzie? Did he tell ya dat he put his foot through her ceilin'? When all she wanted was a light in the attic.'

Paddy laughed as he filled up our kettle. He plonked it on the gas stove and lit the jet, then he gave his mother the grand tour of the house.

While they were upstairs, I quickly hid our old knives and forks, the ones Daddy had brought home from the boats years ago. They had the names of the boats on their steel handles. I didn't want Mrs O'Connor to see them. She'd start again about Daddy taking the house from us.

'Dat's embossed paper; feel it?' I could hear Paddy say, coming back down the stairs with her.

The kitchen door was pushed open and in they walked.

'Yer lucky gettin' him all trained after he's wrecked our places,' Mrs O'Connor said, laughing.

Paddy pulled out a chair. 'C'mon, Mud. Sit down here. Lily has made ya lovely corned-beef sandwiches.'

'Corned beef? Grand.'

'It's silverside. Mammy always bought silverside. She liked a bit of fat on the meat.'

'I buy the tail-end meself,' she said. 'It's dearer but leaner.'

'How d'ya get yer cabbage so tasty, Mud?'

'Cook it in the same water as the corned beef,' she said. 'Add a bit a' bicarb when ya take yer meat out of the pot, den throw yer cabbage in. It makes the leaves lovely an' tender.'

Paddy grinned over at his mother. 'Lily washes every single leaf makin' sure dere are no caterpillars.'

'An' so do I. So do I. What's wrong wit' dat? Me an' yer Aunt Connie were the only ones in the tenements who washed our cabbages at the tap in the yard in the heart of winter. Our hands used t'be blue wit' the cold.'

'An' still a caterpillar escaped ya,' Paddy laughed.

'Ah, get on wit' ya.'

She turned to me. 'Are ya in a ham club, Lily?'

'A ham club? What's that?'

'Ya have t'be in a ham club for Christmas an' Easter. Everyone's in a ham club. Everyone. Ya pay it off weekly. Ya don't feel it. Go t'yer pork shop an' tell dem ya want t'join a ham club. Ya don't miss a shillin' a week.'

Paddy picked up the teapot and gave it a little shake, then marched back into the scullery to make more. 'Can ya tell Lily where to buy the mackerel, Mud?' he called out. 'I haven't had one since I left home.'

'Go to the dealers in Parnell Street any Friday, an' ya'll get some lovely fresh mackerel.' She leant over and gripped my arm. 'Look at the mackerel's eyes, Lily. Make sure dere blue an' not bloodshot. Dat's how ya'll know dey're fresh. It's the dirtiest fish in the sea, but it's the tastiest.'

The thought of asking a dealer in Parnell Street to let me look at the mackerel's eyes to see if they were blue or bloodshot terrified me. What if they weren't blue and I handed the fish back? The dealer would eat the head off me. I hated buying anything from the dealers; they always stuck me with the rotten fruit from underneath their tables.

A fresh pot of tea appeared on the table. Mrs O'Connor gazed around the kitchen. 'I don't see yer Child of Prague anywhere.'

Paddy looked at me and said nothing. He was keeping out of it.

'Oh, I forgot to tell you. I put it on top of the wardrobe for safety. An' what do you t'ink happened? It fell down an' the head broke off. I was ragin'.'

Mrs O'Connor stopped stirring her tea. 'The head broke off?' she said, putting her spoon down. 'Sure dat's when yer luck begins, Lily. Dat's when yer luck begins. It begins when the head breaks off. Show it t'me.'

Paddy raced upstairs and brought down the two broken pieces. Mrs O'Connor stood up, brushed the crumbs off her lap into the grate, took the headless statue and placed it on my cocktail sideboard beside Granny's pink seashell. 'Leave it dere,' she said. 'Dat's where it goes.'

She fetched her bag and pulled out a framed picture of the Blessed Virgin with a verse underneath. 'This is yer house blessin', Paddy. Every Catholic home should have one. Hang it up in yer hall.'

'T'anks, I will,' he said, glancing at the verse.

'Well, I'm off now. Ya can get me hat an' coat, son,' she said, fastening her bag.

She pulled me aside. 'Have ya changed the name of this house yet? It'd be a shame t'lose it after all the work he's done.'

I said nothing. Paddy helped her on with her coat and saw her to the bus stop. I sat down beside the fire and read the blessing.

Immaculate Mary, Mother of God,
We choose Thee this day.
As the Mistress and Lady of this House,
Guard us from the Malice of Enemies.

I went to sleep that night worrying about the malice of enemies. I thought of Daddy. Johnny told me he hated me.

By the morning, I'd made up my mind. Out came Sylvia's bike and down to the Corporation Offices in Lord Edward Street I cycled like mad to change the name of our house. I dragged her bike into the hall and chained it up. Then I stomped up the dusty wooden stairs and into a long narrow room. A man in a grey suit behind the counter served me.

'Now dat yer mother's dead, the house goes to yer father, John O'Shea,' he said.

'It goes to me father?' I said, my heart thumping. 'But it was Mammy's house. My father never even lived in it or paid the rent.'

'Dat's the procedure in the Corporation, I'm afraid. The father gets the house,' he said, examining our file closely. 'It's in his name, *O'Shea*.'

'But he's dead,' I blurted out, my heart beating so loud I was afraid he might hear it. 'That's why I want to change the name to *O'Connor*, me married name.'

The man took off his thick horn-rimmed glasses and stared at me. I recognised him. He lived on our road, a few doors down from my father. He cycled by our house every day on his way to and from work. The look in his eyes told me he recognised me too, but he didn't let on.

'Yer father's dead, ya say?'

I nodded.

Fixing his glasses back on, he studied Mammy's file again, then glanced back up at me. 'I see ya have two brothers,' he said. 'What about yer older brother? He's next in line.'

'He's married. Livin' in Australia.'

'What about the other brother?'

'He goes to sea.'

'When will he be home?'

I bit my lip. 'He's on the boats. I don't know where he is.'

He looked at me and then at the file, his hand to his mouth. 'Ya say yer father is dead?'

'Yes.'

"An' yer big brother has gone t'Australia?'

'Yes.'

'An' ya don't know when yer other brother will be home?'

'No.'

I held my breath as he reached under the counter.

'Sign here,' he said, pushing a form towards me. 'The house is now in the name of O'Connor. Yer married name.'

I was out that door and down those stairs like a flash before he could change his mind. On my way home, I popped into a new little cake shop in Prussia Street.

'How did you go?' Sylvia said, as I wheeled her bike up to our door.

'Mrs O'Connor was right. The house goes to the father. I had to say Daddy was dead. Stick the kettle on. I've got two lovely fresh cream buns for lunch.'

Paddy was relieved with my news, but I wasn't pleased with his. 'I'm on nights next week,' he said, shaking the salt on his sausages.

The nights were awful lonely without Paddy. Sylvia was always next door with her pal, Angela, and Johnny was always out or away at sea.

One evening, I had a terrible cold in my inside. I combed the house, searching for the Baby-Power bottle of peppermint. It was Mammy's cure for colds. You bought it loose in the pub. Having found the bottle, I drained it and fell into bed. I woke in fright.

Thump! Thump! Thump! Someone was pounding off our hall door.

'Jesus, who's that?' I said, springing up.

I heard the letter box lifted. My father's drunken voice bellowed through it. 'Ya changed the name of the house, ya bitch. Ya changed the name of the house, haven't ya? Where's yer fancyman now? Let me in, ya fucken' bitch. It's my fucken' house.'

Bang! Bang! Bang!

I sat there shivering, holding on tight to Aunt Rosie's blankets. He went on swearing and kicking the door, making a holy show of me. Then I heard a woman's voice outside. It was Mrs O'Neill shouting over from across the road. 'Lave her alone. Go on home,' she yelled. 'Get off wit' ya.'

For once I was glad that the neighbours knew all our business.

'Go on home. Get off wit' ya. Go on home,' she shouted.

I knew he'd go now and felt safe. My father was terrified of these tough Dublin women. Our gate banged several times. I slipped out of bed, peeped out the window and saw him staggering off.

IT WAS A WOMAN'S BUSINESS IN THE ROTUNDA

'**D**ERE'S SOMET'IN' WRONG wit' yer stomach. Go up an' see the chemist,' Johnny said, when I dashed to the lavatory to vomit.

But it wasn't the chemist who told me what was wrong with me. It was the women outside the chapel Sunday morning. Seeing me run out of mass and heave against a wall, they stopped talking and took everything in – me in my new coat and hat, Paddy in his new suit. This couple were not long married.

'Take her home, son,' one called over, 'an' make her a strong cup a' tea. Mornin' sickness doesn't last long, t'anks be t'God.'

'You're pregnant,' Dr Kirwan said the following morning. Watching him writing, I wondered if he remembered me. When Mammy was dying, he'd told me off for not getting him sooner. 'I wouldn't let a dog die like that,' he'd said. But Mammy was terrified of doctors and had told me not to get one, and we always did what Mammy said.

Dr Kirwan blotted his paper and looked up. 'Here's a note for the Rotunda Hospital, but you'll need proof to say you're married. Go down to the parish clerk in Old Cabra for a copy of your marriage certificate.'

I cycled down to Old Cabra, over the bridge and past the playground. Leaning Sylvia's bike against the railings, I hurried into the office and handed the doctor's note to the clerk. He threw it down. 'Will dey not let ya into the Rotunda if ya're not married?' he said. '*What the hell business is it of theirs?*'

His outburst surprised me. Made me think. It had never dawned on me that I could question people in authority.

He filled out a certificate. 'I have t'charge ya two shillin's an' sixpence,' he said, stamping it.

The months went by. My skirt got tighter and tighter. Paddy fussed over me; he even got up in the middle of the night to buy me chips. The day arrived for my first appointment.

Clutching the certificate, I marched into the busy Rotunda Hospital, letting on to be brave. A stocky, red-faced nurse, cradling a bundle of files, directed me down a corridor. She pointed to a long wooden bench full of girls. 'Sit over there till your name is called,' she said firmly.

I squeezed in beside them. We chatted away, all the while fixing our loose flowery smocks that draped over our skirts.

As soon as a girl started to show, on went the smock. We were proud to be pregnant, but too shy to show it. And God help you if you did. Older women would make a show of you. 'A brazen rossy,' they'd shout after you in the street.

The girl beside me turned and smiled. 'How many have ya?' she asked.

'It's my first.'

'Yer first? Ah, God love ya. It's nuttin'. Just like goin' to the lav. It's out before ya know where ya're.'

She had me in fits of laughter, telling me stories of babies who fell into girls' knickers in taxis. It all sounded so easy until she gripped my arm. 'Listen till I tell ya,' she said. 'Don't ever go into Holles Street Hospital. I had me first dere. I was in terrible pain an' begged the nuns for gas, but dey wouldn't give it t'me. Dey said Our Lady didn't get gas, so why should I?'

Gas, Jesus. I knew nothing about getting gas.

A group of lanky students, hands deep in their white coat pockets, sauntered by.

'I hope they won't be pokin' round me today,' she said, staring after them.

'Mrs O'Connor?' the red-faced nurse shouted out. 'Mrs O'Connor, you're next.'

'Oh, that's me,' I said, forgetting I was now Mrs O'Connor.

The nurse marched me into a small cubicle and told me to strip off and lie down. She handed me a sheet to cover myself. A small skinny doctor in a white coat pulled back the curtain. A group of students squeezed in behind him. He glanced at my file and began talking about me, his hand stroking his grey pointy beard. The students stood around the bed, gawking at me. The doctor's cold hands pressed my stomach. Then all the students had a go. Without a word to me, the doctor strode off, the students trailing behind him. One glanced back as I pulled up my skirt.

Out of the Rotunda I ran and over to Findlater's to meet Annie.

Annie was also expecting. She was all into this baby stuff, helping me make nappies and baby nighties. Chatting her head off, she rushed me up to Stephen's Green to a posh pram shop where she'd seen a great bargain. A lovely, white, bone-handled pram that bounced along on huge wheels with silver mudguards was going cheap. It had only a few scratches on the side.

'I hope it fits through my gate,' I said, putting a deposit on it.

The shopkeeper knew not to deliver the pram before the baby was born. 'Dat would be flyin' in the face of God,' she said. 'It's up t'God when the baby comes. Time come, baby come.'

A week before I was due, I was sitting in front of the fire, playing cards with Paddy and Sylvia at the table. It was Friday evening. I had just eaten my chips.

'I have a bit of a pain,' I said, gripping my stomach.

'Jesus, we'd better get ya to the Rotunda quick,' Paddy said, gathering up his pennies from the table. 'I need to call a taxi.'

All the way down to the hospital, the taxi driver, a father of eight, gave Paddy great advice on being a father. 'Dey keep ya poor but dere worth it,' he said.

He pulled up outside the pub opposite the Rotunda. 'Good luck,' he shouted after me, driving away.

Paddy kissed me goodbye at the entrance. 'I'll keep ringin' till I hear somet'in',' he said, looking back at me.

Husbands were not allowed past admittance in the Rotunda. 'It's a woman's business,' Mrs O'Connor had said. 'A woman's business.'

I was rushed into the labour ward and nearly died. Rows and rows of stretcher-beds ran up and down a huge room, each bed cordoned off by a skimpy white curtain. Cold glaring bulbs hung down from the ceiling, flooding each bed with light. The air was thick with antiseptic smells, mingling with the moans of women. Nurses in white starched uniforms darted up and down the rows of beds, some carrying little silver dishes covered in white cloths.

'Strip off. Put that on. Up on that bed,' one said, handing me a short white shirt.

Another nurse appeared with a bowl of water, soap and razor. She shaved off all my pubic hair in silence. I didn't know they did that.

A woman screamed in the bed beside me. 'I could fucken' kill ya, Joe Murphy. Fucken' kill ya, ya bugger.'

I lay back, trying not to hear her. Her yells changed to sobbing. I lifted the curtain and peeped over. Nurses were all around her. She was now crying for her mammy, the sweat pouring off her.

Jesus, it's getting worse by the minute. Now she wants her mammy. I preferred it when she was cursing Joe.

Every time a nurse passed, she whipped back my curtain, bent down and listened to my stomach. Without a word, she'd be off.

I didn't know what was happening. We were told nothing about the birth. The little you did know came from other women. Mrs O'Connor told me she was frightened of the knife. She didn't know where the doctor was going to cut her stomach to let the baby out. My mammy said she didn't know she had to take her knickers off.

All night, under the glaring lights, the women moaned. Saturday came and Saturday went. Women were wheeled in and women were wheeled out. Another night of screaming, women calling their husbands every name under the sun. Tired and weak, I was unable to sleep; a horrible taste shot into my mouth. I called a nurse and threw up a black liquid into her silver dish. A doctor appeared. 'How long has this woman been here?' he demanded.

'Fifty-four hours!' the nurse said, reading my file.

'This woman will never have this baby; she is far too high. I want her up in the theatre. She'll have to be forceps.'

Oh t'ank God, I thought, *let me out of this torture chamber.*

When I woke up, I was in a lift with my baby girl tucked up in the bed beside me.

'It's Monday morning,' the nurse said. 'You were lucky. You had Dr Smith. He was in a good mood. He got married last night.'

I was surprised she confided this to me, let alone talked to me. I was even more surprised to learn that Dr Smith had to be in a good mood for me to be lucky.

The nurse wheeled me into a ward with twelve other mothers.

'You were badly torn, Mrs O'Connor,' she said, slipping an inflated rubber ring under me. 'You'll have to sit on this for a while.'

My baby was put in a basket at the end of the bed. Mothers in long homely nighties sat at a large table in the middle of the ward, chatting and tapping cigarette ash into their white saucers.

'Hello, Lily,' one said, coming over. 'Yer Paddy O'Connor's wife, aren't ya? I worked wit' him in Irish Textiles. What did ya have?'

'A girl.'

She peered into the basket. 'Well, Paddy can't deny her. She's the spit of him.' She took a closer look and pointed to small dents on each side of my baby's head. 'She was forceps. Mine wasn't.'

Visiting time was strict. Just one hour in the afternoon. And only husbands for one hour in the evening. No children allowed anytime.

Paddy was the first to run into the ward. Smiling from ear to ear, he hugged me, then stood gazing at our baby. Holding my hand, he told me he'd never stopped thinking about me for three days. 'I was across the road outside the pub in the phone box. I had a stack of pennies beside me,' he said. 'I kept ringin' an' ringin'.'

Visitors began streaming in. Mrs O'Connor, bulging in her best blue coat, pushed by them all, making her way to my bed. She stared into the basket. 'She's an O'Connor all right. She's got Paddy's nose and mouth.' She handed me a christening shawl and a miraculous medal to be pinned onto the baby's vest.

An hour later, a loud bell clanged, waking all the babies. Visiting time was up.

'I'll see ya tonight, love,' Paddy said, holding me tightly.

The ward emptied. I sat happily admiring the seashell pattern on my baby's new woollen shawl. But not for long. Our screaming babies were handed to us to feed. The perspiration poured off me as I tried to balance on the rubber ring and breastfeed. I couldn't do it for the life of me. Lying back on the pillow, I watched the other mothers. They were smiling peacefully, breastfeeding their babies as if they had been doing it all their lives.

'Keep trying, Mrs O'Connor,' a nurse shouted, seeing me lie back on the pillow. 'Keep trying.'

'It's no good, I can't,' I cried. 'Give me a bottle for her.'

'Let me look at you,' she said, squeezing my breast. 'Your nipples are too small.'

She hurried off and was back in a second. 'Use this nipple shield,' she snapped, handing me a cold hard contraption.

I tried to hold this big awkward thing on my nipple. It was no good. The shield slipped all over the place. I gave up, threw the thing down and lay back, sweating. The baby screamed. My face burned. The nurse took my temperature, relented and made me up a bottle to give her.

Every morning, we were told to sit at the large wooden table in the middle of the room. Big bowls of milky gruel would be put in front of us. 'Good for the baby,' the nurses said, handing out spoons. A bottle of stout followed. 'Better for us,' the mothers laughed, pouring it out.

We looked forward to the evening. Seven o'clock sharp we'd be sitting up in bed in clean nighties and best cardigans, hair combed, noses powdered and lipstick on. In came the husbands, running.

On the eighth day, I was let out. On went the new underwear, skirt and jumper. We made sure to look our best when we were leaving, even if we were in bits. The baby was also dressed up to the nines in new christening gown, shawl and bonnet. Eileen's Royalette friend, the smashing knitter, had knit me tiny white matinee coats. She knew the size of a baby at birth. I didn't. My apple-green matinee coats would have fitted a baby elephant. Off to Marlborough Street Church for the baptism and me to be blessed.

Why I had to be blessed, I still don't know.

The following week, I happily bounced Debra in my new high pram down to the Registry Office in the city. The registrar, a small elderly man, was indignant when I told him her name.

'Dat's a film star's name,' he snapped. 'Call her after St Francis. She was born on his feast day.'

I heard the parish clerk's voice in Old Cabra: *What the hell business is it of theirs?*

'She's Debra Ellen,' I insisted, handing him the correct spelling on a piece of paper.

He wrote *Deborah* in his book.

'That's not right,' I said. 'I want it spelt *Debra*.'

His face blazed with anger as he rubbed it out with his rubber.

Six weeks later, it was back to the Rotunda for my post-natal examination. Having stripped off, I was told to climb up onto a chair like a dentist's. The chair was raised and a student examined me internally. He beckoned the doctor. The doctor praised the student.

'What's wrong?' I said, staring at the doctor.

'Your womb is tilted. I'm going to slip a ring in. No intercourse till it's removed.'

'A ring? What kind of a ring?'

'If you don't have this ring inserted, you will have a miscarriage the next time you're expecting,' he said, rolling up his sleeves.

Another six weeks and it was back to the Rotunda to have the ring out. I dropped Debbie off at Lizzie's on my way to the bus. Out came the ring. Another bright student discovered something else.

'You have ulcers,' the doctor said, having praised the student.

'Ulcers?' I said, springing up. 'What caused them?'

Ignoring me, the doctor turned to his group of students. 'What method of treatment should be used for ulcers?' he asked.

The students flicked through their notebooks. 'Cauterise,' they all shouted at once.

'Correct,' the doctor said. He turned back to me. 'Make an appointment. You have to be cauterised,' he said, walking away, his troop behind him.

'Jesus. Cauterised,' I gasped, climbing down from the chair. 'Now they're tellin' me I have to be cauterised.'

Sitting in the bus on the way home, I was worried sick. Cauterise? What in the name of God did that mean?

First off the bus, I sped up Drumcliffe Road and into our house to look up 'cauterise' in a school dictionary Paddy had found on his way home from work. Finding the word, I dropped the book with shock, banged the hall door and flew up Killala Road to Lizzie. She heard her gate go and strolled down her path, carrying Debbie.

'What's the matter wit' ya, Lily? Yer white.'

'Oh, Lizzie, they took out the ring. Now they said I have to be cauterised. I looked up the word in the dictionary. It means to "burn flesh with hot iron". Jesus, what are they goin' to do to me now?'

Lizzie threw her head back and roared with laughter. 'What in the name a' God do you t'ink dey're goin' to do? Stick a hot poker up yer arse?'

Dublin, You Let Your Men Go

IT WAS FOUR in the morning, pitch dark and freezing. Paddy slipped into bed beside me. He had just come in from night work. 'Are ya awake, love? Are ya awake?' he said, nudging me.

'What's wrong?'

'I've somet'in' to tell ya. I'm losin' me job. Irish Textiles are sackin' all the men.'

'What?' I cried, waking up fast.

Debbie stirred in her cot.

'Let's go downstairs,' I whispered.

He slipped his shirt and trousers back on and headed down the stairs into the scullery. I put my cardigan over my nightdress and crept down after him.

'I'm sorry for wakin' ya up, love. I couldn't wait till the mornin'. Sit down, I'll make more tea.'

'Why are they sackin' youse?' I said, watching him strike a match and light the gas.

'Dey're takin' on girls to do our jobs. Dey can pay dem half our wage.'

The rain beat off the window. An icy-cold draught blew under the back door. I shivered, pulling my cardigan tighter. The cup and saucer rattled as Paddy put the tea in front of me.

'They won't sack you,' I said. 'You're their fastest worker.'

'I'll be the first to go. I earn more dan the others. Eight pounds a week on nights.'

'They can't get away with that, can they?'

'We're havin' a meetin' wit' the union tomorra'.'

I looked around our home. We still had to finish the payments on my Singer sewing machine and dining-room suite. And I was expecting again. Like most young couples, we had no savings and lived from week to week.

The next day couldn't go quick enough. 'What happened?' I asked Paddy the minute he walked in the door.

'Bloody union can't do a damn t'ing,' he said, thumping the wall with his fist. 'I've been payin' me union fees for feckin' years.

Ya know what dey said? Dey said we're lucky dey didn't sack us before Christmas.'

The very next Friday all the fellas in Irish Textiles were sacked. No payout. No nothing.

First thing Monday morning, Paddy was up early, cycling all over Dublin, hounding the factories for work. He wandered down backyard lanes, in and out of knitting dumps, begging to be put on. Friday evening, he burst through the door.

'I got a job,' he said, grabbing Debbie up.

'T'ank God. Where is it?'

'It's on the south side. Two rooms in a tenement house. A woman runs it. She has a few old machines. I'll soon get dem goin' for her.'

All weekend, Paddy went on and on about his new job. The great future he had. No longer would he be just a number in a big factory; he could help this woman expand her business.

'T'hell wit' Irish Textiles,' he said, cycling off Monday morning.

But his dream didn't last. He didn't get home till all hours that night. I heard my bike being thrown against the wall.

'She's a slave driver,' he said, banging the door behind him. 'Expects me to work miracles on her awl crocks of machines for little or nuttin'.'

He tried another backyard factory in a converted stable. Again, he was expected to work like hell on old rusty machines only to be thrown a few bob. Day after day, he pounded the pavements of Dublin, knocking on factory doors, chancing his arm, letting on he could do jobs he couldn't. But bosses could pick and choose who they wanted and pay them a pittance. There was a glut of unemployed men standing around every corner in the city.

Two weeks went by and Paddy watched me piling the last of the cinders onto a miserable fire. We had to sit on top of it to get a bit of heat. He leapt up and flicked his cigarette butt into it. 'I'm goin' to England.'

'England? You're not goin' to England?'

'Dere's feck all work here. How d'ya t'ink I feel not havin' a job? We can't go on like this. We have to pay our rent. The HP bills will mount up. An' we have to eat.'

He gave the fire a good kicking, trying to get some life into it.

Debbie was playing with her colourful wooden bricks on our black rug. She stopped, looked up at Paddy and began to cry. He bent down, picked her up and walked around the room, holding her tightly.

I watched him. I'd miss him terribly if he went. And so would Debbie. Without fail, every Sunday morning after mass, he'd dress her up in her little blue coat, red jumping-jack boots and a big bow of ribbon in her hair. He'd proudly carry her down to his mother's in Gardiner Street. Mrs O'Connor and Eileen made a fuss of her. Debbie would come home all excited, a bag of sweets clutched tightly in her hand.

'Somet'in' is bound to turn up,' I said, clearing the delft from the table.

'If I wait any longer, we'll go further into debt.'

'What about the Labour Exchange?'

'Have ya seen the queues outside it, Lily? Dey go right up Gardiner Street. Even if I was lucky enough to get it, we couldn't live on it.'

'What are the other fellas from Irish Textiles doin'?'

'Dey're doin' the same as me, leavin' Dublin while dey still have the fare. Dey can pull the plug out of Ireland for all I care.'

There was no good arguing with him. Once Paddy made up his mind, there was no changing it.

'Where will you stay in England?'

'Sammy will put me up in Bedford till I find a job an' lodgings. I'll send ya money as soon as I can.'

It was drizzling rain that February morning in 1956 when he fastened up his old battered case. 'It won't be for long,' he said. 'Just till the work picks up. Go around to Lizzie's if ya need help.'

I handed him his Crombie. He kissed Debbie and me goodbye. 'Mind yerself an' Debbie for me,' he said, his eyes full of tears. 'Go to the Rotunda for yer check-ups, love, won't ya? I'll write as soon as I'm settled.'

I pulled back the curtain and watched him disappear down Drumcliffe Road. *Please God, he'll be all right and come back safe.*

The Postman Cycled Right By

It was Monday morning. Debbie sat happily sucking her crust in the pink high chair Mrs O'Connor had bought her. I was up to my eyes in the scullery sink, washing buckets of nappies and baby nighties with Lifebuoy soap. One kettle after another was boiled for hot water. By the time I'd finished, my hands were red and chapped, my fingernails cracked. A loud rap on the hall door sent me hurrying towards it.

'Sign here,' the postman said.

Drying my hands on my apron, I signed for the registered letter. It was from Paddy. Only a week gone. I tore it open. Four pound notes fell out.

> Dear Lily,
> Hope everything is all right. Sorry for not writing sooner. I waited till I had money to send you. The boat was packed coming over with men like meself. We all stood staring back at Dublin disappearing. Some went into the bar, got drunk then sick over the side. I never made it to Sammy in Bedford. I got off the train at Luton by mistake and walked straight into a job at the Luton Knitting Company. Luton is full of Irish. I'm lodging in a boarding house. I've a poky room with a lumpy bed and gas cooker. The landlady packs the Irish in. Mind yourself and give Debbie a hug for me.
> I love you,
> Always, Paddy XXX

Sylvia burst through the door for dinner that evening, all excited. It was her first day in Irish Textiles. Paddy had made sure to get her into his factory before he left.

She heard all about my day, wheeling Debbie into the city to put a pound deposit on a hot-water geyser. Now that Paddy was sending me money, I wouldn't miss five shillings a week. 'He'll be delighted with it when he comes home.'

'Runnin' hot water,' she said, filling up a kettle. 'That'll be great. We won't have to wait for the kettle to boil to wash our-selves.'

Johnny traipsed in from a trip at sea a week later. He picked up the poker and stabbed the turf into the fire, sending up sparks, saying nothing.

'What's wrong?' I said.

'How's Paddy goin' in Luton?'

'Don't' tell me you're t'inkin' of goin' to England as well?'

'Ah, I'm fed up wit' the sea. It's no life.'

'Are there no jobs in the paper?'

'There's nuttin' here,' he said, throwing the *Herald* over to me. 'I don't want t'leave Dublin, but I'm gettin' off the boats.' He snatched up his overcoat and stomped upstairs to bed.

Within a month, Johnny and his girlfriend left Dublin for Luton, where they both walked into jobs.

I wrote to Paddy several times a week, telling him all the news: how Debbie sat in her high chair chewing a rasher rind till it went white and how she loved going to the shops every day. The shop-keepers spoiled her. I'd sit her up on the counter, and Mrs Flynn would pop a lump of cheese into her mouth. It was the same in the pork shop; a lump of black and white pudding would be put in her hand.

I lived for Monday. Paddy's registered letter would arrive with-out fail. I'd scan it for news on when he was coming home. He'd send me as much as he could to see me through the week.

One Monday, I got the fright of my life. The postman cycled right by.

'Where's me letter? Jesus, I've no money left,' I said, dropping the curtain.

Debbie was asleep in the pram outside the hall door. I grabbed the key and banged the door behind me. The pram's big wheels bounced out the gate. I tore down Drumcliffe and caught up with him on Dingle Road.

'Excuse me,' I panted. 'Where's me registered letter? O'Connor? Drumcliffe Road?'

'Drumcliffe? I've done dere,' he said, pointing behind me.

'I get a letter every week from me husband in England. You must have it.'

'I've done yer road,' he said, cycling on.

I hurried after him with the pram, Debbie crying. 'Will you look again? Please.'

He stopped and turned around. 'I don't have yer letter.'

'Yes, you do. He always sends it.'

He sighed, leant forward on his bike and went through his bag thoroughly. 'O'Connor, Drumcliffe. Be Gad, yer right. Here 'tis. Sorry about dat.'

'I knew you had it,' I said, tears burning my eyes.

I Can't Keep Two Homes Goin'

'HOPE YER NOT goin' t'have it in me taxi,' the driver said, as I fell into his car.

'I t'ink ya better hurry,' Nora laughed, struggling in behind me.

The taxi sped down Parnell Square to the Rotunda. Nora rushed me in and gave me a big hug. 'Don't worry about Debbie, Lily. She'll be fine with Sylvia. I'll ring Paddy's work in England.'

I was hurried into the noisy labour ward and had Paul, a tiny baby, the image of Paddy.

No trauma this time with feeding. The nurses handed me the bottle with no fuss. But not all the rules had changed. Children were still not allowed to visit at any time, and only husbands could see you of an evening.

After our tea, I sat up in bed, watching the other girls getting ready for their husbands. On went the clean nightdress, lipstick and powder. All the fathers came racing in, dead on the dot of seven. I hid behind a magazine, letting on to be reading it. A nurse walked in and handed me a telegram. I tore it open.

Thanks, Honey. See you tomorrow, Saturday, 21st July. Love Paddy.

Under the covers I slid and sobbed.

Paddy beamed when he strolled into the ward the very next day. 'I'm sorry I couldn't get here yesterday, love,' he said, giving me a kiss. He peeped into the basket at the bottom of the bed. 'T'ank God everyt'in' is all right. Did ya get me telegram? I timed it so ya'd get it at visitin' time.'

'I was the only one in the ward with no husband.'

'I had to wait for the factory to break up for the holidays. Dey've paid me the full two weeks' holiday money, even though I haven't been dere all year.'

'Have you seen Debbie?'

'Ah, Lily, she's a real little girl. I opened the gate this mornin' and dere she was sittin' on the doorstep wit' a ribbon in her hair. I grabbed her up, but she yelled to be put down.'

'She hasn't seen you for five months.'

He slipped his hand under the covers and touched my leg. 'I haven't seen you for five months either,' he said. 'I've missed ya terribly.'

'Well, you're home now.'

The smile left his face. 'I have to go back.'

'You're not stayin'? You're goin' back?'

For the rest of the hour, Paddy talked about his job and Luton. How he was no longer just a knitter. His boss was training him to be a textile mechanic. How much better off we'd be in England.

'I don't want to go,' I said. 'The house is all fixed up. You haven't even mentioned the hot-water geyser I'm buyin'.'

'Ya wouldn't be able to buy it if I wasn't workin' in England.'

'You promised me you'd stay. You wouldn't go back.'

'Dere are no jobs here. It's worse dan ever.'

'How do you know?' I said, sitting up straight. 'You haven't even looked.'

'We'll discuss it later,' he said, smiling at the nurse nearby.

But the nurse didn't smile back. She reached for her bell. 'Visiting time is over,' she shouted to everyone, staring at Paddy.

I thought my eight days would never be up to get out of the Rotunda and have it out with him.

'Debbie's wit' me mudder,' he said, when he came to fetch me.

The nurse handed me my new baby, Paddy took my bag, and we walked out of the hospital and down Parnell Street towards Gardiner Street for Debbie.

'Ah, let's have a look at the babby,' Mrs O'Connor said, opening her door to us. She peeped into the shawl. 'Ya can't deny him, Paddy. He's the spit a' ya.'

'Where's Debbie?' I asked.

'She's playin' in the coal-hole.'

'In the coal-hole?' I said, handing Paddy the baby.

The coal-hole door was wide open. Debbie was fast asleep, lying on the coal.

'She screamed after Paddy dropped her off,' Mrs O'Connor said. 'I couldn't shut her up, so I let her play in the coal-hole wit' the bucket an' shovel.'

Debbie heard my voice and ran to me, crying.

'God, she's black,' I said, brushing the slack off her dress. I wet the corner of a towel and washed her little black face.

'Divil the bit a' harm it'll do her,' Mrs O'Connor said. 'It's only a bit a' dirt.'

Paul woke up whimpering. I went to fetch him. Debbie clung to my legs. 'Put baby down. Put baby down,' she whinged.

Paddy tried to lift her up but she yelled, clinging to my new skirt.

'She's still only a babby, Lily,' Mrs O'Connor said, tidying up her kitchen. 'Don't go havin' any more for a few years. Whenever he wants it, give him a shillin' an' send him up to the Phoenix Park.'

Paddy burst out laughing. 'I t'ink dey might be wantin' a bit more dan a shillin' now, Mudder.'

'I needn't worry anyway,' I said. 'He's goin' back to Luton.'

'He has t'go where the work is,' she said. 'An' so will you.'

As I patted Paul on the back, I thought about England. All the violence and murders over there. I felt safe in Ireland.

'What about all me friends here?' I said.

'Well, I'm losin' all me sons t'England. Even Chris, me youngest, has gone. Men have t'go where the work is. An' ya have t'go wit' dem.'

I looked over at Paddy. 'We'd better go now. I have to feed the baby.'

Mrs O'Connor gave Debbie a big kiss and a little bag of sweets.

'Would ya like to mind Debbie again, Mud?' Paddy said, gathering up our things. 'I'll bring her down to ya tomorra'.'

'Ahh no. Now dat I've seen her, I'm satisfied. Dat'll do me for a good long while.'

For the rest of the week, I heard nothing else from Paddy but how wonderful Luton was. Even on the morning he was leaving, he was still going on about it. 'Ya'll love it, Lily. It's a little village in the heart of England,' he said, packing his case.

As I sat feeding Paul, I looked around the room. 'I'm happy here, Paddy. Look at all we've done an' all the t'ings we've bought. Mammy always said it was easier to break a home than make one.'

'We're not breakin' up a home,' Paddy said, collecting his shaving gear. 'We're takin' everyt'in' wit' us.' He pointed to my pink shell-shaped lampshade hanging from the ceiling. 'Ya can even bring dat flycatcher wit' ya,' he laughed. 'Ya can bring the blue-bottles in it an' all if ya like.'

'What about the geyser I'm payin' off?'

'I'll buy ya another.'

'An' what about Mammy's grave?'

'Well, we can't take dat wit' us, can we?'

With his case packed, and jacket on, Paddy was at the door, leaving. He looked over at Paul asleep on my lap, Debbie playing on the rug, her stack of bricks getting higher and higher.

'I can't keep two homes goin' at once, Lily,' he said. 'A fortune dat woman charges me in Luton for a crummy little room. An' she's Irish.'

IF SHE DIES, MISSUS, CAN I HAVE HER ROCKIN' HORSE?

'JESUS, WHO'S THAT knockin' on the door?' I said, as I changed Paul's nappy on my lap. 'I bet it's that Cissie wan again.'

Cissie, a bold little six-year-old, the youngest of eight, lived at the back of us. Every day after school, she'd slip in under a wire that separated our gardens. You'd see the top of her red head dashing through the weeds. Her pinched little face with big green eyes would pester me to let her mind Debbie. One day, I did. Debbie was back in a minute, banging off the back door. Her silver bracelet that Sylvia had bought her was missing. 'Girl took it,' Debbie said, pointing at Cissie. 'It wasn't me, Missus,' Cissie said, crossing her heart. 'The devil made me do it.' From then on, no more playing with Cissie for Debbie.

The knock on the hall door grew louder. I put Paul back in the pram and opened the door. It was the postman. He'd come early with my registered letter.

> Dear Lily,
> Johnny's getting married. He's asked me to be best man. You have to come over for the wedding. Sylvia will look after Debbie and Paul. Catch the night boat next Friday and I'll meet your train in London Saturday morning. I've done a bit of overtime. Buy yourself a new coat and hat with the extra money.
> All my love,
> Paddy XXX

'Go, Lily,' Sylvia said, over dinner that evening. 'It's only for a weekend. I'll look after the two of them.'

'Are you sure you can manage a new baby with Debbie?'

'He sleeps all the time, an' Debbie's delighted with that little red rocking horse.'

Sylvia was right. Paul was never awake; a few sucks of his bottle and he was unconscious. And Debbie loved that horse Lizzie gave her. It belonged to Charlie, her youngest. Debbie saw him rocking on it and screamed for it. Lizzie dragged him off it and put it on my pram to take home. I felt sorry for poor Charlie. 'He's a big boy now,' Lizzie said, wiping his eyes. 'He'll have another pile of toys next Christmas.'

I looked over at Paul, fast asleep in the pram, then at Debbie, rocking like mad on that horse. I made up my mind.

Paddy ran up the platform and hugged me in Euston Station Saturday morning.

'Ya look smashin',' he said, admiring my new beige figured coat and white hat.

The day held out for the wedding. Paddy and Johnny stood proudly in double-breasted suits, white carnations pinned to their lapels. Helen, the bride, a slim pretty girl, looked radiant. Her cream outfit showed up her jet-black curly hair. Like Johnny, she had a quick, easy smile. A circle of girls hovered around her, chatting and giggling.

'Dey've only been in Luton for a while, Lily,' Paddy said, 'an' look at all the friends dey've made.'

'T'anks for comin',' Johnny said, giving me a kiss.

'Are you settled in Luton?'

'I have a good job in Vauxhall.'

Paddy was in great form at the reception. He joked about his mother's wise advice. 'Me Mudder told Lily not to be havin' any more for a while. She said whenever I want it to send me up to Phoenix Park wit' a shilling. Me poor mudder doesn't know dere's t'ings ya can buy over here in England dat ya can't buy in Dublin.'

Paddy couldn't wait to show me around Luton after the reception.

'Look at the big white town-hall clock,' he said, walking up George Street. 'An' dere's lots of parks an' playgrounds for the kids. C'mon, love, I'll show ya Wardown Park.'

We dawdled along New Bedford Road, admiring the big houses. Paddy led me into a well-kept park with a pond. Families, with real English accents, were sitting having picnics, their children throwing bread to the ducks.

'What's wrong?' Paddy said. 'Yer gone very quiet.'

'I'm worried leavin' a new baby for the first time, an' Debbie's not even two.'

'Ya haven't abandoned dem,' he said. 'C'mon, I'll buy ya some chips.'

Paddy sneaked me into his lodgings that night and into his bed. He reached for his jacket and took a small packet out of his wallet.

'What's that?' I said.

'French letters. Ya can buy dem in the barber's.'

After a lot of fumbling with a little packet, trying to tear it open, he was ready. I didn't fancy this rubber thing going inside me and was glad when it was all over.

'Oh God, Paddy, I hope that t'ing came out of me.'

'Of course it did,' he said, slipping back into bed. 'I've just flushed it down the toilet.'

Next morning, I trained it up to London with Paddy. 'Here's yer money for this week,' he said, handing me his pay packet. 'Have a safe trip back home, love.'

The train trip to Holyhead took forever. It was dark and icy cold by the time I hopped on the overnight boat. The foghorns moaned as we drew close to Dublin Monday morning. A thick eerie mist hung over the city like a suffocating blanket as I hurried down O'Connell Street for the 22. The bus crawled up towards Phibsborough and home. Sylvia was staring out the window, an anxious look on her face.

'T'ank God yer home, Lily,' she said, opening the door. 'I was expectin' you ages ago.'

'The ferry was late with the fog,' I said, taking off my coat.

'I'm late for work,' she said, wheeling her bike out. 'He won't take his bottle an' she won't stop coughin'.'

Paul was screaming. I heated up his bottle and tried to feed him, but the milk shot back. He lay tucked up in his pram, wheezing. Debbie was hanging out of me in her flannelette nightie, whingeing and coughing. After I'd washed and dressed her, she fell asleep on the fireside chair.

I lit the fire and sat, worrying. *Should I take them to the doctor or not? God knows what he'll charge. Maybe I'll take them to the chemist or wheel them down to the children's hospital. I wish to God Paddy was here.*

Knock. Knock. Knock.

'I hope to God it's not that young wan.'

I ran to the back door. It was.

'Can I mind yer little girl, Missus?' Cissie begged.

'No, she can't go out; she's very sick.'

Cissie squeezed in, her little granny face staring all around. 'If she dies, Missus, can I have her rockin' horse?' she said, pointing to it.

That was it. I shoved her out, slammed the door, wrapped Debbie up and squeezed her into the pram with Paul. Then, grabbing my purse with Paddy's wages inside, I ran up to the doctor on Navan Road.

'They've got croup,' he said. 'It's that damn fog. We've had it all weekend. Keep them in. I'll give you something. They're not going to die.'

Just a Fella I Met at the Canal

IT WAS A misty autumn morning. Out the door I inched the pram, Paul fast asleep under the hood, Debbie sitting up in her new red ski suit Paddy had sent her. Her little hand grabbed the silvery cobwebs spread over our hedging as we went out the gate.

We strolled up Killala Road, past Lizzie's house. No sign of her or little Charlie. I carried on up and crossed the road towards the chapel. Ten o'clock mass had just finished. The big wooden doors swung open, and the women streamed out, blessing themselves. Mrs O'Neill spotted me and rushed down the steps, waving.

'Dere's Holy God's house,' she said to Debbie, pointing behind her. 'Say hello t'Holy God. An' when's yer daddy comin' home? He's a bold daddy, isn't he? Stayin' away in England? He should be here wit' you an' yer mammy, shouldn't he?'

'Tell Paddy that,' I said, laughing.

But Mrs O'Neill wasn't laughing. 'Dere's nuttin' as vulnerable as a woman on her own,' she said, trotting off to the shops for her messages.

The mist lifted and a pale watery sun came out. I didn't want to go home.

'We'll go for a walk up to the canal,' I said, undoing Debbie's little red hood.

My pram bounced along the narrow country roads towards Broom Bridge. Holding on tight to the handle, I steered it down the grass slope to the canal, making sure not to wake Paul.

The swans glided by, their long white necks bobbing up and down in the water, searching for food.

'Look at the lovely white swans,' I said to Debbie. I put the brake on and lifted her down.

She ran like mad to the edge. 'Stop,' I screamed. 'Don't go any further.'

A fella, who was gazing down into the water, looked up and saw Debbie heading for the canal. He rushed over and grabbed her.

'T'anks very much,' I said. 'I'll murder her.'

He took off his cap and crammed it into his pocket. 'It's lovely an' peaceful up here, isn't it?' he said.

'Are you not workin'?' I said, keeping an eye on Debbie rolling down the grassy embankment.

'I've been laid off for the winter. Slackness.'

'My husband's factory sacked all the men. He's gone over to England.'

'The da doesn't want me t'go t'England,' he said, kicking a stone into the water. 'He said I'd be called up. No son of his is fightin' for the English. Yer husband will be called up, ya'll see.'

'Called up? No he won't. He's Irish.'

'Once he's workin' in the country, he has t'fight for it.'

Paddy had mentioned nothing to me about being called up.

'I'd better go now,' I said, taking Debbie's hand.

'Show, let me help ya.'

He grabbed the handle of the pram and pushed it back up on to the road again.

Jamie walked me right back to my house, still holding the handle. He opened the gate while I wheeled the pram through.

'Do you go up to the canal every day?' I said.

'It's better dan being at home on top of the fire,' he said, fixing his cap on. 'I have t'get out; otherwise I'd go mad.'

'I know what you mean. I'm goin' mad not havin' anyone to talk to.'

He waved goodbye to Debbie, then walked off, whistling away.

Before I went out the following day, I found myself changing into my good skirt and putting on a bit of lipstick. With the messages done, I wandered up to the canal. There he was, cap on, staring down deep into the water. He bent over and scooped up a few pinkeens, then threw them back in. Brushing his hands, he waved.

Debbie ran up to him. Jamie took her hand to hold her back from the canal, then he peeped in at Paul, fast asleep.

'He's a great little fella,' he said. 'What's his name?'

We strolled along the canal, chatting about the pictures and the dance halls we went to.

'Just imagine, you were dancin' in the Elite when I was,' I said. 'Maybe I danced with you.'

The time flew by. Before I knew where I was, he was holding my gate back while I inched the pram in. 'Does dat baby never wake up?' he said, laughing.

Someone was watching from over the road. It was Mrs O'Neill. Out she came to sweep her front path.

'Day-day,' she sang over to Debbie, glaring at Jamie.

He glanced over, lifted his cap and smiled. She looked down and swept the dirt from her path on to the road.

'I'll let you go now,' I said, taking my key out.

The weeks went by. The housework got done quickly. And so did the messages. Debbie didn't know herself seeing the swans every day. Jamie was good company. He'd push the pram while I chatted and hummed the tunes we'd danced to.

One day we arrived home to find Paddy at the door, waiting. Jamie put his cap back on, nodded to him, then hurried off.

'What's wrong?' I said, opening the door.

'Nuttin's wrong, love. I'll tell ya inside.' He turned and looked after Jamie. 'Who was dat?'

'Ah, just a fella I met at the canal.'

A Moneylender is Our Only Hope

'I DON'T WANT TO buy a house in England,' I said, feeding Paul. 'It sounds too final.'

'It's a great opportunity, Lily. I have to get three hundred pounds for the deposit. The boss will back me up for a mortgage wit' the bank.'

'I don't want to borrow all that money.'

'A moneylender is our only hope. Me mudder will know one.'

Paddy was on the first bus down to his mother's the next morning. My mind was a hell to me all day, thinking about this big decision he was forcing me into. I'd only got them to bed when the hall door burst open and Paddy rushed in, his face flushed red with excitement.

'Sit down, Lily,' he said, taking his Crombie off. 'Sit down at the table. I've got the money.'

I said nothing and pulled over a chair beside him.

'We're very lucky,' he said quietly. 'Me mudder took me around to see this dealer, a moneylender.' He put his hand in his jacket pocket and out came a thick bundle of rolled-up notes.

'Jesus, Paddy, wait,' I said, jumping up and dragging the curtains across. 'You never know who's watching. Next door's meter was robbed last week.'

Neither of us had ever seen so much money in our whole lives. His hands shook as he unrolled the bundle and counted out three hundred pounds onto the table.

'If it hadn't been for me mudder's good name, we'd never have got it,' he said, gathering up the notes. 'We have to pay the moneylender back three pounds a week. She's chargin' us two an' six in the pound interest.'

He rummaged in his pocket, took out his pencil and added up the interest on the back of his cigarette packet. 'Dat's nearly forty pounds extra we have to pay.'

'Jesus, that's a lot,' I said, biting my nails.

'We'll be broke for a couple of years, but we'll manage.'

The notes were rolled up and the pair of us crept upstairs

shaking, looking for somewhere to hide it. I found a small hole in
the corner of my pillow and stuffed it in among the grey flock,
then sewed it back up.

It was me that tossed and turned on the three-hundred-pound
pillow that night. Not Paddy. He was in dreamland.

He sprang out of bed next morning. 'Let's enjoy Christmas,' he
said. 'I'll run to the shops an' get a little Christmas tree for
Debbie.'

'Wait till I dress her. I'll come with you.'

'We can't leave this house on its own, Lily. Someone has to mind
the money.'

'Don't forget to pick up the ham from the pork shop. I've paid
it off.'

'Awl Jack's comin' up for Christmas dinner an' the gang are
comin' up Christmas night for our sing-song. I'll get a few bottles
in an' the makings of the puddin'.'

It was an O'Connor tradition that the man of the house made
the Christmas pudding. Well, that's what Paddy always said, and I
was happy to go along with it.

Christmas morning, I pulled back the curtains. The sky was
laden with snow. We wrapped Debbie up and went to early mass.
Sylvia looked after Paul, the house and the three-hundred-pound
pillow.

Our tiny tree glistened with tinsel and nursery-rhyme lights. Awl
Jack came up for dinner. He shook my hand, sat down and never
moved. He was shy with the women all right; he had nothing to say
to me. He left straight after dinner.

'Dat was a great puddin', Paddy,' he said, heading for the door.
He tipped his cap to me and was gone.

All the O'Connors turned up Christmas night and did their
party pieces.

'What's the matter wit' ya, Lily?' Awl John said. 'Ya didn't give
us yer "Cheating Heart" tonight.'

'She's upset because we're leavin' Dublin,' Paddy said.

'Sure, the way t'ings are goin', we'll all be joinin' ya in Luton,'
Awl John said, laughing.

When everyone left, Paddy and I went into the scullery and got
stuck into the washing-up. He washed while I dried.

'Dey were all in great form tonight, weren't dey?' he said, wringing out the dishcloth.

'I don't want to buy that house, Paddy. It's too final.'

He threw down the dishcloth and stormed into the kitchen. I followed him. He sat down on a fireside chair and lit up. I sat opposite him and poked the sinking fire.

'Ya have to go where the money is, Lily. I want the kids to have all the t'ings dat I never had.'

'They'll be all right. We hadn't much when we were little, an' we were happy.'

'Just listen t'me, will ya? One Christmas I hadn't even a pair of shoes to wear, never mind a toy. Me mudder didn't want anyone to see me in me bare feet Christmas morning. She called me for six o'clock mass. I flew all the way to Marlborough Street Chapel. It was pitch-dark and freezing. The path was like glass. Me feet were blue wit' the cold. I ran into the chapel an' up into the balcony. Two nuns were behind me. After mass, dey tipped me an' told me to follow dem to the convent. Me eyes nearly fell out of me head when dey handed me a brand-new pair of boots. Dat was the best Christmas I ever had.' He threw his cigarette into the fire and laughed. 'I tell ya what, Lily, I never called the nuns the hooded horrors again. I wore those boots till dey fell off me, an' I swore no kid of mine would ever go barefoot.'

We were up early in the morning, unpicking the pillowcase, glad to be rid of this money. Paddy had a long day ahead, travelling back to Luton.

'Have you got that money safe?' I said for the hundredth time.

'Don't worry. I won't take me hand off it.'

He lifted Debbie up, kissing her till she squealed to be put down. Grabbing up his strapped case, he opened the hall door and hugged me. 'Whoever t'ought dat we could buy our own house, Lily?' he whispered. 'I'll write as soon as I can, love.'

I watched him hurrying off into the cold morning air, his collar up, his free hand dug deep into his coat pocket, holding the money.

I'll Be Back

'So ya're off t'England?' the removalist said, when I opened the hall door.

'It's only till the work picks up. I'll be back.'

'Nah, ya won't. Yer husband won't come back. Dere's nuttin' here.'

Sylvia dressed Debbie and Paul and took the pair of them next door to her pal, Angela, while I scurried around, giving the house a good sweeping.

'Do we take everyt'in'? Even the pram?' the removalist said.

'Everyt'in'. Don't forget me bucket, floorcloth and scrubbin' brush. Everyt'in'.'

'Yer furniture will be in Luton Saturday,' he said, leaving.

I shut the hall door behind me and carried our bags down the path. Then I stood at the gate gazing back at the house, remembering all the things that had happened there. The happy times, the chats with Mammy around the fire, my feet up on the fender. The advice she gave me about boyfriends and work. Telling me to stand up for myself. And the sad times. Mammy staying in. Losing the will to live. Coughing up blood all night in that little back bedroom where she died. *Now look at the house. It has returned to its bare bones. It looks just like the day we moved in. Its eyes are gone; the windows are stripped of their floral curtains. Even the garden is gone.* The hedging had left. It was now living next door with my neighbour. I had let her come in last night and dig it up with her fork.

'Mammy, Mammy,' Debbie shouted, running down the road towards me.

Sylvia hurried after her, carrying nine-month-old Paul.

'C'mon,' I said, taking Debbie's hand. 'We're goin' on the bus to Nanny's.'

Mrs O'Connor was very good. She'd offered to put us up for our last few days in Dublin. She even borrowed a cot from her neighbour for Paul. Debbie slept with her. Sylvia and I shared Paddy's old bed in her spare room.

'How will I fix up with you?' I asked, taking out my purse.

'Don't give me anyt'in, Lily. Just look after yerselves. We all have our own little tinpot way. Our own little tinpot way.'

She fussed around her kitchen, rinsing out cups and saucers. Sylvia took off to say her goodbyes to her pals. It was time for Debbie and Paul's sleep. I put them down, then hurried over to the Corporation Offices in Lord Edward Street.

'I'm movin' to England,' I said to the clerk behind the counter. 'I'm handin' in me keys to our house an' this week's rent.'

He looked surprised when I counted out the thirteen shillings and sixpence onto his bench.

'Yer a good girl,' he said. 'Most people leave Dublin wit' months of arrears.' He bent under the counter for his book, then picked up his pen. 'When ya come back, ya'll be given another house. Ya won't have t'go on the end of a queue.'

'Oh t'anks very much,' I said. 'T'anks very much.'

I skipped down those stairs, two at a time, hugging myself. Down O'Connell Street I sprinted, past Nelson's Pillar, across the road and into Parnell Street. Then a mad dash down to Gardiner Street and up the stairs and into the flat.

'They're givin' me a house when I come back,' I said, panting. 'Isn't that great?'

Mrs O'Connor looked up from her pan. 'Lily, houses are only bricks an' mortar. Ya can make a home anywhere. As long as youse are all together, dat's all dat matters.'

Sylvia slipped in. I slipped out for fish and chips, then fell into bed exhausted.

The following morning, I rinsed out a bucket of napkins and baby clothes.

'Hang dem out here,' Mrs O'Connor said, pulling up her back window. 'Dey'll be dry in a minute.' She pegged all the clothes on to a rope then pushed them out her window with a long pole.

'T'anks,' I said, putting her bucket away.

'Not at all. Dolly clothes, dat's all dey are, Lily, dolly clothes.' She pulled a chair over and sat next to the window. 'I could sit here all day, lookin' at yer washin' blowin' in the wind.'

That night, when I had the two of them tucked up in bed, Mrs O'Connor called me into her front room overlooking the street. The room was dark. The light was out.

'Get yerself a chair,' she said, making room for me in front of an open window.

I pushed a chair over, squeezed in beside her and looked down into Gardiner Street. It was all lit up, alive with voices and laughter. Couples, arm in arm, sauntered along. Fellas hung around doorways smoking, watching people scurrying by. A mother, dressed up to the nines, stepped out of the flats opposite. She crossed over and waved up.

'Tell Eileen t'anks for the tickets,' she shouted up.

'Enjoy the show, Bernie,' Mrs O'Connor called down.

Mrs O'Connor knew everyone in the street. No wonder women like her never left the city. In the city, you could sit in front of open windows, call down and be part of city life and never be lonely. In Cabra West, you sat in front of your laced curtains, just watching, saying nothing.

Easter Sunday, after mass, I packed our bags ready to go. Mrs O'Connor handed Debbie and Paul little egg cups with Easter eggs in them. She pointed to my scruffy old slippers on top of my small bulging bag. 'Don't take dose awl t'ings wit' ya, Lily,' she said. 'Dere's holes in the toes.'

'I like them. I've worn them for ages. They're comfortable.'

We said goodbye, then taxied it down to the docks and scrambled up the ramp of the boat. Into the bar we went for a bit of heat. The usual fog of smoke hit us. Men, balancing pints of Guinness on trays, cigarettes stuck to their bottom lips, winked at us.

'It's awful in here,' Sylvia said, picking up our bags. 'Let's go outside.'

A loud moan from the boat's horn and off we steamed.

To this day, I can still see myself in 1957 sitting on that long wooden bench, staring out to sea, huddled inside myself, trying to hold on to Dublin, my pals and everything I ever knew. It was my city and my life, and I was having to leave it. I made a vow then: I'd be back.

Paul wriggled on my lap. I tucked a small rug around his skinny little legs. Debbie jumped up on the seat beside me. *Thank God I made her wear her warm coat.*

Hours later, passengers pushed in front of us. Across the ramp they hurried towards the waiting train, struggling with battered old cases, wanting to grab the best seats. As the train puffed out of

Holyhead, Debbie and Paul fell asleep on our laps. Sylvia and I gazed blankly out into the darkness. Our carriage clickity-clacked all night long down through Wales and England to London and Paddy.

PART TWO

From Luton to Torquay and Back Again

Sit Down, I've Somet'in' to Tell Ya

WE STAGGERED OFF the train at Euston Station. Paddy came charging down the platform and nearly squeezed me to death.

'C'mon, give me those bags,' he said, rushing us towards a taxi. 'I have to get youse to St Pancras.'

The taxi rattled out of Euston and into another big station.

'Quick, Lily, here's the Bedford train,' he said, rushing us along.

I struggled on, Paul asleep in my arms. Sylvia lifted Debbie up. The porter slammed the doors and blew his whistle. We collapsed into an empty compartment.

'It's great to see ya, love. I t'ought I'd never get ya here.'

He talked non-stop about how lucky we were to get this house. 'Nuttin' needs doin' to it. It has a lovely big back garden for dem to play in. An' the shops are just around the corner from ya.'

The train pulled in to Luton. We gathered up our things and crawled into another taxi.

'Leagrave, Limbury Road,' Paddy said to the driver.

Sylvia and I sat silent, staring out the window. Old red-bricked houses flashed by as the taxi sped along. We turned into a tree-lined road, then stopped outside a sad-looking, semi-detached house. Dark green paint flaked off its small bay windows. Rusty drainpipes dangled from its roof. Its little wooden gate hung on its ear next to a small picket fence.

'God, it's very old, isn't it?' I said.

'It's over a hundred years old, but solid,' Paddy said proudly.

The tiny front garden was covered in crazy paving. Long skinny weeds poked out of its cracks. I peered into the front room, delighted to see my pram. At last I could put Paul down – my arms were hanging out of me.

Paddy's brother, Chris, yanked the door open. 'Hello,' he said. 'It's good t'see youse. Isn't the house great?'

Down a long dark hall we all trailed into the kitchen. Our modern cocktail sideboard looked so out of place in this old house. I sat Paul down on the bare floorboards. Sylvia and Chris stood chatting. Two stone steps led down into a little room off the kitchen.

'The scullery's been added on to the house,' Paddy said, stepping down into it.

I followed him and looked around. A mouldy wooden draining board hung next to a stone sink under a little sash window. My frying pan sat on a grimy old gas cooker. My delft and Liam's canteen of cutlery were in a box on the floor. Our kitchen cabinet stood in the middle of the room, looking awkward.

'We'll have to get rid of dat,' Paddy said, banging its door. 'Dere's no place for it.'

'You're not gettin' rid of me good kitchen cabinet,' I said. 'It's all I've got to put me food in.'

Another room led off the scullery, the bathroom.

'Dere's yer hot-water geyser, Lily,' he said, pointing to a big white-enamelled thing hanging over the bath.

I bent down and turned on the tap. Gushes of steaming hot water spluttered into the bath.

'That's grand,' I said. 'I can bath both of them at the same time.'

'C'mon, I want to show ya outside,' he said, turning the tap off. He pulled the back door open. 'Dere's yer coal shed. I got ya a bag a' coal to keep ya goin'. Dere's bundles of sticks in dere too.'

A narrow concrete path ran right down the centre of the garden, disappearing under a mound of weeds.

'It's a great garden for the kids to play in, isn't it?' he said. 'But don't expect me to do it.'

A loud scream went through me. Debbie ran out. 'Paul's fallen down the big steps, Mammy,' she shouted.

'God, I forgot all about him,' I said, tearing back into the scullery.

I grabbed him up and held a wet towel to the bump on his forehead.

Paddy took him from me. 'C'mon, Lily. I'll show ya upstairs.'

We went back down the hall and climbed up the bare wooden stairs, Debbie behind me, gripping each stair as if it was a ladder. Paddy had everything worked out, even the bedrooms. 'Dat's Chris's room. He's stayin' wit' us. He's workin' in Vauxhall,' he said, pointing to a door on the right. 'Sylvia has the back room. We have the front room.'

Debbie charged ahead of me and jumped up onto our bed. I hardly recognised my dressing table. Its sides were pushed in, leaving jagged edges like a shark's teeth.

'It had a rough crossin',' Paddy said, putting Paul down beside Debbie. 'We'll shove it up against the wall. Ya won't notice it.'

'The room smells damp,' I said, walking over to a window.

I tried to pull it up. It wouldn't budge. I stood gazing out. A row of semi-detached houses opposite looked old, deserted and lonely. There were no children playing outside in this street like Cabra West. No women talking at corners.

Paddy sat down on our bed, lit up and inhaled deeply. 'Listen, Lily, sit down, I've somet'in' to tell ya.'

'Tell me now? What?'

'I've changed me name.'

'You've changed your name? Jesus, Paddy, what do you mean you've changed your name?'

'I'm due to be called up. Once yer workin' in the country a year, ya have to fight for it. Do yer National Service. I'm here over a year. So I had to change me name.'

He was right. I had to sit down.

'I wish to God you hadn't,' I said, holding on to Paul on the bed.

'I'd be bloody conscripted if I didn't. Ya don't want to be left here on yer own, d'ya?'

'Jesus, Paddy, you're after gettin' me over here. Now you're tellin' me I could be left here on me own.'

He drew hard on his cigarette. 'The Irish have to change their names. Don't worry about it.'

'Supposin' they find out.'

'Dey're not goin' to find out, are dey? Unless you tell dem.'

I sat, trying to take it all in.

'I'm hungry,' Debbie moaned.

'C'mon, I'll give ya a lovely bath,' Paddy said, taking her hand.

Debbie didn't know herself getting all this attention. He hurried her down the stairs and, within minutes, had her in a lovely bath of bubbles. Singing away, he whipped her out, wrapped a towel around her and dried her. He fed Paul his dish of Farex, then made up a small bed and cot in our bedroom. An hour later, I crawled into bed, jaded tired. Paddy fell in beside me.

'What name did you change to?' I said, turning around to him.

'George. All the Irish do it. Dey change from Paddy to George. Half a' Vauxhall have done it, Lily.'

'So I suppose there's millions of Georges walkin' around Luton now with Irish accents?'

He laughed and grabbed me. 'Just let me do the worryin'. It'll be all right.'

I fell into a deep sleep that night, feeling safe and warm beside Paddy. The next thing I knew, he was standing in front of me, fully dressed, handing me a cup of tea.

'I'm off now, love,' he whispered. 'I'll see ya tonight.'

I heard the hall door close. I slipped out of bed and peeped out the corner of the bay window. Paddy skipped out the gate, his Crombie collar turned up. He disappeared into a heavy mist. I turned around. Two small faces smiled over at me, Debbie and Paul, wanting their Farex.

'Right,' I said. 'Now to get youse two dressed an' fed. I've loads to do.'

In no time at all, I had Paul tucked up in the pram and Debbie all buttoned up outside, exploring her new back garden. Then it was up with the sleeves and on with my scruffy old slippers from Cabra. Now to find a place for my kitchen cabinet in this little cold scullery.

'Where in the name a' God will I put it?'

A watery sun shone straight through the window into a dark corner recess that had once been a fireplace. God must've heard me and guided me to it.

'Sylvia, can you give us a hand?'

We lifted the cabinet up with all our strength, then inch by inch, we pushed it backwards into the corner recess as far as it would go. Perfect. I couldn't stop looking at it, delighted with myself.

'Let's have a cup a' tea,' I said, filling the kettle.

We didn't sit for long. Sylvia went searching for the shops with Debbie. I went in search of my bucket, scrubbing brush and floorcloth to get stuck into this house.

That evening, Paddy hurried down the hall and gazed around the kitchen. A big smile spread across his face. Paul was in the high chair, nibbling on a Farley's rusk. Debbie was lying on our astrakhan rug, colouring her picture book. My two green fireside chairs had found their place each side of the glowing fire. The Irish Textiles clock ticked away on the mantelpiece, Granny's seashell and our few ornaments arranged around it, the little personal things that make all the difference.

'Come an' see what I did in the scullery,' I said, stepping down into it.

'Ya've found a spot for dat cabinet,' he said in amazement. 'Ya've turned a house into a home.'

LILY IN LUTON

I INCHED THE pram out the back door and up into the garden. Debbie followed me, dragging her coat.

'Don't wake Paul up,' I whispered, pulling up the hood. 'I want him to have a little sleep while I do the washing. Then we'll go to the shops.'

'I want to go now,' she begged.

I bent down and buttoned her up. 'Play with Lally. We'll go later.'

Desperate for someone to play with, Debbie had invented an imaginary friend, Lally. She'd play with her for hours in the back garden. But not today.

'Lally's gone to the shops with her mammy. I want to go too.'

'I won't be long. Let me finish,' I said, rinsing the floorcloth out in my bucket.

She kicked the back door. 'I want to go now,' she shouted.

'Don't wake him.'

She disappeared up the garden. Paul let out a loud scream. Debbie popped her head around the back door. 'He's awake now. Can we go?'

I sent the floorcloth flying towards her. She scarpered around the side entrance to the front of the house. I propped Paul up in the pram and stuffed a rusk in his hand.

A few minutes later, three hard knocks banged off the hall door. *Jesus, if that's her, I'll murder her. She has me heart scalded.*

Down the hall I marched and whipped the door open. A well-groomed, grey-haired lady stood back.

'Excuse me,' she said politely. 'I'm Mrs Stewart, your neighbour. Your dear little girl with the plaits is up the road talking to builders. You should not let her.'

I tore up the road, grabbed hold of Debbie's hand and ran her home. 'Stay in there,' I said, throwing her down on a chair. 'Let me wash me face an' comb me hair, then we'll go to the shops.'

Off to the shops on Leagrave Road we dawdled, Paul sitting up in the pram, Debbie trotting beside me. Dying for a chat with someone, I gazed around. Not a neighbour to be seen. The houses were quiet and private, their dusty windows draped in heavy curtains. Nobody looking out.

'Mind the pram,' I said to Debbie outside the grocer's. 'I have to go in here.'

I took my place behind a queue of women holding baskets. They looked immaculate, dressed in their best Sunday coats, hair neatly tucked under tiny smart hats. They waited patiently to be served. This was new to me. I was used to Dublin where you didn't queue. You pushed your way to the counter and called out what you wanted.

I tightened the scarf on my head and buttoned my coat. 'It's a terrible long queue, isn't it?' I said, turning to the lady behind me.

She smiled then faced the front again. A shopkeeper, not a speck of dirt on his brown wrap-around coat, was weighing vegetables on his scales.

'Yes, Madam?' he said, when it finally came to my turn.

'Can I have five potatoes, two carrots an' one onion, please?'

'We only sell them by the pound, Madam.'

'I always bought them loose in Dublin.'

'Sorry, only by the pound.'

'How many potatoes in a pound,' I said, opening my purse.

He threw a pile on his scales and emptied them into a bag.

'Can you put some more in, please?' I said, counting them.

He threw another couple in, weighed them, flicked the bag over a couple of times, twisted the corners and rung up his till.

Next it was the hardware for pegs. I had a pile of washing to hang out.

'I want to come in,' Debbie shouted, as I put the pram brake on outside the shop.

'No, stay there with Paul. Mind him. I won't be long.'

A minute later, I was out with a cardboard strip of pegs. Debbie was rocking the pram, trying to stop Paul from crying. I handed him the pegs to play with.

Now for the butchers. Debbie squeezed in the door behind me. The butcher busied himself arranging his meat on trays. Not a spot of blood on his white-starched coat and apron, fresh sawdust spread evenly on his floor. While I was waiting to be served, Debbie bent down and gathered the sawdust up into little piles. The butcher glared down at her. I gave her a dig to stop. She went running out with a handful of his sawdust.

'Can I have a piece of silverside, please?' I asked.

'Do you mean beef?'

'No, I want corned beef.'

The butcher pointed to rolls of beef in the window. 'You mean beef or pork for roasting?'

'Beef soaked in brine, corned beef,' I said, hoping he had some out the back in a bucket.

'I don't have any.'

'How come I could get it in Dublin?'

'This is not Dublin.' He turned to serve the woman behind me.

'I'll have a pound of stewin' steak then, please.'

While he chopped up the meat, I kept an eye out the window. Mothers were crowding round my pram, admiring Paul. Debbie darted in and tugged the bottom of my coat. 'Mammy, Paul's crying; his finger's hurting.'

I paid the butcher, took the meat and shot out. The mothers parted each side, making way for me. Paul held up his finger, sobbing.

'He has a peg on his dear little finger,' one of the women said.

I undid the peg, rubbed his finger better, then stuffed the cardboard strip into my pram bag. All the women moved off, except one.

'Promise me,' she said, coming close to my face, tears in her eyes, 'that you will *never* give your baby pegs to play with again.'

Ashamed of my life, my face burning, I snatched Debbie's hand and rushed away. I missed my turn into Limbury Road and ended up lost.

'A park,' Debbie said, galloping through two big iron gates.

I raced after her and couldn't believe my eyes. A red merry-go-round, a yellow see-saw, and brand-new swings were waiting for children. But there was only one little girl to be seen. Her mother stood close by, watching her.

'Will you be me friend?' Debbie said, swinging beside the girl.

The pair of them jumped off the swings, spun on the merry-go-round and climbed onto the see-saw.

'It's a lovely park, isn't it?' I said to the mother.

She nodded.

'In Dublin, this park would have been swamped by children fightin' to get on the swings day an' night.'

She smiled and called her little girl. 'Emily. Emily. We have to go.'

Emily ran up. 'Mummy, I need to go to the toilet,' she said, holding her behind.

Emily's mother threw a look at her daughter. 'Did you make a rude noise, Emily? Say excuse me in front of this lady,' she said, gripping her hand.

'Excuse me,' Emily said, looking up at me.

I stood, smiling after them, thinking how different Emily was from Cissie back in Cabra. Cissie wouldn't have said 'excuse me', that's for sure. And she certainly wouldn't have said 'rude noise' either.

Paul began to suck the corner of the pram cover.

'Come on, Debbie. We'd better find our way home before he starts.'

'One more swing.'

'Now,' I said, glancing back at the empty park. 'We'll come tomorrow.'

She ran up behind me. 'This is my swing park, isn't it?' she said.

'It might as well be. No one else wants it.'

Sylvia opened the hall door. She was smiling. She had a job in Skefko, a ball-bearing factory in Luton.

Over the stew that night, Paddy and Chris fell over the place laughing when I told them about Debbie talking to the builders, Paul pegging his finger and Emily excusing herself.

'I wish there were a few kids around here for Debbie to play with,' I said.

'The children don't play in the streets here, Lily. Yer not in Dublin now.'

Four Healthy Children, a Wringer and a Brand-New Fridge

'IN THIS COUNTRY,' Dr Hall said, 'our mothers only have their first in hospital. The rest are home births. A midwife will be around to see you. She'll deliver the baby.'

Dr Hall fixed his thick-rimmed glasses up on his nose and scribbled out a list.

'What if the midwife is out when I go into labour?'

'Don't worry, Mrs O'Connor. Here's an emergency list of seven. They won't all be out.'

The midwife, a tiny woman with tired eyes, knocked on my door a few weeks later. She looked over the house and settled on the empty front room for me to have the baby in. 'Put a single bed in there,' she said. 'That will be fine.' Without another word, she was gone.

That sounds easy, I thought, closing the hall door.

Over the months, Sylvia and Chris fell in love and married. They stayed on with us to save up for their own place. Annie wrote to me from Dublin to say she was missing us terribly and was coming over to Luton with her Paddy and their two little boys, Roddy and Gordon. I found her a flat to rent at the end of our road.

One afternoon in May, Sylvia was in the scullery preparing a stew for Chris. Paul was digging holes all over the garden with his new spade. Debbie was playing with Annie's little boys. And I was showing off my new wringer to Annie outside the back door. She couldn't take her eyes off it.

'Where did Paddy buy it?' she asked.

'In the hardware. Only ten bob. I don't know meself being able to wring out the blankets. We couldn't afford a washin' machine, but listen till I tell you. We're savin' up for a fridge. The milk keeps goin' off.'

'I'd love a wringer,' she said, turning its big iron handle.

I whipped the soaking wet floorcloth out of my bucket and gave Annie a demonstration. She watched as I turned the wringer's handle. Its two white rollers squeezed every drop of water out of my cloth.

'God, that's great,' she said. 'It's nearly dry.'

I collapsed the heavy rollers and pulled up its enamelled table top. 'The table's great for me bucket,' I said, gripping my stomach.

'Are you all right, Lily?'

'I t'ink you'd better ring the midwife. The pains have got worse. There's a phone box down the road.'

She threw her coat on and fled out with my midwife's number and my emergency list of seven. I made my way down to the front room and struggled to make up the single bed. *T'ank God I got Paddy to carry the bed down last night.*

Annie's face was white when she returned. 'I've rung every one of them, Lily. They're all out. What'll I do?'

'Get the doctor.'

Off she dashed while I searched for a rubber sheet.

A car screeched up outside. Dr Hall's lanky legs galloped in with Annie. He put down his bag, took off his jacket and examined me. 'Get undressed,' he said. 'The baby's coming. I need plenty of boiling water.'

He rolled up his sleeves and charged down the hall to the scullery. I heard him shouting to Sylvia. 'Get that dinner off. I need boiling water.'

Annie slipped into my room. She grabbed my rubber sheet and struggled to put it under me. The doctor appeared. 'Too late for that,' he snapped, flinging the sheet across the room. 'I need a scrubbing brush.'

'Where's your scrubbin' brush, Lily?' Annie said.

'Outside in me bucket.'

She raced off and was back in a second and handed my brush full of fluff to the doctor.

'Not a scrubbing brush for the floor,' he yelled. 'I want a scrubbing brush for my nails.' He dashed out for more water. 'Who keeps putting that dinner back on?' I heard him roar.

The perspiration poured off me. The doctor reappeared, bent down, fixed his glasses up tight on his nose and gently guided Bryan out.

'You have a healthy boy,' he said, standing up.

Without another word, he took the baby over to the window and held him up to the light for ages, as if this birth was a miracle. Then he wrapped him up and laid him in my pram.

'Didn't the midwife give you a list of instructions for the birth?' he said, stitching me.

'No, she told me nuttin'.'

He packed his bag and left. Annie brought me in a cup of tea. We laughed about the scrubbing brush and the missing midwives.

'Just imagine, Lily, dey were all out. You were very lucky I caught the doctor just in time. He was in his driveway about to go shoppin' with his wife. I was beginnin' to t'ink I'd have to deliver it meself.'

'I'm glad that's over,' I said, sipping my cup of tea. I put the cup down just as quick. 'Annie, look! There's two spoons in me saucer. That means I'll be havin' another one next year.'

Annie burst out laughing. 'Well, you can't say you're not gettin' great wear out of that pram,' she said, looking over at it.

Sure enough, one year later, I was having my fourth. This time, no trouble. A different midwife, plenty of boiling water and a brand-new nail brush. The songs of *Housewife's Choice* sailed up to my bedroom while Steven was being born.

'Your wife and baby are fine, Mr O'Connor,' the midwife said, when Paddy looked in. 'Not a stitch or anything. He's a lovely big boy.'

The midwife packed her bag, trotted down the stairs and saw herself out. Paddy sat on the side of the bed. 'God, we're doin' great, Lily, all the same, aren't we? We've four healthy children, a wringer and a brand-new fridge. What more could we want?'

HOMESICK

'WE CAN'T TAKE Debra this year,' the headsister of St Joseph's said. 'They have to be five before September.'

'But she's ready for school,' I said, praying to God she'd take her. 'She's five in October.'

'I'm sorry, Mrs O'Connor. That's school policy.'

She looked at Debbie sucking her plaits, Paul whining, clinging to my legs, Bryan bouncing on the floor and Steven, the new baby, wriggling on my lap. She examined her book again.

'Seeing as you have four under five,' she said, 'we will make an exception and take Debra this September.'

'T'anks very much, Sister. That's great.'

She glanced up and smiled. 'How long have you been in England?'

'Two years. I miss Dublin. Everyone here keeps to themselves. Back home, if you went to the shops, you'd always meet someone. People talk to you in Dublin, even if they don't know you.'

The headsister wasn't interested. She closed her book and jumped up. 'We'll see Debra in September,' she said, walking me to the door.

Gathering them all up, I dawdled out and tucked Steven up in the pram.

I was missing Annie. She and her Paddy had moved out of Luton to a new house in Basildon, near the sea. 'Luton's very old an' full of factories,' she'd said, packing up. 'An' the lime in the water has destroyed me good kettle with thick chalk.'

I didn't see much of Sylvia either since she and Chris had moved out. She was flat out looking after David, her baby. Never a moment for a cup of tea or a chat.

I fell into a routine that summer. It was messages in the mornings, Debbie's park in the afternoons. At night, when they were all in bed, the mountains of nappies and rompers were washed, wrung out and hung on the line.

At last, it was September. The first day of school. Debbie held my hand, singing to herself all the way to St Joseph's, her new school bag swinging off her shoulder. As soon as we entered the classroom, she claimed a desk, took out her pencils and paper, and began writing her name.

Other children were dragged in, sobbing. I lingered, wishing Debbie would cry so I could talk to the other mothers. But she was glad to get rid of me.

'Go!' she said, waving me goodbye.

Each day was the same. I dropped Debbie off to school in the morning, her dress clean and fresh, then picked her up for lunch, her dress filthy dirty. After a sandwich, I scrubbed her face, redid her plaits, changed her dress and galloped her back to school till three-thirty.

The weeks went by and it was Debbie's birthday. I stood outside the school gates at home time, waiting for her. The headsister was busily talking to mothers picking up their children in the playground. Dying for a chat, I wheeled my pram up to her.

'Hello,' she said, bending down to Paul. 'And what's your name, young man?'

Paul was lost in his own world as usual, his tongue out, curved up, touching his nose.

I nudged him. 'Tell Sister your name.'

'Faul O'Tonnor,' he muttered.

'Paul,' I said. 'He means Paul. He can't pronounce "p".'

She patted his head. 'I like your red dicky bow. Where are you going all dressed up?'

'I'm goin' to a farty.'

'He means party,' I said, grabbing his hand. 'It's Debra's birthday. I've bought ice cream an' wafers, an' set a bowl of strawberry jelly for her.'

Sister moved on to the next mother. I tore out the gate, Debbie skipping behind me.

'Right,' I said to Paul, dragging him along. 'It's off to the doctor with you, I can tell you. You're makin' a show of me.'

I marched him into the surgery the very next morning. 'He's three an' not talkin',' I said, pushing Paul forward.

'What's your name, young man?' the doctor said, bending down.

'Faul O'Tonnor.'

The doctor picked up a torch-like instrument from a shelf, pulled Paul towards him and peered into his ears.

'Mama! Mama! Mama!'

'He can say Mama all right. He's no trouble with that.'

Paul shot back to me like a stone out of a sling.

'He's a lazy talker. Make him pronounce his words,' he said, writing up my file. 'Anything else worrying you?'

I pointed to Bryan, bouncing around on the floor. 'Could you look at him? He won't walk.'

'How old is he?'

'Sixteen months.'

'He's a lazy walker.'

As I was leaving, I looked back at the doctor. 'Can I have an iron tonic, please?'

'Why do you need an iron tonic?'

'I have a pain in me side.'

He pulled back a curtain. 'Up on the couch. I'll examine you.'

My stomach was pressed this way and that way. Then I sat up and he tapped my back. 'Big breath, please. Good.' After a few more tests, he whipped his stethoscope off and strode back to his desk.

I climbed down from the couch and sat opposite him.

'I can't find anything physically wrong with you, Mrs O'Connor,' he said, leaning back in his chair. He clasped a hand under his chin and studied me through his glasses. 'You seem lonely.'

That was it. A door inside me opened. 'I am lonely. I miss talkin' to someone. No one talks to you here, not even the butcher or the dustmen. Back home in Dublin, everyone talks to you.'

I went on and on. He tried to interrupt me several times, but for the life of me, I couldn't stop talking.

'*Please* let me speak,' he said, putting his hand up.

My face burned with embarrassment.

'You're homesick,' he said. 'Tell your husband you need a holiday. It's the best tonic on earth.'

Paddy heard all about it in bed that night. 'We can't afford a holiday, Lily. Not until we finish wit' dat moneylender.'

'Do you t'ink she'd mind if I postponed her payment for two weeks?' I said, putting my cold feet on his hot ones.

'No harm in askin' her. Write her a letter. Tell her what the doctor said, dat ya need a holiday.'

THE MONEYLENDER'S SON

'DOES A PADDY O'Connor live here?' a young fella asked, when I opened the hall door.

'I'll get him.'

Paddy raced down the hall and looked over my shoulder.

The fella's face lit up. 'Hello, Paddy, I'm Matt. Me ma loaned ya money. She knows yer mother.'

'C'mon in, Matt.'

Matt picked up his case and a wet paper parcel and followed us down the hall. I hurried ahead and made a clean sweep of everything. I pushed the clothes horse of nappies and the basket of ironing out of the way, then bent down and scooped up Paul and Bryan's millions of bricks and threw them into a box.

'The ma told me t'give ya dat,' Matt said, handing Paddy a parcel.

Paddy unwrapped the wet paper. 'Corned beef,' he said, sniffing it with delight. 'Tell yer mudder t'anks very much, Matt.' He passed it to me.

'You're very good carryin' that big lump of meat all the way over,' I said, staring at it. 'Would you like a cup a' tea?'

'I'd love a cup, Missus, t'anks.'

'How was yer trip, Matt?' Paddy said, clearing a chair.

'Rough.'

'Are ya after work?'

'Dere's nuttin' in Dublin.'

'Ya'll get work in Vauxhall. All the Irish work dere.'

I stepped down into the scullery and put on the kettle. *I won't have to buy any meat now for Sunday*, I thought, rubbing the bits of paper off the corned beef under the tap. A loud scream came from behind. Debbie jumped down after me. 'Paul's broken me crayons again.'

'No, I didn't,' Paul said, climbing down. 'Bryan's eating them.'

'When are we goin' to my park?' Debbie said, opening the back door.

'Soon,' I said, drying my hands. 'Now go out an' play, you two. An' don't wake up Steven. He's asleep in the pram.'

I put the lump of meat onto a plate and shoved it into the cold oven. Paddy came down into the scullery for Matt's cup of tea.

'Do you know him?' I whispered.

'He's the moneylender's son.'

He shovelled three heaped teaspoons of tea into our big teapot.

'She's very good sendin' us the corned beef, isn't she?' I said, rinsing out cups.

'She didn't send dat for the love of us, Lily. She wants me to put her son up.'

'Put him up? We've no room. No beds. Where would he sleep?'

'He'll sleep on the two fireside chairs in the kitchen. He won't mind. One more won't make any difference.'

'I can't manage any more,' I snapped, throwing the plates in the sink of sudsy water. 'We've never been on our own. Never.'

He pulled the scullery door over. 'Quiet, Matt'll hear ya.'

'That's what I mean. I couldn't talk to you in front of Sylvia an' Chris. In bed, you're too tired to talk to. Now, you're bringin' another one in.'

'Right,' he said. 'I'll find him lodgings in Downs Road. But his mother's not goin' to like it. Ya can forget dat holiday.'

Paddy was right. Matt's mother didn't like it. She wouldn't let me postpone one week of her money. There was no holiday for Lily that year.

STOP THE BUS, PADDY WANTS TO WEE-WEE

'ETHEL FROM WORK has invited us to the British Legion Club tomorra',' Paddy said one Friday night. 'It's just around the corner on Leagrave Road. We won't stay long. It'll do ya the world a' good to get out.'

'I'm not leavin' them on their own. We've no babysitter. We've no one to ask.'

'Just for an hour. We won't go till they're fast asleep. We'll take Steven wit' us in the pram. Dey'll be all right. Dey never wake.'

Paddy did everything for me that Saturday. He cleared the table, washed up, hung out the nappies and went for the messages.

I raced into the bathroom and filled up the basin to wash my hair. The shampoo bottle was empty, so I grabbed the Tide washing powder, shook some on my hand and rubbed it into my wet hair. My hair went sticky and hard. I was sorry the minute I did it. It was murder trying to wash the Tide out.

'Yer hair'll be fine,' Paddy said, unpacking the shopping.

'Can we go to my park, Mammy?' Debbie begged. 'You promised.'

'I can't. My hair's wet.'

'I'll take dem,' Paddy said. 'I'll tire dem out.'

A few hours later, they all traipsed in, jaded tired, starving for tea. Paddy bathed and fed them, and had them in bed and fast asleep by seven. I searched our wardrobe for something decent to wear.

'Hurry up, Lily,' he said quietly, dressing up in his best suit.

I found a jumper and skirt that still fitted me and laid them on the bed. Down to the bathroom I ran, stripped off and looked in the mirror. *What the hell will I do with my hair? It's like straw, dull, dry and lifeless.* The comb wouldn't go through it. I gave up, had a quick wash and flew out of the bathroom in my bra and knickers to dress upstairs. Two complete strangers faced me in the kitchen. They smiled and nodded.

I folded my arms in front and stormed down the hall. 'I'll murder Paddy for not tellin' me they were callin' in first. I'll kill him.'

He raced up the stairs after me. 'Are ya nearly ready?' he whispered, coming into the bedroom. 'Ethel an' Fred are waitin' downstairs.'

'God, Paddy, you're awful. You didn't tell me they were callin' for us.'

'Ethel has to sign us in. Don't worry. Ya made Fred's day.'

On went the old skirt and the last bit of lipstick, and down the stairs I trotted. Ethel was peeping in the pram at Steven.

'I could run away with your baby,' she said, turning around. She looked immaculate, not a hair out of place, back brushed and well lacquered. And not a crease in her pale blue summer coat, nor a speck of dirt on her brown high heels.

Fred stood up and held out his hand, his gold cufflinks peeping out from under his navy-blue blazer. 'Nice to meet you, Lily,' he said. 'You'll like the club.'

'I don't like leavin' them on their own,' I said, bending down to turn off the oil fire.

'Leave it on,' Paddy said. 'It'll be nice an' warm when we get back.'

'Turn it off,' Ethel said, grabbing her gold-clasped handbag. 'The papers are full of houses being burned down by oil fires.'

Paddy and Ethel, linking and laughing, marched in front along Leagrave Road towards the club. Fred, a quiet Englishman, walked beside me, smiling at me, then at the pram.

The doorman of the club held up his hand. 'Sorry, love, no prams. Don't want people falling over.'

'We'll sit at the back,' Paddy said, grabbing the handle and wheeling it in.

I was disappointed. I couldn't see a sign of the band and could barely hear them. The smoke sailed over the millions of tables. Couples, drinking and laughing, were having a grand time.

I sipped my bitter-lemon drink. Paddy lowered his ale. Ethel caught his sleeve. 'What do you get up to down the cellar with Mona?' she said, teasing him.

'Nuttin',' Paddy laughed. 'The girl's nuts.'

'I see lipstick on your face when you come up.'

'Who's Mona?' I asked.

'Ah, dat girl I told ya about. The one who wears the big brown rosary beads. She t'inks it's a necklace.'

Ethel grabbed his sleeve again. 'It's the factory's excursion next Saturday, Paddy. We're going to Clacton.'

'It's a smashing day,' Fred said. 'Plenty of free drink on the coach. You have to come.'

A slow waltz began. Couples pushed their way to the floor. Paddy tapped the table and sang along with the band. Steven began crying. The doorman of the club glared at me.

'I'm goin',' I said. 'I'm worried about the others on their own. One of them could be cryin'.'

'Ya don't mind if I stay, do ya? I won't be long.'

I raced home, bouncing the pram up and down kerbs, worried sick. Did I turn that oil heater off or not? Up Limbury Road I sped and dragged open our gate. The house was deathly quiet.

Thank God everything's all right, I thought, inching the pram in.

After I'd checked the other three, I gave Steven his bottle, changed him and put him in his cot, then fell into bed. It wasn't long before I heard the stairs creak and our bedroom door open.

'Did ya enjoy yerself?' Paddy whispered, slipping in beside me.

'I'm not leavin' them on their own any more. Bryan's still only a baby. He could've woke up cryin', wakin' the others. Debbie would've run outside looking for us.'

No more was said about the club or the excursion for the rest of the week.

'I'm goin' to Clacton,' Paddy said Friday night, making himself a sausage sandwich. 'The boss expects us all to go. It'll look bad if I don't.'

I said nothing. He washed up and wiped down the high chair, and even swept up the crumbs around it.

Saturday morning, he was up early. 'I'd better run, love,' he said, kissing me goodbye. 'The coach is outside.'

The coach dropped him home late that night. No mass for Paddy Sunday morning.

'How was it?' I said, when he finally sauntered down.

'Ya missed nuttin', Lily,' he said, knocking back a few aspirins. 'Ya missed nuttin'.'

'What did you do?'

'We were in the coach all the time.'

The week went by. Saturday evening came, and so did Ethel and Fred.

'I'm not goin' to the club, Paddy,' I said. 'I'm not leavin' them on their own again.'

'Ya don't mind if I go for an hour, d'ya?' he said, flying up the stairs to get dressed.

Ethel sat down beside me while Fred stood smiling.

'Did Paddy tell you about Clacton last week, Lily?' she said. 'It was ever so funny. Mona sat beside him on the coach. Every time he stood up, she sang out, "Stop the bus, Paddy wants to wee-wee. Stop the bus, Paddy wants to wee-wee."'

I Didn't Need Much Encouragement

'How would ya like to live in Torquay?' Paddy said, walking in the door one night.

'Torquay? What do you mean Torquay?'

'Dere's a job goin' down dere wit' a house.'

'A house an' all?'

I didn't need much encouragement, I can tell you. The house in Limbury Road was the same as the day I walked into it: the front room still empty, the floorboards still bare and the house still crying out for a coat of paint.

Our house went straight on the market. It hadn't improved one penny in three years. We came away with just our deposit, the three hundred pounds. But thank God we'd finished with the moneylender.

The alarm clock rang and danced on the chair beside our bed the morning we were leaving. I ignored it and rolled over in bed. It was pitch dark and freezing, and I was dead to the world with all the packing. Paddy nudged me. 'Get up, Lily. Get up. It's five o'clock. We've a lot to do. We can't miss dat Cornwall train. You dress an' feed the kids. I'll take the beds down an' roll up the beddin' for the removalists.'

I wrapped the wet nappies and rompers in the rubber cot sheets, then stuffed them into Paddy's battered old case. Two tins of Heinz baby soup and Farley's Rusks with clean nappies were packed in my shopping bag. Paddy herded us all out, then dropped the hall-door key into my neighbour's letter box. Mrs Stewart was letting the removalists in.

We shivered in the cold frosty air on Leagrave Road. The six o'clock double-decker bus rumbled in. Paddy climbed on and shoved our case and pusher under the stairs. The conductor banged the bell and the bus began to move.

'Will ya hold on, for Christ's sake,' Paddy shouted. 'Dey're not on yet.'

The conductor hit the bell twice to stop. We clambered on. Grumpy-faced workers looked up from their papers.

'Dere's a seat, Lily. Beside dat man. Go an' squeeze in.'

The man moved his briefcase reluctantly. I sat with Steven on my lap, Bryan squatting down on the shopping bag at my feet.

'Hold the back of the seats,' I said to Debbie and Paul, as the bus swerved around corners.

We drew up sharp outside Luton Station. The workers pushed by and ran for their train. Over the station bridge and down to the draughty platform, we trailed behind them. We huddled together, saying nothing. Debbie skipped around the case, keeping warm. She was delighted with herself; we were going somewhere for once. I looked at Paul whimpering, his skinny little legs trembling. Why the hell hadn't I put his warm trousers on? Bryan's hands clung to my leg for dear life. Steven, all rugged up in my arms, was fast asleep.

The London train roared in.

'Quick, Lily. Ya have to push yer way on wit' the kids. I'll find youse after I put our t'ings into the luggage van.'

Holding Steven, I squeezed into a seat. I smiled over to the other three, squashed between workers, reassuring them. Paddy, standing in the corridor, lit up his last cigarette. It was drizzling rain when we arrived in London.

'In this taxi, quick,' Paddy said. 'I'll be happy once I get youse to the next station.'

The Cornwall train was waiting for us at Paddington.

'There's an empty compartment,' I said, as we hurried down the platform.

I put Steven and Bryan on opposite seats by the window, ready to be fed. Paul sat opposite Debbie by the door, swinging his legs, warm and happy.

'Breakfast is now available,' the conductor said, poking his head into our compartment.

'Give me those tins of baby soup, Lily,' Paddy said. 'I'll get him to heat dem up.'

Within a minute, he was back with my tins of Bone and Veg opened and hot. An elderly couple outside on the platform pointed into our window. They were laughing at me feeding Bryan and Steven like two little birds, shoving the spoon into one mouth then the other.

Paddy glanced at his watch. 'I won't be a minute, just gettin' cigarettes an' the paper,' he said, disappearing into the corridor.

The whistle went. We were off. The train puffed out beyond the platform. *Where the hell is he?*

'Here's Daddy,' Debbie said, peeping out the door and down the corridor.

Sure enough, in he came, smiling, with little bags of sweets and comics.

The faster the train sped, the more my heart lifted. I felt I was going on a holiday.

We were staying in a hotel for a week at the firm's expense. The house that came with the job wasn't ready. Sipping my hot cup of tea, I beamed over at Debbie and Paul who were happily munching the jam sandwiches that I had made up with the last of the bread.

The train finally pulled into Torquay. We stood waiting on the platform for Paddy to fetch our belongings from the luggage van. The cries of the gulls took me back to Dublin. I took a deep breath. It had been three years since I'd had a smell of the sea. I glanced up at the sun elbowing its way out through the clouds.

A taxi pulled up and beeped.

'Babbacombe Hotel,' Paddy said, hurrying us over.

Even though we were all in one room in the hotel, it was a godsend not having to do housework. I had never stayed in a hotel before. I could sit back, relax and enjoy the week. The boys didn't know themselves, rolling around on the hotel's thick carpet instead of bare floorboards. Debbie ran after the maids in and out of the rooms, persecuting them with questions. 'Why do you change the sheets every day? Have the people wet the bed again?'

LIVING BY THE SEA

'IT'S A HAPPY house, isn't it?' I said, pulling back the bright yellow curtains. 'The boss is very good lettin' us have it.'

'We're not gettin' the house for nuttin', Lily,' Paddy said, banging the arms of our chairs back in. 'He's stoppin' the rent out a' me wages, ya know.'

Outside the hall door, Steven was fast asleep in my high grey pram, knocked out from the warm sun and sea air. A high hedging of golden privet protected the front garden from the path outside. Double iron gates closed off the driveway.

I danced up the stairs and ran from room to room, marvelling at the wide modern windows. 'It's so sunny and cheery,' I sang out.

Paddy stomped up the red-carpeted stairs with his toolbox. 'I'd better put their beds up,' he said. 'Or dey'll have nowhere to sleep tonight.'

'Have you seen the back garden? It's full of big flowerin' shrubs an' small trees. Daffodils are peepin' up everywhere.'

'Where are the kids?' he said, glancing out the window.

'They're playin' out the back with the boxes the removalists left.'

'Well, I don't see dem.'

I ran down and out the back door. 'Debbie? Debbie? Where are youse?' I shouted, flying around to the front of the house.

The two iron gates were wide open. Not a sign of them. I galloped up the road and spotted an opening into a field. 'A park. This is where Debbie will be,' I said to myself, walking inside.

Sure enough, there she was, kicking a ball to Bryan. He was speeding after it towards the sea. The ball suddenly disappeared from view.

'Get back,' I screamed, sensing danger.

Debbie ran over. 'I found a lovely park, Mammy.'

'Where's Paul?' I said, trembling.

She pointed to the sea. I rushed over and nearly collapsed. Paul was sitting on the edge of a steep cliff, his skinny little legs dangling over the side.

'Jesus, Mary an' Joseph,' I cried, grabbing him up.

I couldn't believe it. No fence. No warning. No nothing. Just a sheer drop to rocks.

An elderly couple stood close by, enjoying the view out to sea. They smiled when they saw me snatch him up. 'We were getting a little worried about him, dear,' they said.

'You'd t'ink they'd have it fenced,' I said, holding on to him.

'Oh no, no, no. That would spoil the natural beauty of Torquay. This is a scenic lookout.'

I gripped Debbie's hand hard. 'Don't you ever come up here again without me,' I said, shaking her. 'Do you *hear* me?'

I chased the three of them home.

'God, Paddy, I could have murdered her. They could have fallen over those cliffs.'

'It's not my fault,' Debbie cried, rubbing her eyes. 'They ran out the gate after me.'

'She couldn't see the danger, Lily,' Paddy said, picking her up. 'Ya can't put an old head on young shoulders. Dat's what me mudder always said.'

The very next morning, I marched Debbie off to the nearest Catholic school.

'We'd be pleased to have Debra,' the elderly headsister said. 'We have plenty of places. She can start tomorrow.'

'Great, I'll get her here as quick as I can in the mornin'.'

Sister flicked through her book. 'One of our senior girls lives close to you,' she said, looking up. 'I'll arrange for her to collect Debra in the mornings and take her home in the afternoons.'

'T'anks very much, that's grand,' I said, hurrying out with them all.

Off we strolled to the few little old-fashioned shops for the messages. Everywhere I looked, men were hanging out of ladders, painting up B&Bs, guesthouses and hotels for the summer. Colourful buckets and spades dangled from shop doors and windows. Gardeners whistled happily as they trimmed their hedges and mowed their lawns. The trees were budding and the roads were spotless. With a pram-bag full of shopping, I rambled home to get their lunch.

'I can't wait for the summer,' I said to myself, opening the hall door. 'I'll take them to the seaside every day.'

A letter lay on the mat in the hall. I picked it up. It was from the local council.

ATTENTION:
The hedging of this property is overgrown and
encroaching on the pathway. If it is not trimmed before
Easter, the council will cut it and you will be billed.

Paddy gave out hell that evening. 'The cheek a' dem,' he said, throwing the letter in the bin. 'Just forget it, Lily.'

'I'll cut the hedgin',' I said, washing up. 'T'ank God I brought my shears with me from Cabra West.'

Paddy threw down the tea towel. 'The rich retire down here wit' nuttin' better to do.'

The boys were in bed early that night. Out the back door I went with Debbie and resurrected my shears from under the coal in the shed. Paddy walked out after me with my butter dish. 'Here, give me those old shears; dey're rusty,' he said, plastering the blades with butter.

He stood smoking, watching me clipping away. 'Dey wouldn't get away wit' dat in Luton, Lily. Just imagine worryin' about a bit a' hedgin' stickin' out of yer garden.'

'I'm glad they're proud of their town,' I said. 'I love living by the sea, even though I've only had a smell of it.'

Debbie threw down the bits of hedging and looked up. 'When are we going to the seaside, Daddy?'

'We'll go next Monday. It's Easter. I'll be off work.'

I opened the curtains Easter Monday. The sun streamed in the window, lighting up the whole kitchen. Paddy gave them their Farex while I made up a few sandwiches with the leftover chicken.

'C'mon,' he said, sitting Bryan in the pram beside Steven. 'We'll walk down to Babbacombe Cove. I'll buy dem buckets an' spades on the way.'

I wheeled the pram outside and pulled up its canopy to shade the pair of them from the hot midday sun. Paddy grabbed the handle and pushed it up and down those steep Babbacombe hills. Debbie and Paul skipped along, swinging their shiny new buckets and spades. In no time at all, we were looking down at Babbacombe Cove and the sea. Our faces dropped.

'My God, it's black with people,' I said, lifting Bryan out of the pram.

'You take the handle, Lily. I'll hold the back.'

We struggled with the pram down the narrow path to the Cove. The other three trailed behind, Debbie holding Bryan's hand, Paul clutching his bucket and spade for dear life.

'Don't move, any of you,' Paddy said firmly when we reached the bottom. 'I'll find a space.'

He picked his way along the sea edge in search of a vacant spot. I gazed around at the couples dozing on deckchairs, newspapers on heads, boxes of sweets on laps, and flasks of tea beside them.

'C'mon, quick,' Paddy said, grabbing the pram. 'I've got a good spot. Me jacket's on it. I'll hire out a deckchair for ya.'

Debbie stripped off and changed into her new seersucker bathing suit.

'I want to go into the sea,' she pleaded.

'Wait till we're settled,' I said, stuffing her clothes in the pram.

'I'm hungry,' Bryan moaned.

The sandwiches came out, and every crumb was eaten. The diluted baby orange juice was passed around in plastic beakers and drained. Steven, still in the pram, devoured his tin of baby soup then fell asleep, holding on to his bucket of pebbles. Debbie ran out to the lapping waves. Paddy, shoes off, trousers rolled up, hobbled on the pebbles after her. Bryan sat happily dropping pebbles in and out of his bucket. Paul dug like mad with his spade, frantically searching for a bit of sand. I sat back in the deckchair and relaxed in the sun. 'T'ank God we came here. The sea air will do them the world of good.'

PADDY THE MAGICIAN

'I'LL HAVE TO dip into the deposit money,' I said to Paddy one morning. 'Debbie needs a new jumper, an' your wages are all gone.'

'Don't do dat, for God's sake, Lily. We'll be goin' backwards,' he said, pulling on his jacket. 'I'll speak to the boss today. He owes me a rise.'

That night, Paddy opened his coat and pulled out a child's red woollen jumper. 'Would dat fit Debbie?' he said.

'God, it's lovely. It's brand new. Where did you get it?'

'The mean bugger wouldn't give me a rise, so I took it. I've never robbed a boss in me life but now I have to. He's not payin' me what he promised.'

'Oh God, Paddy, don't start takin' t'ings.'

'He has me over a barrel. Dere's no work down here an' he knows it. Dey're all robbin' him. Don't worry about it.'

As the days passed, more and more woollens appeared from under Paddy's jacket. By the end of the week, the children were dressed up to the nines in new red cardigans, jumpers, hats and leggings to match.

'Oh God, Paddy, I wish you wouldn't,' I'd whisper each time he opened his coat and did his magician's trick.

'We can't touch dat deposit money. He won't pay me what I'm worth.'

I looked down at my new green woollen cardigan. 'Jesus, Paddy, I'm even wearin' one of his.'

'Give us a shout when me tea is ready,' he said, laughing. 'I'll be in the front room readin' the paper.'

Saturday morning I went out for my messages and strolled into a bread shop, proud of them all in their brand-new woollens. Debbie pointed to plates of colourful iced cakes displayed in a glass case under the counter. 'Will you buy some of those, Mammy, please? You never buy cakes,' she begged, pulling out of my cardigan. 'Please, Mammy, buy some.'

'Quiet,' I said, embarassed in front of the other customers.

A tall, well-groomed lady standing in the queue whispered something to the shop assistant. A bag of small iced cakes was passed down to Debbie.

'It's just a little present,' the lady said, smiling.

I thanked her, paid for my bread and pushed Paul and Bryan out before they started. Debbie skipped after me clutching her bag of cakes.

Paddy heard all about the cakes the minute we walked in.

'Mammy never buys us any,' Debbie said. 'So a lady in the shop did.'

'What's she on about?' Paddy said, closing the hall door. 'What lady?'

'Go an' play outside in the garden, Debbie.'

Paddy whipped out the chair and sat down. 'So other people are buyin' us cakes now, are dey?'

'I know,' I said, taking down two cups. 'I could have peacefully strangled her.'

'I should be able to give ya more money. Dat bugger's under-payin' me.'

'It won't do them any harm not havin' cakes or biscuits.'

He picked up his paper and sauntered off into the front room. He was back in a flash. 'Dere's a weekend job advertised in the paper. I'm goin' after it.'

'What is it?' I said, spreading jam on their bread for lunch.

'A photographer wants an assistant.' He slipped on his jacket and was out the door heading for the nearest phone box. Within minutes he was back.

'I start tonight. He's pickin' me up.'

'What will you be doin'?'

'He's loanin' me a camera to take pictures.'

'But you've never takin' any photos.'

'He doesn't know dat, does he?' he laughed, sticking on the kettle. 'Would ya like another cup a' tea? I've bought a few fig rolls.'

PADDY THE PHOTOGRAPHER

I WATCHED PADDY straightening his tie. 'You're wearin' your good suit?' I said. 'I wish I was goin'.'

'I'm not goin' out to enjoy meself,' he said, pressing his hair into a quiff. 'I'm goin' out to earn money.'

A car beeped outside.

'Dere's the photographer. Bye, love. Shouldn't be late.'

Four hours later, I heard a car pull into our driveway. Our hall door opened and closed, and Paddy raced up the stairs.

'What was it like?' I said.

'It's easy money. Walkin' around dance halls, takin' photos of couples sittin' at tables.' He emptied his pockets and dropped a bundle of change on the bed.

I sat up straight and counted it. 'Thirty bob. That's great. I can get the week's shoppin' with that.'

He switched the light off and climbed into bed.

'What was the band like?'

'I didn't notice,' he said, yawning.

'Will you be goin' every Saturday?'

'An' Sunday.'

'Sunday as well?'

'He wants me wit' him in Newton Abbott. If ya want to live here, Lily, I have to work weekends as well.'

Summer arrived in Torquay. Paddy was in a great mood, dressing up and going out weekends. The photography business was thriving. I invited my sisters and their families down for their holidays.

Annie and her Paddy, and their two little boys, were first. We struggled down to Babbacombe Cove every day with all the kids for a picnic.

'Oh, Lily, it's beautiful here,' Annie said, looking around at the cliffs and sea.

'I know. I just wish Paddy's job paid more. Everyt'in' here is so expensive.'

The week flew by, and soon they were packing.

Sylvia and Chris were next. They trained it down with their little boy, David. The weather dropped and they were freezing. But Paddy the magician was back. New woollens appeared from under his jacket for the three of them.

'What's the band like?' Chris said, watching Paddy dress up Saturday night.

'Dey play the latest tunes. Why don't youse come? Yer on yer holidays. Might as well enjoy yerselves.'

Sylvia and Chris looked at each other.

'Dere's plenty of room in the photographer's car. Lily'll look after David.'

They ran upstairs and changed.

Sunday morning over breakfast, Sylvia joked with Paddy about the previous night.

'He doesn't be takin' photographs all the time, you know, Lily,' she said. 'He asks girls up to dance as well. It's a pity you can't go.'

T'ink of Torquay as a Holiday

'THE DANCE HALLS were empty tonight,' Paddy said, throwing a few bob on the bed. 'The season's finished.'

'Ah well, you got a good run out of it. It helped us over the summer.'

The months slipped by. It was harder and harder to make ends meet. I missed the photo money terribly.

Christmas week, Paddy handed me his pay packet. 'All the overtime I did for dat stingy bugger an' the miserable git didn't even give me a Christmas bonus.'

'We'll manage.'

It was a quiet Christmas. No turkey or the O'Connor sing-song.

'Why is he limpin'?' Paddy said, watching Bryan chasing Debbie down the hall.

'It's his shoes. I got them cheap in a sale.'

He stabbed out his cigarette.

'Throw dem in the bin, Lily. We can't stay here.'

He was right. The deposit money was going, and he couldn't keep robbing woollens from work. That couldn't go on.

One night in the New Year, Paddy burst through the door. 'Dere's a job in the paper. Dey're lookin' for a knitwear mechanic. I've rung dem.'

'Where?'

'Luton. Dey want to see me tomorra'.'

'Back to Luton?'

I had to sit down.

'At least I know Luton,' Paddy said.

He ran round the room, tidying up the children's toys. He stopped and looked over at me.

'T'ink of Torquay as a long holiday, Lily. Eighteen months ya've had down here. It's been a great break for ya.'

The following morning, he was on the first train up to London, and he got the last train back that night.

'Did ya keep me a bit a' dinner?' he said, walking in. 'I'm starvin'.'

'What happened? Did you get the job?'

'He wants me immediately. He's payin' all movin' expenses. Wages are twice as much. I can buy ya dat twin-tub washin' machine ya have yer eye on. Ya won't know yerself not havin' to wash everyt'in' in the sink wit' yer bare hands.'

The pork sausages were pricked and rolled on the pan with a scoop of dripping. I mashed the leftover potatoes and turnip with a lump of butter, and fried it on the pan to give it a brown crispy skin, the way he liked it.

'Did you see Sylvia?' I asked, sitting down.

'She's expectin' again an' delighted ya're comin' back. Dey're all in Luton now. Liz an' her gang. Frank an' his family. An' Phil an' Mike have a lovely flat near the station.'

'God, they're all comin' over.'

'I've somet'in' else to tell ya,' he said, buttering his bread. 'I found a great house for two and a half thousand pounds. Hope to God ya still have dat deposit money.'

'I wanted to see this house, Paddy, before we put down a deposit.'

'Wait till I show ya,' he said, digging his hand into his coat pocket. 'The agent gave me a picture of it. It's a great house on a hill wit' big bay windows overlookin' Luton. Sylvia t'inks it's like a doctor's house. Ya're only two doors away from her.'

'Is it close to the shops?'

'Ya can walk into Luton in ten minutes.'

'What about the schools?'

'Dere's a new Catholic one up the road, St Margaret of Scotland.'

'When do we have to go?'

'As soon as possible. I'll have great pleasure tellin' dat awl bugger tommora' to stick his job an' his house.'

Within a month, we were all packed up and ready for Luton. The removalists knocked on the door at seven in the morning. Debbie sped out, skipping behind them. 'We're moving to Luton,' she told them.

'Are you joining the Luton Girls' Choir?' one said, pulling her plaits playfully.

I ran around the garden, gathering up their buckets and

spades. Then, after a march to the toilet, they were ordered to stand at the gate and wait. The key to the house was left on the draining board. The door banged behind us.

'T'ank God they're all trained,' I said. 'I don't have to worry about nappies.'

'T'ank God dey're all walkin',' Paddy added. 'I don't have to worry about prams.'

Get Rid of Dat Pram

MRS O'CONNOR CAME over from Dublin for Debbie's First Holy Communion. Paddy met her in London and brought her home to our house in Meyrick Avenue. She looked no different – short, smart and round, her grey hair tucked neatly under a felt hat that matched her blue buttoned coat.

'I'll put yer case upstairs, Mud, in our room,' Paddy said, walking her in.

Slipping her coat off, she bumped into my pram in the hall. 'Is dere anyone in dat pram now?' she asked.

'No. Steven's two an' Bryan's three.'

'Get rid of dat pram, Lily,' she said. 'As long as ya have it, he'll fill it.'

'Me pram? I couldn't get rid of me good pram.'

Paddy came back down the stairs. We followed her into the kitchen.

'Where's me First Holy Communion girl?' she said, beaming.

Debbie, clutching her little white handbag, stood smiling in front of her.

'Ah, God love her. Look at her lovely white dress, veil an' all,' she said, opening her large black handbag. 'Here's yer medal an' prayer buke, an' here's money for yer purse.'

Paul marched up to her, hands stuffed in his short trouser pockets, his eyes on her bag.

'Here ya are, Paulie,' she said, handing him his bag of sweets and patting him on the head. 'I've seen Debbie an' Paul, but I haven't seen Bryan Boru and Stevie.'

Bryan and Steven hid behind me. Paddy pushed them forward. 'Go an' say hello to yer Nanny. Go on, say hello.'

'Dey're O'Connors all right,' she said, giving them their little bags of sweets. 'Dey've got the O'Connor nose.'

We trailed up to St Margaret of Scotland's Church for Debbie's communion. The two front rows were reserved for the communion children, girls on one side, boys on the other. The little brides sat, hands joined, too terrified to move. The headsister was watching. The boys sat stiff in their new bottle-green school blazers. They didn't dare move either. Sister was watching. After communion, they stood up and sang 'On Our First Communion Day'. Their innocent voices had us all in tears. Then it was out onto the lawn to watch them having their plates of cakes and drinks on long trestle tables. Paddy ran around taking pictures.

'Dat was a lovely mass,' Mrs O'Connor said later, making herself at home in my kitchen.

I sliced up Debbie's special cake. Paddy sat smiling at his mother. 'T'anks for comin', Mud.'

'T'ank God youse are all in Luton. Dat's all I can say.'

'I hated movin' again,' I said, clearing the table. 'All that packin'.'

'Paddy's a gypsy, Lily. It's a caravan he should've bought, not a house. He'll be off again before ya know where ya are.

'No he won't. I really like this house. It's modern, with a view all over Luton.'

Paddy lit up and leaned back on his chair. 'D'ya ever see Awl Jack, Mud?'

'Poor Awl Jack died.'

'Ah God, I'm sorry to hear dat,' he said, lighting up. 'I wished I'd got back to see him. I loved hearin' about his travels.'

'Ya have t'settle down sometime. Ya have a lovely family. Ya're doin' well.'

'Show her yer twin-tub, Lily.'

I wheeled it out from under the sink and pulled off its lid. 'I don't know meself,' I said, reaching in for its wooden tongs. 'I have me washin' done in no time at all. All you have to do is lift the scaldin' hot clothes from one tub with your tongs an' put them in the other to rinse an' spin.'

But Mrs O'Connor wasn't interested. 'Where's the wringer ya bought? I hope ya didn't get rid of dat.'

'It's out in the backyard.'

She followed me out to examine it. 'Don't throw dat out, will ya?' she said, turning its iron handle. 'It'll last forever.'

'C'mon, Mud, I'll show ya upstairs,' Paddy called out.

Climbing the stairs, she eyed the pram again. 'Get rid of dat, Lily. D'ya hear me?'

I threw Paddy's Crombie over it and followed her up into our bedroom.

Paddy opened the airing cupboard. 'This is the immersion heater,' he said. 'Ya switch it on for yer hot water. Isn't dat great? It's all electric now.'

'England's been good to youse, son,' she said. 'Every one of youse is doin' well over here.'

Paddy fussed over his mother all weekend. And she spoiled her grandchildren with endless bags of sweets.

It was back to school for Debbie on Monday and off to work for Paddy. After breakfast, Mrs O'Connor said her prayers, opened her bag and out came her deck of cards.

'Put the boys out to play an' sit down, Lily,' she said, shuffling them. 'Dere's me penny. I'm out. Where's yers?'

No beds were made that morning. No washing was done. A pile of delft waited in the sink. Four cups of tea later and my pennies had vanished.

I jumped up. 'Do you want another cup a' tea?'

'I know what I want,' she said, gathering up her cards and her pennies. 'I want t'go into Luton t'buy ya a pot for yer ham at Christmas.'

A quick scrub of the boys' faces and we were out the door and up the road to the bus stop. Mrs O'Connor clambered on and handed the conductor all her winnings for the fares. The three boys squeezed onto the seat behind us.

Straight into Gibbs and Dandy we went. She bustled around, ignoring assistants, examining every pot in the shop. 'Dere's the one I want,' she said, pointing to the largest.

'This is Sheffield Steel, Madam. Five pounds.'

'That's too much,' I whispered.

'Ah, get on wit' ya. It's for yer ham.'

Out of the hardware and into the sweetshop we trailed after her. 'Dere youse are,' she said, handing out more sweets.

Every morning was the same: it was in with the prayer book and out with the cards. With the pennies she'd win, she'd buy sweets. The week went by. The boys hated seeing her leave.

Paddy carried her case out. 'C'mon, Mud. We'll miss the train.'

She buttoned her coat and looked back at me. 'Get rid of dat pram, Lily,' she said, tapping its handle.

I closed the door and looked at the pram. She was right. It took up the whole hall, and the children were forever bumping into it.

I gave it a good scrubbing that night till every little crumb was cleaned out. Its body and mudguards shone with the polish. Its rain cover was washed, dried and carefully clipped back on.

The following morning, I sauntered down and put an advertisement in a shop window at the end of Meyrick Avenue. I was only in the house when someone rapped hard on my hall door. A big coloured woman, holding her baby, faced me. Another two little ones with black curly hair looked up to me. I smiled at them then wheeled the pram outside.

'It's a good pram,' I said, rubbing its bone handle. 'The springs are still perfect. I bought it in Dublin.'

The woman didn't even look at it, but plonked her three on top of its rain cover.

The cover sank under their weight.

'Just what I need, Mam,' she said, opening her purse.

With the few bob in my hand, I closed the door and ran to the front-room window. There was my high grey pram bouncing down Meyrick Avenue. A part of me went with it that day.

It's Up to Your Own Conscience

It was midnight, a week before Christmas. Paddy couldn't stop talking about the assassination of President Kennedy. I couldn't stop talking about my pains; they were getting worse and worse.

'Wait as long as ya can, love,' he said. 'The angels are gettin' ready to send down the baby. It's a long way.'

'Forget the angels, Paddy,' I said, holding my stomach. 'Ring the midwife.'

He leapt out of bed and hurried up to the phone box at the top of the road. He was back in a minute and up the stairs. 'She's on her way, love,' he said, tidying the room up.

A soft knock came to the door. A young midwife walked into my room, smiling. 'Would you like your doctor to be present?' she said, examining me.

'Yes, I would,' I said, feeling relieved.

This surprised me. I had never been asked this before.

Dr Hall's long legs came flying up the stairs and into my room, his pyjama top peeping out from under his pullover.

'Would you like your husband with you for the birth?' he said, opening his bag.

'Oh, no,' I said. 'An' he wouldn't want to either.'

This was also new. I never dreamt I'd be asked this.

I held my mouth tightly closed, turning my head from side to side, determined not to make a sound. I didn't want to wake the children. The doctor struggled to give me gas, but the mask kept slipping off my face. Four hours later, Carol came into the world screaming.

'Finish now. No more,' the doctor said. 'Five is enough.' He poked his head out the door. 'You can get me that cup of tea now, Father,' he said to Paddy, who was sitting on the stairs.

Dr Hall packed his bag and left. The midwife cleaned up and saw herself out. Paddy got the children up for school. After their breakfast, he lined them up outside my door to see their new little sister who had come in time for Christmas. One by one, they tiptoed in.

'C'mon,' he said, ushering them all out again. 'Youse'll be late for school.'

'Paddy,' I called after him. 'Make sure they're all rugged up in their duffel coats an' gloves, won't you? An' tell Debbie to hold Bryan's hand crossin' the road.'

'Don't worry,' he said, hurrying down the stairs after them.

A little head peeped back around my bedroom door. It was four-year-old Steven. He was feeling left out because he was no longer the baby.

'You can come in,' I said. 'But be quiet; the baby's asleep.'

I heard the hall door close and Paddy coming back up the stairs. 'Dere all gone now. I have to go to work, love,' he said, handing me a cup of tea. 'I'll go up the road an' ring a home help for ya.'

An hour later, the letter box rattled. Steven, dressed in his short pants, knee socks and green jumper, jumped off my bed, trotted down the stairs and opened the door to the home help. He led Mrs James upstairs. A country-looking woman with a round freckled face and red hair walked into my room.

'It's like an oven in here,' she said, turning my two Dimplex heaters off.

'The doctor said he lost a lot of babies last year from the bitter-cold winter.'

'That was last year.' She stared out the window. 'Are they allotments out there? It's ever so nice here, isn't it?'

Carol stirred in her basket across two chairs beside my bed. Steven climbed in beside me. 'Can you ask the lady to make me toast?' he whispered.

'There's no more bread,' I said, looking around for my purse. 'Mrs James, can you get me some messages, please?'

'I finish at three o'clock,' she said. 'Home helps only do basic things like tidying, making lunch and washing up. But seeing it's Christmas week, I'll do it as a favour.'

'An' can you take Steven with you? He needs to get out for a bit of air.'

I handed her the money. The stairs creaked as she trotted down.

'Put on your duffel coat and gloves,' I said to Steven. 'An' ask the lady to tie your laces. Go on, hurry down after her.'

Steven leapt off the bed and galloped down the stairs. The hall door slammed shut. Mrs James was out and back in no time. A crash in the kitchen made me jump. Steven was up to me like a rocket. 'Mummy, do you know that lady downstairs?'

'Yes. Why?'

'She dropped your good kettle. The lid's all broke.'

'It'll be all right. I'll stick it with Bostik.'

'And she's eating all our custard creams. The ones Daddy bought.'

'That's all right. Leave her.'

'Shall I go down and count them?'

'No, see if *Play School* is on.'

For the rest of the week, Steven watched Mrs James like a hawk. Up he'd run, reporting her every move. 'Mummy, Mrs James is sitting down. She's made another cup of tea and she's smoking.'

The sweat poured off me. I was glad when the week was up and Mrs James was paid and gone. Now all I had to do was face the doctor to be allowed up.

'You can get up Christmas Day,' Dr Hall said, peering at his thermometer. 'But Father must make dinner.' Closing his bag, he hesitated. 'I know you're a Catholic, Mrs O'Connor, but I strongly advise you to think about taking the pill. I'll see you in six weeks' time.'

I discussed it with Paddy that night in bed. 'I don't fancy goin' on the pill,' I said.

'Don't worry about it. Dere's t'ings I can buy in the barber's.'

Paddy did everything that Christmas. Having made the pudding, he took the boys down to Woolworths and bought a big artificial Christmas tree, more flashing lights and a white-feathered fairy for the top. Christmas Eve, he soaked the dry marrowfat peas, peeled heaps of potatoes and boiled the ham in his mother's five-pound pot. Christmas morning, he was up early, stuffed the turkey and popped it in the oven, then took them all up the road to nine o'clock mass.

New Year's Eve came and went. I was invited to attend the Catholic mothers' meeting in the church. I brought up the subject of contraception.

'The Catholic religion forbids it,' the president said firmly.

Mrs Ryan, a down-to-earth Cork woman, took me aside after the meeting and gripped my arm hard. 'Listen, Missus,' she whispered. 'Dere's the rhythm method. He can only do it certain times of the month. The rest of the time, he has to hold his hand on it or pull out in time.'

I laughed and gave her a look that said *I can see that working.*

Mrs Ryan nodded. 'I tell ya what t'do,' she said, dunking her biscuit in her tea. 'Go t'confession an' ask the priest. If he says it's okay, den let him take the blame.'

Saturday night I was off to confession.

'It's up to your own conscience,' the priest said in his English accent. 'God will see inside your soul. Now, make a good Act of Contrition.'

I said my prayers, genuflected, blessed myself and buttoned up my long heavy coat. I walked along Bolingbroke Road and down Meyrick Avenue, crunching down hard on the slush in my fur boots. I couldn't wait to tell Paddy what the priest had said.

'The Catholic Church leaves it up to your own conscience. Fancy that,' I said, heating my hands near the fire.

He turned off the telly. 'I've a confession to make too, love.'

'What?'

'Ya know I did the Christmas dinner.'

'Yes. Why?'

'I didn't tell ya. I stuffed the turkey an' cooked it. An' I forgot to take out the plastic bag a' giblets.'

THE LUTON LABOUR CLUB

'I CALLED IN to see our Phil,' Paddy said one Friday night. 'She's invited us to the Luton Labour Club tomorra' night. Ya'd love it, Lily. It's full of Irish. Dere's dancin' after the bingo.'

'I'd really like to go out, but who'll babysit?'

'I'll ask Sally next door. She's doin' a mothercraft course. Dey'll be fine. Dey know her.'

Paddy was up early, singing his head off as he did his Saturday jobs. He trotted around the house with his toolbox, Bryan trailing behind him. The doorknobs were tightened, a new plug was put on my twin-tub and the worn flex on my Russell Hobbs kettle was finally fixed. After lunch, he cleaned out the fire and lit it, then relaxed watching the wrestling, cheering on Mick McManus. I sat beside him, knitting pullovers for the boys, all the same colour, royal blue.

Five o'clock came and the bath was filled. 'You wash. I'll dry,' he said, wrapping a towel around his waist.

One by one, they were washed and dried. Then in flannelette pyjamas and tartan dressing gowns, they charged downstairs for their tea, boiled egg and toast cut up into soldiers.

'Be good now, won't youse?' I said, when I finally got them to bed. 'I'll bring youse back crisps.'

Sally knocked on the hall door dead on the dot of eight. Debbie let her in.

'C'mon, let's go while the goin' is good,' Paddy whispered, closing the hall door quietly behind him.

We hurried down Meyrick Avenue and into Luton.

'How much do you think we'll need?' I said, holding on to his arm.

'A pound should do us for the night,' he said, patting his jacket pocket.

A short stocky man stopped us at the door of the club. 'What's yer name?' he said, in a flat Dublin accent.

'Paddy O'Connor. Me sister Phil an' her husband Mike are inside.'

'Yer Phil's brother? Ah hello, Paddy. She's signed ya in. Go on in. Ya'll catch the last game of bingo.'

We found our way down a narrow hall, past two draughty toilets and into a huge room buzzing with chatter. Paddy scanned the tables for Phil and Mike. I couldn't take my eyes off the well-polished dance floor. A cloud of smoke floated in the air. Chubby-faced women in bright-coloured blouses and cardigans glanced over at us. Men in their best Sunday suits jumped up and headed to the bar, grumbling, giving out hell about the bingo numbers. The whiff of strong aftershave nearly knocked me out as they brushed by.

I followed Paddy up the hall to the stage.

'I've kept youse seats,' Phil said, removing her long beaver coat from two chairs.

She looked immaculate as ever in her grey woollen suit. Her nails were manicured, and large diamond rings sparkled on her fingers. She had no children.

Paddy gave her a big kiss. We were introduced to her Dublin friends sitting beside her: Betty, a round, homely looking woman, and Joe, a serious thin-lipped fella.

'Did ya have any luck, Phil?' Paddy said.

'I was waitin' on all the fours,' she said, showing Paddy her cards. 'Mike was bad news. Couldn't get a number. Betty was waitin' on legs eleven and two fat ladies.'

There was screaming and laughing at the table next to us where a couple were having a grand time. Phil directed me to them with her eyes. 'See dem, Lily? Dey're always winning. She's eight an' one. Ya wouldn't t'ink it, would ya? An' he's all the eights.'

Bingo talk was another language to me.

Phil's Mike appeared, balancing a tray of Guinnesses. 'Ah, be Gad, dey've come,' he laughed, putting the tray down carefully.

Phil leant over to Paddy, her back to Betty and Joe. 'Paddy,' she whispered. 'Mike an' I have a kitty. We put a pound in. If any of our gang show up, dey have to put dere pound in as well. Dat way we all have t'pay our round.' Her eyes told me that Betty and Joe were not included. This was a family thing.

Paddy handed over his pound then headed back to the bar with Mike.

'It's a good club, Lily,' Betty said. 'Dey give the children a great party at Christmas. In the summer dey take dem t'Wicksteed Park.'

A Babycham appeared in front of me. 'Ya'll like dat,' Paddy said. 'It's nice an' sparkly, an' ya get a cherry in it.'

I picked it up and admired the little deer on the glass.

'What's dat yer drinkin', Lily, sugar an' water?' Phil said, knocking back her Scotch.

A committee member climbed up onto the stage beside the bingo wheel. The last game was about to begin. The five-pound jackpot.

'Get yer cards, Paddy, quick,' Phil said, sharpening her pencils.

He flew up and got one for himself and one for me. Phil passed over pencils.

'Eyes down,' the committee member shouted.

A hush fell over the room.

'This is the big one,' Phil said, her eyes glued to eight cards.

The bingo wheel was spun and spun. The numbers were called. I crossed them off and stared around at the serious faces fixed on their cards.

'All the sixes. Clickity-click.'

'Give it a good spin, Sean,' somebody shouted.

'Shush,' Phil said.

'Seven an' six. Seventy-six. Was she worth it?'

'Bingo!' a voice screamed.

The game was over. They all leaned back and lit up. Phil took my card. 'Lily, ya had all the sixes, sixty-six. Why didn't ya shout bingo? Ya missed the jackpot, five pounds. We could have had a free night on dat.' She jumped up and headed to the bar for consolation.

Paddy laughed. Betty looked away. Her Joe shook his head in disbelief.

'Ah, be Gad, Paddy,' Mike said. 'Don't buy *her* any more cards; she's a dreamer.'

I sat twirling the cherry inside my Babycham, letting on not to care. Two men up on the stage behind me struggled with the bingo wheel, making room for the band. They lost their grip. The wheel slipped and tumbled down, hitting my shoulder and crashing onto our table.

The hall fell silent.

'Sacred Heart a' Jesus,' Betty said. 'Are ya all right, Lily?'

I couldn't stop shaking. A committee member ran from the bar with a huge glass of brandy. 'Here ya are,' he said. 'Ya'll be grand now.'*

'She doesn't drink anyt'in' dat strong,' Paddy said, taking the glass and knocking it back himself.

Betty opened her handbag and took out a plastic bottle in the shape of Our Lady.

'It's Holy Water from Lourdes,' she said. 'I keep it in me bag just in case. Rub it on yer shoulder tonight. Ya'll be right.'

The band arrived. The drummer set up his drums and the guitarists tuned their guitars. The singer tapped his mike.

'Look at the band,' I said to Paddy. 'They're all guitars. Nuttin' like the bands we danced to back in Dublin.'

The drums rolled. The guitars strummed. The singer came close to the mike and sang, 'Well I walked up to her and I asked her if she wanted to dance.'

I leapt up. 'It's me favourite song, Paddy, quick.'

He took a gulp of his pint and joined me.

We led the floor for every dance. Before we knew where we were, it was eleven o'clock and time to run.

BACK HOME TO DUBLIN

'I WISH I could take the kids back to Dublin for a holiday, Paddy,' I said, watching Dave Allen telling jokes on the telly. 'If only Mammy was still alive, I could go back to her.'

'Eileen will get ya a place,' he said, wiping his eyes with the laughing. 'Write an' ask her.'

Eileen answered immediately. She'd found a flat for us to rent in Parnell Street for the whole of the summer school holidays. I hugged myself with delight and danced around the kitchen.

As soon as they broke up from school, we were on our way.

The boys were first off the boat when it docked in Dublin. Down a long ramp they ran, duffel bags slung over their shoulders. Paddy pushed my new folding pram with his case on top. Debbie and I sauntered behind them. Carol, in her little red dress, toddled along happily, sucking her red lollipop.

'Straight ahead,' a short skinny man said, waving his cap towards an exit. He bent down to Carol and stuck out his tongue. 'Give us a lick of yer lollipop?' he said. 'Go on, give us a lick.'

I laughed back at him. *I'm home*, I thought. *It's taken me eight years, but I'm back. I swear to God, I'll never stay away this long again.*

A taxi dropped us off in Gardiner Street. Mrs O'Connor and Eileen were hanging out the window, watching for us. After hugs and kisses, Paddy's mother handed out her little bags of sweets. Eileen grabbed Carol up. 'I could eat ya,' she said, kissing the face off her.

'T'anks for gettin' us a flat, Eileen.'

'The flat's not much, Lily, but it's all ya need. Somewhere t'put yer head down an' make a bit a' dinner. An' dere's a playground round the corner from ya.'

'I can't wait to take them to the seaside. We'll go every day.'

'Where's the flat, Eileen?' Paddy said, stabbing his cigarette out.

'Over Paddy's Pet Shop in Parnell Street. Ya know it. Mrs Byrne owns it. I told her youse are here for six weeks. She's lettin' ya have it very cheap.'

'If dere's not enough beds,' Mrs O'Connor said. 'Bring Bryan Boru around. He can sleep wit' me.'

'We'll be fine, Mud, I'm only here for the week. I have to get back to work.'

It was a warm sunny day as we walked down Parnell Street past Kennedy's Bakery to Paddy's Pet Shop.

'Here's it is,' Debbie said, staring in a window at all the puppies.

The boys galloped up the bare wooden stairs next to the shop's entrance and into the flat. Debbie followed them. 'I can hear the birds,' she said.

'I can smell them,' I said, taking Carol's hand.

After our case was unpacked and the beds decided on, it was time to think about dinner. A shopping list was written.

'I'll get lovely fresh bread in Kennedy's,' Paddy said, making for the stairs.

Half an hour later, Hafner sausages sizzled on a pan. A plate of Archer's black and white pudding sat waiting to be thrown in. I opened the oven. A mouse strutted out as if he owned the place.

'Jesus! Paddy, a mouse. Don't tell me there's mice here.'

'I'll get a mousetrap after tea,' Paddy said, rolling his sausages. 'Don't worry. I'll catch him.'

That night he set the trap with a chunk of our red tasty cheese. I woke up the next morning and was delighted to see we'd caught him.

They all had to have a look at the mangy old thing in the trap.

'Blood's coming out of its mouth,' Steven said, touching it.

Paddy snatched up the trap. 'Out of the way, all of youse.' He opened the back window and flung the mouse out to the wild-looking, scabby-eyed cats that were scurrying around on the roofs. He then set another lump of my good cheddar cheese in the trap. 'Better make sure he hasn't got a missus,' he said, laughing.

Breakfast over, down Parnell Street we rambled and into O'Connell Street. Families inched around us. It was great hearing Dublin accents again. A mother pushing her pram smiled at the three boys marching by in their blue pullovers.

'Are dey triplets?' she said, looking back at me. 'Did ya knit their jumpers yerself? Dey're lovely.'

I nodded to her.

In Dublin with five children, I felt at home. In England, I was the Irish mother with all the kids.

'All the same, Paddy, there's nowhere like Dublin, is there?'

'It's all right if ya have a job.'

Debbie straightened her new glasses and tried to read the Irish names over shop windows. She bumped into a woman wheeling a pram, with a gang of kids behind her. Paddy apologised to the woman, then stood chatting to her.

'This is Bernie, Lily,' he said. 'She worked wit' me in Irish Textiles.'

She caught hold of my arm. 'It's very hard t'manage, Missus, isn't it, when he's unemployed?'

A small man, his hair slicked back, stood aside with the children. Paddy turned to him. 'Ya'll easy get a job in Luton,' he said. 'Come over an' I'll help ya.'

'I'm not leavin' Dublin for England. I'm no renegade.' He moved on with his kids.

'Well, mind yerself, Bernie, won't ya?' Paddy said. 'I hope t'ings pick up for ya soon.' He dug his hand in his pocket and handed her a few bob. 'Buy a few sweets for the kids,' he said, patting the baby's head.

'Was that your girlfriend, Daddy?' Debbie said, looking after the family.

'I went out wit' her a few times, yes.'

'She sounds like she's had it very hard,' I said.

'He's out a' work, but he won't leave Dublin.'

'I can understand him not wantin' to leave. Not everyone wants to leave.'

Back in the flat, the trap had sprung again. Cheese gone, but no sign of the mouse.

'How in the name a' God did he get the cheese an' not get caught?' I said.

'These are city mice, Lily. Dey know all the tricks.'

'What will we do?'

'Well, dey're not gettin' any more cheese, dat's for sure. Dey'll t'ink every day is dere bloody birthday.'

We made the most of the week. If it wasn't the Botanical

Gardens, it was off to the seasides, Dollymount, Portmarnock or Bray.

Paddy didn't waste his nights either. He found a babysitter – ten-year-old Debbie. He bribed her with a new Enid Blyton book every night to look after the others.

'We won't go far,' he reassured me on our first night out.

We went from pub to pub on the quays. But they were all packed with teenagers, laughing and joking.

'How come there are no married couples in here?' I said, sipping my bitter lemon. 'Where are they all?'

'Dey've married an' moved out of the city like we did. Dey're drinkin' in their locals.'

It was the same every night. We'd go to a pub on the quays and sit on our own, chatting together. Two pints later, we'd stroll back to the flat and drop into bed.

Paddy packed his bag Saturday morning.

'Mind yerself an' the kids for me. I'll send yer money to me mudder every week.'

'What about the mice?'

'I can't take dem back wit' me,' he laughed. 'Ignore the buggers, love. Ya'll never get rid of dem. As Eileen says, yer over a pet shop an' next door to a bakery. I'll be back in five weeks to take youse all home.'

DON'T BE MINDIN' DESE AWL WANS

'I'M GOING DOWN to the playground to meet my friend,' Debbie said, slipping on her blue shorts one morning.

The boys lay on their bed, reading scruffy old second-hand comics they'd bought for a penny. They weren't interested in the playground. 'The kids are too rough,' they said. 'They push us off the swings.'

Carol dawdled around the room, chatting to Wow Wow, her new toy dog, while I cleaned up and washed their T-shirts before we went out.

All of a sudden, an unmerciful scream shot up the stairs. 'Get dat child away from me good lace curtains. D'ya hear me?'

I got such a fright. I ran to the window where Carol was standing, pulled her back and stared down into Parnell Street. A short fat woman was glaring up at me, shaking her fist.

'God, that must be Mrs Byrne, the owner,' I said, straightening her curtains.

The next thing I knew, Debbie was on the stairs, crying.

'Jesus, what's wrong with you?'

'A horrible granny followed me home shouting at me to cover my legs. I'm not wearing these shorts any more. I want to go home.'

'The cheek of her. The cheek of her,' I said, banging down my bucket of washing. 'C'mon, we're goin' out. You belong here too. I was born here. You were born here. Me mammy's buried here. She wasn't like that awl granny. She loved children. We'll go to her grave in Mount Jerome, that's what we'll do.'

I made up jam, spam and salad-cream sandwiches, all their favourites. Debbie changed into a dress and carried our picnic in her duffel bag.

Rambling down Parnell Street with them all, I bumped into my old neighbour from Cabra West, Mrs O'Neill.

'Is dat Lily O'Shea?' she said, peering into my face through her thick glasses.

'It's great to see you,' I said, gripping her arm.

'God, yer the spittin' image of yer poor mammy. Lord have mercy on her. Have ya come back t'live?'

'I wish I was.'

She looked at the five faces gazing up at her. 'Are dese all yers, Lily? Dey're lovely, God bless dem.' She opened her purse and gave them a penny each, all the while asking their names.

We chatted on about Mammy. The boys charged to a red bingo-looking machine on the path outside a sweet shop.

'Mum,' Paul shouted, shaking the machine, 'we put our pennies in but our gobstoppers won't come out.'

The door of the sweet shop burst open. A roly-poly shopkeeper waddled out. 'Are dey yers?' she shouted, pointing to the boys.

I nodded.

'Would ya mind tellin' dem to leave dat machine alone.'

'It's not workin',' I said.

'It was a minute ago till dey t'umped it.'

'Why didn't they get their sweets then?'

'Yer afta' askin' me an' I'm afta' tellin' ya,' she said, heading back into the shop.

Mrs O'Neill saw my face. 'Ah, feck her, Lily.'

I burst out laughing. 'I used to say *feck*. It made me feel better. But when I moved to Luton, people stared at me as if I was cursing. It's been knocked out of me.'

The boys started fiddling with the machine again.

I sat Carol up in the pram. 'I'd better let you go,' I said.

'Mind yerself now,' she said, hurrying off.

As I dragged them all across Parnell Street, one of the pram's little wheels wobbled off.

'Leave it,' I said, holding Paul back.

A van screeched to a stop. The driver climbed out and fetched it. 'Is this yer wheel?' he said, looking at the pram.

I couldn't believe it. It was an old friend of Paddy's, Christy Brennan.

'How are ya, Lily?' he said. 'How's Paddy?'

'God, Christy, am I glad to see you.'

We chatted as if I'd seen him only the day before instead of eight years ago. I found myself telling him about Mrs Byrne and her curtains over Paddy's Pet Shop, the shopkeeper and her gobstopper machine, and the granny who had chased Debbie home for showing her legs in the street.

'Ah, don't be mindin' dese awl wans, Lily,' he said, laughing. 'Feck dem.' He stared down at Paul kicking the wheel back on. 'What's wrong wit' it?'

'It keeps fallin' off.'

Bending down, he examined the axle. 'The t'reads have worn.' He fetched a hammer from his van. There on the path, he belted the wheel back on. 'Dat won't come off again,' he said, spinning the wheel.

Cars beeped his van. 'I'd better get back t'work or I'll be joinin' Paddy in England,' he said, galloping off.

'Was that *your* boyfriend?' Debbie said, grinning.

'He's a very good friend. He lived beside me in Cabra West.'

'Did your mammy like him?'

'My mammy liked everyone,' I said, moving them along. 'She was very kind an' soft. She loved children.'

'Are we nearly there?' Steven said.

We tore across the road to Mount Jerome Cemetery. I bought a bunch of chrysanthemums, Mammy's favourite flowers, from a dealer outside the gate, then walked them straight up to her grave.

'Here it is,' I said, lifting Carol out of the pram.

I bent down and brushed the dirt off the small flat stone that Annie and I had bought from the cemetery stonemason for five pound. 'I'll do it as a nixer,' the stonemason had said, making out he was giving us a bargain.

'Alice O'Shea. Is that her name?' Debbie said, reading the stone.

I laid the flowers down and blessed myself.

'Say a prayer for your nanny,' I said.

'Where is she then?' Steven said, staring around. 'I thought you said she was here.'

'She's buried there,' I said, pointing to the grave.

They stood silent, their eyes fixed on the flowers lying on a pile of rubble.

'Can we go now?' Steven said.

'Can we go to Dollymount?' Bryan said, pulling me away from the grave.

There wasn't a word said as we strolled back down the path. It was my own fault. I hadn't explained that Mammy had died. They were expecting to see her with little bags of sweets for them all. They'd never been inside a cemetery. The day wasn't turning out at all the way I'd thought it would.

Paul sat down on a seat near the tombs. 'I'm tired,' he said.

'Okay, we'll have our picnic here.'

'I'm thirsty,' Bryan said. 'Did you bring any drinks?'

'Right,' I said, grabbing his arm. 'See that little path? Go straight up there till you come to a rubbish bin full of dead flowers. Next to it, you'll see a little tap. Turn it on an' put your mouth under it. That's what I did when I was a kid an' needed a drink.'

From then on, it was Dollymount.

Every morning, with buckets and spades, we walked down to the quays, onto the bus and off at Dollymount Strand. Summer showers didn't worry me; they'd be brief and I made sure to sit near a shelter.

The weeks went by and it was time for Paddy to fetch us.

'God, youse are all lovely an' brown,' he said, walking in Saturday morning.

They hung out of him. They hadn't seen him for five weeks.

'I missed youse,' he said, kissing them. 'The house was like a morgue wit'out youse.'

Debbie couldn't wait to tell him she'd nearly drowned in Dollymount.

'What's she on about?' he said, picking up Carol.

'I forgot there was swally holes in Dollymount. She fell down one. A man pulled her out. She's all right.'

'How d'ya go wit' the mice?'

'I ignored them. They ran in an' out of that open fireplace every night, playin' to their hearts' content. An' I let them.'

'Did ya catch up wit' yer friends?'

'They all said I'm gone very serious. An' they were right. That's what happens when you stay away from Dublin too long. You become too serious. I'm comin' back next year, I can tell you.'

Things Happen in Threes

'YA BETTER GET up, Lily,' Paddy said, handing me a cup of tea. 'It's snowin' an' the power's gone.'

'The power's gone? Jesus, not again. That's the t'ird time this week.'

'I took the milk in before the birds pecked the tops,' he said, dropping Paul's torch on the bed. He hurried down the stairs and went out the hall door.

I jumped up, dragged the curtains back, scraped the frost off the glass with my nails and peeped out into the dark. Flecks of snow were blowing against the window. The double-decker bus, dimly lit, dragged itself up the hill. The tall street lamps were still glowing amber. Paddy pulled up the collar of his new Gannex coat and hurried down Meyrick Avenue for his train. 'Be careful,' I said, watching him skid on the icy pavements.

He was now working in London in a small factory run by Mr Stein and his son. He preferred working in a small place. 'Ya get to know the boss, an' the boss gets to know you. In big factories, ya're just a number.' That's what Paddy always said.

On with the dressing gown and slippers, and down the stairs I went with the torch. First, the fire had to be lit. The cinders were still warm, so with Paddy's paper and a bit of rex coal, I soon had it blazing. I balanced a big pot of milk on it, then hurried out to the bottom stair and called them. They were going to school, no matter what.

It wasn't long before I had four bowls of hot Ready Brek on the table. 'Hurry up, eat your breakfast,' I said, as I rushed around, polishing their shoes.

I opened the hall door and an icy gale blew in. They pulled up the hoods of their duffel coats and ducked as I tried to smear Vaseline on their lips. Sylvia's David, all wrapped up, was waiting at our gate for Steven.

'Don't slide on the ice,' I called after them, as they hurried off with brown leather satchels swinging off their shoulders.

After Carol was dressed and fed, I stuck a piece of bread on a fork and held it close to the fire to toast. I sat thinking of Mammy and how we all sat around the fire, toasting thick pieces of bread, telling her all our worries.

'Can we go now?' Carol said, handing me my coat and scarf.

I tucked her up in her pusher and picked my way down Meyrick Avenue over the slippery path and into Luton.

It was Wednesday, the day for triple Green Shield stamps in Tesco. In no time at all, I'd have two books filled to get that blue and white rack for my potatoes.

With my shopping bag on top of the pusher, I hurried home, up that hill, praying to God the power would be back on.

Debbie was waiting at the hall door.

'What have you forgotten?' I said, opening the gate.

'You have to come up to the school immediately,' she said, smiling so as not to worry me. 'Paul's had an accident.'

I stared at her, my hand to my mouth. 'What's happened to him? Did he slip on the ice?'

'He fell off the horse doing leapfrogs during PE and broke his arm. His bone is sticking out.'

'Jesus. His bone's all stickin' out?'

I dropped Carol into Sylvia and raced off with Debbie, my shopping bag still in my hand.

The ambulance was waiting for me when I arrived. I climbed in beside Paul, and we went off to Luton and Dunstable Hospital. Then the long hours began, waiting for his wrist to be X-rayed and set in plaster.

It was pitch dark by the time the ambulance dropped us back. Paul fell into bed half-unconscious, looking like death.

One by one, they trotted in from Sylvia's. They were all very good. They didn't have to be reminded to hang their duffels up in the cupboard under the stairs; even their shoes were stacked up neatly on the rack. Each one went upstairs, had a quick look at Paul, then tiptoed downstairs, looking worried. After their dinner of hot stew and dumplings, they slipped into the front room to watch television. Debbie went up to do her homework. I threw another bucket of Phurnacite on the fire, drew the curtains and switched on the lights. I had no worries getting them to bed that night. As soon as it was half-six, they crept up with hot water bottles under their arms.

The seven-fifteen bus droned up the hill. I peered out the window, expecting to see Paddy jump off, the *Daily Mirror* sticking out of his pocket.

Where in the name of God is he? I thought, heading back to the kitchen. I was anxious to tell him about Paul. The train must have been late with the snow.

I turned his sausages slowly, browning them all over, the way he liked them, then shoved his dinner in the oven to keep warm

Steptoe and Son was on, but I couldn't enjoy it. Every time a bus passed, I ran to the window and pulled back the curtain, hoping to see Paddy.

A car door banged. I peeped out the window to see a taxi drive off. The letter box rattled. It was Paddy, his arm in a sling, white as a sheet and smelling of antiseptic.

'What's happened to you?' I said, seeing his shirt full of blood.

'I've had an accident at work. I've been in the hospital all day.'

He stumbled down the hall and collapsed on a chair, his eyes nearly closing.

'God, you look terrible.'

'It's nuttin', love. Me arm got caught in the motor belt. Just a few stitches, seventy-two.'

'Jesus, seventy-two stitches? Imagine the boss lettin' you go all the way home on your own.'

'Lily, it was me own fault. I left the guard off the machine. I'm lucky I didn't lose me hand.'

'God, Paddy, that's the second t'ing that's happened today. Paul's had an accident too. He's up there on his back with a broken arm.'

'Is he all right?'

'He'll be fine. Do you feel like your dinner?'

'I have to go to bed, love.'

'Do you want me to help you?' I said, turning off the oven.

'I'll be right. Dey gave me painkillers.'

I followed him down the hall and watched him struggling up the stairs, taking one step at a time.

In a daze, I went into the kitchen and dragged a few chairs into the front room. I circled them in front of the sinking fire and hung the duffels on the backs of the chairs to dry overnight. Shoes were lodged on the fender along with a pile of soggy mittens and gloves. I pulled out the television plug, then bolted the back door, top and bottom, turned off the lights and went up to bed.

Paddy was sitting up in bed, drinking water, taking one painkiller after the other.

'I hope nuttin' else is goin' to happen,' I said.

'What are ya on about?' he moaned, trying to lie down.

'Well, you know how they say t'ings happen in t'rees? What else is goin' to happen?'

MRS O'CONNOR DIES

'AFTER I SAW me mudder in the morgue,' Paddy said, sitting down, 'I tramped the back streets of Dublin all night long, past the dumps of factories I'd slaved in, tryin' to make sense of it all.'

Paddy had been over to Dublin to bury his mother, who had died unexpectedly of a hernia. He was in bits.

'How's Eileen takin' it?' I said, putting on the kettle.

'She an' Mick are comin' over here to live.'

'God, I never t'ought Eileen'd leave Dublin. She was part of the city.'

'What's dere in Dublin for her now, Lily? The Royalettes are gone. Me mudder's gone. We're all over here.'

The boys appeared in the kitchen and stood staring at him. 'Are we still going to Dublin for our holidays?' Bryan asked.

I pushed them out the door. 'It's time for bed. Go an' get undressed,' I whispered. 'You can read in bed for a while.'

Having seen them off to school the next morning, I combed the paper, searching for a place to rent in England near the sea. *We need to go somewhere*, I thought. It'd do Paddy good. I found a bungalow in Hastings.

July arrived. The schools broke up. The boys were up early, dressed in beige pullovers, brown shorts and sandals, ready to go, eager to get on the train.

I sped around the house, leaving it spotless. That was my one consolation returning from a holiday, seeing the house clean and tidy, even if it didn't last long.

The train pulled in to Hastings. It bucketed down, freezing cold rain.

They'll be all right, I thought. *They've got their brown anoraks.*

We found the address. It was no bungalow like the ad in the paper said, just a big white box on a bleak windy hill near caravans.

Paddy's face dropped when he opened the door and saw how cold and miserable it was inside, no heater or anything. 'How much did ya pay for this place?'

'It'll look better in the mornin' when the sun shines,' I said. 'It's very handy to the sea an' shops.'

He dumped the cases, picked up an old booklet on Hastings, skimmed through it, then threw it down. 'Nuttin' in dat.'

'What are we going to do?' Debbie said.

'We'll go out an' find somewhere nice to eat,' I said. 'What do you t'ink, Paddy?'

'Whatever ya like,' he said. 'It's up to you.'

The boys galloped ahead, exploring the town centre. The steamy smell of fish and chips sailed out of warm, cosy cafés.

'Let's go in here,' I said. 'They've lovely white tablecloths.'

A tall, thin-faced waiter squeezed seven of us around a small table. We studied the menu and ordered sausages and chips with a big plate of bread and butter and a pot of tea. Soon the boys were making up bulging chip sandwiches, pouring on the tomato sauce. The waiter sat a pot of tea on our table. His face dropped at the sight of the red sauce spots on his snow-white tablecloth.

'Use yer knives and forks,' Paddy snapped at the boys.

'They're on holidays,' I said. 'Leave them.'

'Dey've no manners. Did ya see Bryan on the train, dunkin' his doughnut in his tea? Ya let dem away wit' murder. Don't ya ever check dem?'

'The world will beat them time enough,' I laughed, tipping him playfully, trying to get him into a holiday mood. 'Isn't that what your mother always said?'

After Knickerbocker Glories had been licked clean with long spoons, it was back to the unit. We sorted the beds and unpacked the cases, then fell into bed jaded tired.

We woke up to the rain lashing off the windows the following morning.

'What are we going to do, Mum?' Bryan complained, opening and closing the door to see if the rain had stopped.

'Get your anoraks on,' I said, washing up. 'We'll go down an' have a look at the sea. It's only a summer shower.'

Paddy walked along the promenade with Debbie, talking all about his mother, how much he'd miss her. The boys climbed down onto the beach, firing pebbles into the murky green sea. We passed a dull, grey, ancient-looking building.

'It's an indoor pool,' Paul shouted. 'Can we get in?'

Debbie went over and read the sign. 'It's a saltwater pool.'

'Paddy, can you take them back for their bathers, while I let Carol have a little sleep in the pram?'

'Whatever ya like.' He walked after them back to the unit.

I wandered off in search of a café, a hot cup of tea and a dough-nut. Delighted I was when I found one. Slipping my coat and scarf off, I settled on a seat in the corner. Carol slept in the pusher beside me. Before I had a chance to glance at the menu, a surly-faced man tipped me on the shoulder. 'Excuse me, Madam, did you not see the sign?' he said, pointing to the door. *No Prams or Pushers Allowed Inside.* 'Would you mind leaving?'

I reached for my coat and said nothing.

The rain had stopped. Carol woke and I sat her up. A green wooden bench near a patch of grass looked inviting. I put my coat on the seat and sat down. A gardener cutting the edges glanced at Carol running on his grass. Clearing his throat, he straightened up a *Please Do Not Walk on the Grass* sign.

'C'mon, Carol,' I sighed. 'They should be out of the pool by now.'

The pool door sprung open and the boys charged out towards me, their eyes red, their wet towels rolled up under their arms.

'It's a massive pool, Mum. Old and smelly but great to swim in,' Paul said, his teeth chattering.

'Where's Debbie?'

'Getting dressed.'

'Zip up your anoraks,' I said, looking at them all shivering.

Debbie sauntered out, her hair dripping down her back.

'Did you see any sign of Dad?'

'He's coming.'

'What's wrong with him?' Steven said. 'He just floated around on his own, saying nothing.'

'It's because Nanny's died,' Debbie whispered.

It rained every day. So it was down to the pool in the morning and strolling around Hastings in the afternoon. The highlight of their day was dinner of an evening, when they could choose what-ever they liked from the menu.

But by the end of the week, they were fed up with the pool, and going out for dinner was no longer a treat.

'What can we do today?' Debbie said, flipping through the Hastings booklet. 'We've seen the Battle of Hastings and the Smugglers' Cave. What about the Fisherman's Museum? We haven't seen that yet?'

'Right, anoraks on.'

The museum was a small grey-stone church. I held Carol's hand as we queued up behind families. A smell of fresh paint filled the air inside. Not a spot of dust on the floorboards. Pictures of old-fashioned boats hung on the walls, but the boys had no time for them. Their eyes were fixed on a large wooden boat, *The Enterprise*. We followed a rope that circled it. A short, serious-looking man in a dark suit instructed us with his hand to keep moving around it.

'It's twenty-nine foot, Dad,' Debbie said, reading a small plaque.

'How did they get it in here?' Paul asked.

'They broke down the wall,' she said.

Steven bent under the rope and touched *The Enterprise*. The dark suit pounced on him. 'Can *you* not read?' he shouted, pointing to a piece of brown cardboard up against the boat.

The queue halted. People glanced back. Paddy, his face red, apologised to the man.

'He didn't do any harm,' I snapped. 'He's only seven.'

I grabbed Steven's hand and headed to the exit. I looked back and was furious – Paddy was dropping all his loose change into the donation box.

Outside he let Steven have it. 'Couldn't you see dat sign?' he said, gripping his arm.

'He barely touched his bloody awl boat,' I said. 'Was he supposed to read "Do Not Touch" scribbled on a bit of awl cardboard? I'm fed up with these cranky awl buggers. You can't *touch* this, you can't *touch* that. You can't *sit* here, you can't *walk* there.'

'He shouldn't have gone under the rope.'

'T'hell with that awl fella, Paddy. Your mother wouldn't have listened to him.'

'Lily, the Irish have a name over here of being ignorant an' stupid. An' dat's how we looked in front of those people.'

'Feck 'em, Paddy. You can't put an old head on young shoulders. That's what your mother always said. You would have listened to her all right.'

Paddy lit up and inhaled deeply, then patted Steven's head. 'Okay, let's find somewhere to eat. Sorry, love, for being an awl crank. T'ank God I've got you an' the kids.'

ME BRAINCELLS ARE DYING

'PADDY, DON'T FORGET I'm startin' that typin' class tonight, will you?'

'Be ready to go when I get in from work,' he said, giving me my cup of tea in bed.

I was waiting at the gate when he jumped off the seven-fifteen bus that night, the *Mirror* sticking out of his pocket.

'They're all in bed waitin' for you to go up an' kiss them good-night. Your dinner's in the oven.'

'Good luck wit' the class,' he said, closing the door.

Clutching my new typing book, I hurried up Meyrick Avenue to Debbie's school. Having left school at fourteen, I was nervous. *I hope to God I'm able to do it*, I thought, picturing myself in front of a typewriter, tapping away.

Schools are strange places at night: dark, lonely and cold. I tip-toed in through the half-lit front entrance. Teenage girls, heavily made up, pushed by me. I followed them to a classroom, all lit up. The girls settled down, chatting away as if they knew each other. I slipped into a back seat in front of a big black typewriter with rows of white letters and numbers.

The tall, thin teacher marched in, brushing chalk marks from his dark suit.

'Good evening, girls,' he said, handing out blank sheets of paper. 'Books open at page ten.'

Why is he starting on page ten? I wondered, flipping through my book.

'Now, load your paper, girls,' he said, polishing his glasses.

The girls loaded and lined up their sheets with no bother. I tried my best to slip the paper into my machine, but for the life of me I couldn't do it.

The dark suit moved from girl to girl, up and down the rows. Without saying anything, he bent down, loaded my paper, then drifted back down to the front.

'When you finish page ten, continue with the next exercise, girls,' he said, looking up at the clock.

I struggled with the keys, which kept jamming. By the end of the night, my fingers were black with the ink. But I didn't care, I'd completed page ten and showed it to him.

He scanned my smudgy sheet and said nothing.

Determined to be better the following week, I hired out a type-writer from a shop in Luton and wheeled it home in Carol's push-er. Every spare minute I had was spent in front of that typewriter, loading the paper, watching my fingers and tapping the correct keys. I raced along to the next class, delighted with myself. I had conquered one exercise, not a spelling mistake to be seen.

'Exercise twenty, girls,' the teacher instructed, handing out blank sheets of paper.

Twenty, Jesus. What about the other exercises?

'Speed is the essence, girls,' he kept muttering to the class.

He floated from girl to girl, praising them. 'Keep up the good work, Deirdre. You're doing well, Mary.'

I put up my hand. 'Can you help me?' I said, smiling. 'They're really good, they don't even have to look at the keys.'

'This is touch type,' he said, walking up to me. 'You're not sup-posed to look at the keys.'

'I find it hard to type the right letters without lookin'.'

He came close and bent down. I listened intently. I thought he was going to say, *it's only your second lesson, Lily. You'll soon pick it up.*

'Mrs O'Connor,' the dark suit whispered. 'It's because your brain cells are dying.'

'What?' I said, my heart thumping. 'Me brain cells are dyin'?'

'As you get older,' he continued, 'your brain cells begin to die. You can't learn anything new.'

He straightened up and pointed to the other girls. 'They are younger than you. They can pick it up.'

I looked over at them, their long manicured nails click-clacking away on the keys.

Deirdre beckoned him. He was gone without further comment. I sat staring at the typewriter, my hand to my mouth, my face burn-ing. Closing my book, I picked up my coat and crawled out. No attempt was made to stop me leaving. As I slunk home in the dark, I wiped my eyes. I didn't know what to believe. One thing I did know: he didn't want me in that typing class.

I discussed it with Debbie when she came home from school the following day.

'Yes, that's right,' she said. 'I learnt that at school. Your brain cells die when you turn thirty. So yours are dying.' She picked up her satchel and carried on upstairs to do her homework.

I ran after her. 'It's funny how those girls in the class all know each other.'

'They're in my school, Mum. He teaches them typing during the day.'

'Then what the hell are they doin' there at night?'

'Building up their speed.'

Over sausages and mash that evening, I asked Paddy what he thought.

'I read somet'in' about dat in the *Mirror*,' he said, handing me his plate to be washed. 'It's hard to learn new t'ings after a certain age.'

I threw the delft into the sink. 'I don't believe that,' I said. 'That bugger didn't want me there, Paddy. He only wanted those young wans.'

'Never mind, love. Yer a great mother.'

The next morning, the house was cleaned from top to bottom, savagely. *Is this all I'm good for? Havin' babies an' cleanin' the house?*

Thank God, Helen, my Irish friend, was coming for lunch that day. I needed a laugh.

Just as I finished shredding the cheese for our bread rolls, she pulled up in her yellow Ford Anglia. After lunch, we sat beside the fire, chatting.

She put down her knitting.

'How is the typing going, Lily?' she said.

'The teacher said me brain cells are dyin'. It's too late to learn.'

She roared laughing. 'Don't be minding him. You're not the only one he has put off. I know others he said the very same thing to. They paid the fee and bought the books, just like you did.'

Little Canada Holiday Camp

'WELCOME TO THE Isle of Wight,' a young lad in a blue blazer said, taking our case. 'We're here to make sure you have a good holiday.'

This was our first holiday camp. My next-door neighbour heard all about Hastings and the rain. 'Go to a holiday camp,' she told me, giving me her brochure. 'You don't have to worry about the weather. The kids will love it.'

We traipsed behind the Bluecoat down a narrow hilly path towards log cabins shaded by tall forest trees. Fourteen-year-old Debbie, looking all grown up in her mini-skirt and white stockings, chatted to him about John Lennon and Yoko Ono's *Make Love, Not War* campaign on the island. We pulled open the door to our cabin. Paddy and I sank down on our bed. Debbie and Carol shared one room; the boys argued over their bunk beds in another.

'We're off to explore the camp,' Paul said, walking off, the others close behind.

'Wait for us,' I said.

Paddy lay back on the pillow, his hands clasped behind his head. 'Dey're safe in the camp, Lily. It's all fenced in.'

'Look after Carol,' I shouted.

I picked up the menu and studied it. 'Listen, Paddy, it's fish an' chips tonight. Steven doesn't eat fish. Just leave him. I don't want any arguments.'

'I won't say a word,' he laughed. 'C'mere to me an' stop yer worryin'.'

The door burst open. 'We want our bathers!' they shouted. 'The pool's heated, and there's a fantastic fountain.'

'Where's Debbie?' I said.

'She's talking to boys in the hall.'

The fun began Monday morning, immediately after breakfast. The boys ran to the pool. Paddy and I trailed after them. The fathers were asked to throw money into the water for the children to dive in and collect. Steven nearly drowned himself trying to pick up the most. I worried sick watching him crawling on the bottom like a crab, gathering up every penny. I thought he'd never surface.

After the pool, it was into the hall. A Bluecoat asked the children to come up onto the stage, one at a time, to sing for a stick of rock. The boys queued up with Carol. They did their party piece and handed me their sticks of rocks to mind. They queued up again and again for more sticks of rock, singing the same old song over and over. I was ashamed of my life and was glad when it was finished.

Then it was outside for the wheelbarrow race. Paul fell to the ground; Bryan gripped his two skinny legs. The pair ran like mad, Paul's wiry arms galloping like a bandy spider. Next, it was the sack race.

Paddy took my arm and pulled me back from the crowd. 'C'mon, we'll sneak off. Let dem get on wit' it. We'll go an' get a cup a' tea.'

But Carol had other plans for us. She dragged us towards a whole load of old donkeys, lined up to race. Paddy chose one and placed his bet. 'Now, hold on tight,' he said, dumping her on it.

Everyone's donkey moseyed off, except ours. Ours wouldn't budge, no matter how much we pushed him. The men cheered theirs on, their children hanging on for dear life. Paddy gave up when the race finished and took Carol down. Off she went running, looking for the boys.

Just as we were escaping, a Bluecoat announced a fancy dress on the loudspeakers all over the camp. Debbie appeared from nowhere with Carol. She dragged us back to the cabin to dress Carol up as Yoko Ono. Debbie was in her element, cutting up long strips of black crepe paper and sticking them into her big red sunhat for Yoko's hair. Carol pulled on the hat, climbed into her white pyjamas and put on my black round sunglasses.

With her Yoko Ono smile, she climbed up onto the stage. The boys clapped, whooped and whistled. She showed us her prize, a milkshake voucher. Then off she trotted with the boys.

'C'mon, we'll go to the bar,' Paddy said, hurrying me away. 'I'll teach ya how to play snooker.'

'God, it's great here all the same,' I said. 'Not havin' to worry about the kids.'

Paddy took pains in teaching me the rules of snooker.

'I t'ink I need practice,' I said, as the balls took flight from the table.

'Let's try darts den.'

Men standing close by let on to duck as my darts shot all over the room.

'I'm not very good at this game either,' I said, collecting them.

'D'ya mind if I have a game wit' one of the fellas?'

I slipped out of the bar to see what the boys were up to. They were in the hall where a show was going on, having a grand time. The seats were packed with fathers, their little ones on their laps. I squeezed by them, sat down beside Paul and stared up at the stage to see what they were all laughing at.

A tall, serious-looking man in a suit was blowing up long thin balloons, making sausage dogs for the kids. A little girl was up on the stage being silly. I nearly died. It was Carol. She kept running behind the man, pushing a long skinny balloon between his legs. He tried to stop her, but closed his legs too late. The fathers fell over the place laughing at the sight of the man's face looking down at the skinny balloon sticking out between his legs.

'Jesus, Mary and Joseph, she's gettin' carried away with herself,' I said to Paul. 'For God's sake, go up an' get her.'

The days were for the kids, but the nights were for the mums and dads. On went my Marks and Spencer's apple-green dress and white lacy cardigan. Paddy straightened his maroon silk tie and slipped on his best navy-blue suit. 'C'mon, Lily,' he said, 'or we won't get a table.'

The ballroom was ablaze with coloured lights. We hurried across its well-polished floor and took up a whole table near the stage.

'I'll get youse Tizers,' Paddy said, strolling off to the bar.

'Creamy soda, Dad,' Steven shouted after him.

He was back in a minute, balancing a wide tray of drinks. The games began. A Bluecoat swaggered down the hall, tossing his mike from hand to hand. He stopped, switched on his mike and scanned the hall. 'I'd like two volunteers,' he said.

'Go on, Dad, go on,' the boys cheered.

'No, Dad, don't,' Debbie said. 'Don't.'

'Don't mind her, Dad. Go on,' Paul said.

But Paddy needed no encouragement from anyone. He gulped down the last of his Guinness and sprang out of his chair.

Two large rubber balls with ears for handles appeared on the floor at the front of the stage.

'Get on your Spacehoppers, gentlemen,' the Bluecoat announced. 'To the end of the hall and back. On your marks, get set, go.'

Carol and the boys were out of their seats, jumping up and down, clapping him on.

Debbie was nowhere to be seen. Paddy bounced to the end of the hall, swung around and bounced all the way back to the stage.

His face beamed with his prize, a pint for himself and a Babycham for me. But just as he put down the drinks, his feet skidded from under him. He went flying on his back, kicking the table over. I couldn't stop his full pint of Guinness sliding across the table and into my lap. A stage spotlight zoomed over, beaming on us.

'Oohhh,' the hall went.

Paddy stood up and took a bow. The hall clapped and roared with the laughing.

'Are you all right, sir?' the Bluecoat asked.

A staff member appeared from nowhere with a bucket and mop. Paddy took the mop from him and proceeded to wipe the floor. The hall cheered him on. I froze under the glare of the spotlight. My face burned as the Guinness soaked through my dress and down my legs.

'Are ya all right?' Paddy said, straightening his chair.

'I'll have to change,' I said through my teeth. 'Give me the key.'

It was still bright as I sneaked out of the hall. The night patrol was out, listening for crying babies. I dodged them and let myself into our cabin.

I peeled my dress off and washed the sticky Guinness from my legs. Sitting down on the bed, I looked in the mirror at my red, angry face. Then I reminded myself I was on holiday. And if I was going to enjoy this holiday, I needed to let myself go and join in with the fun as well. Out came the red mini-skirt, white blouse and black sandals. On went the lipstick and powder, a spray of Tweed, and out that door I marched.

As I entered the hall, they were calling for one more volunteer. I glanced at our table. There was Paddy with one hand up, the other stubbing his cigarette out. Without thinking, I raced past him. The spotlight flashed over to me and three men on the floor. Four shiny miniature bikes were wheeled over.

'Okay, take a bike each.'

We struggled onto our bikes.

'Not so fast, ladies and gentlemen.'

Four large sacks, full of balloons, appeared beside us. The hall broke up into cheers.

'Into the sacks, then onto your bikes and wait.'

I jumped into my sack and was on my bike, my heart thumping. What in the name of God was I doing? The men, whipping their jackets off, struggled into theirs, falling all over the place.

'On your marks, get set, go.'

I peddled like mad down to the end of the hall. As I turned my bike around I caught sight of Debbie's face. She made for the door, a boy behind her.

I marched back to the table, all smiles, carrying my prize.

But no one was interested. Paddy lowered his pint. 'C'mon, Lily,' he said, grabbing up his cigarettes. 'We have to get these back to the cabin an' into bed. The dancin' is about to begin.'

I stood my vase on the table. 'Look what I won,' I said proudly.

'Why didn't you let Dad go up, Mum?' Paul said.

'Am I not to have any fun?'

'You're Mum. Dad's fun,' Bryan said.

'Don't mind dem, Lily. Just enjoy yerself.'

And I did. For the rest of the week, it was on with the mini and up on the floor with the rest of them.

Back to Vauxhall for Browny

'SYLVIA'S HOUSE HAS been broken into. Her landin' window is wide open,' Paddy shouted in the back door to me.

'She's been robbed? Jesus, no,' I said, dropping the tea towel.

It was Sunday morning after mass. Sylvia and Chris had left the day before with their two, David and Cheryl, for a holiday camp in Clacton.

The police arrived and banged off our hall door. Paddy led them into Chris's house. They combed the windows for fingerprints, then returned to our place to take down particulars.

'It happens this time every year when Vauxhall breaks up,' they said. 'We never know where the burglars will strike next. Last night, it was Meyrick Avenue. Tonight, some other street.'

'How come they didn't touch our house?' I said.

'They did,' one said, pointing to fresh marks on our kitchen window. 'What was on your table?'

'Cigarettes and matches,' Paddy said. 'Me jacket was on the back of dat chair.'

'They knew you were in.' He closed his notebook. And that was it. They left.

Paddy and I examined the fingerprints on our window.

'Do you think you should ring Chris at the holiday camp?' I said.

'What's the point? Let dem enjoy their holiday.'

I felt awful all week. I was the one who'd persuaded Sylvia to go to a holiday camp, telling her she wouldn't have to worry about the weather or the kids.

Paddy watched out for Sylvia and Chris all Saturday morning. He was out like a shot when a taxi drew up outside their house.

'Not much is missin',' Sylvia said, coming in for a cup of tea. 'But it's horrible knowin' a stranger's been rummagin' t'rough your t'ings.'

David and Cheryl became very nervous. They kept imagining a burglar was coming through their landing window. Sylvia couldn't get them to sleep at night.

'Chris is gettin' me a dog so they'll feel safe,' she said one morning. 'A fella in Vauxhall is givin' him a pup.'

The pup arrived a few days later. I heard all about Browny from Steven – how funny he was, spinning in circles chasing his tail.

The first chance I got, I popped in to see Browny. Sylvia opened her hall door. A gangly brown pup galloped out. He charged up and down the driveway, his long tail wagging. We stood chatting at the door, watching him. He was having a grand time, digging up her flowerbed, plants going everywhere. Finished with the garden, he lapped up the muddy puddles in the driveway.

'Ah God, he's thirsty,' I said.

Sylvia fetched his lovely new dish, filled with fresh water, and slid it in front of him. Browny wasn't interested. He kicked it over with his back legs, sped around the yard and continued lapping up the puddles.

'See what I mean?' Sylvia said. 'He's a real mongrel.'

'He's all right.'

'Look at his long skinny tail, Lily. I hate it.'

'Why don't you have it chopped off?' I said. 'Do you remember how Daddy used to make a few bob foxing dogs' tails back home? He'd hold the tail on the stool an' give it a good whack with the hatchet. We'd run out screamin', the dog behind us with a bit of rag on his tail.'

'I don't know anyone who'd do it here. An' how much would it cost?'

'There's a vet on Bedford Road. I bet he'd do it. I'll drop in an' ask him when I'm takin' Carol for her swimming lessons.'

'T'anks, that'd be good. It might make him look a bit better.'

I called in to the vet the following Wednesday. An elderly man in a white coat looked up from a desk in a tiny waiting room. 'How can I help you?'

'How much does it cost to fox a dog's tail?'

'Pardon?'

'How much do you charge to chop a dog's tail off?'

He removed his glasses and gave me a look that said *You stupid Irish woman.*

'Docking a dog's tail is a barbaric practice,' he said. 'They might do it in Ireland. We do not do it in this country.'

He stood up and shut the door behind me. I grabbed Carol's hand, walked slowly home and broke the bad news to Sylvia.

Browny got his marching orders the very next morning. Back to Vauxhall for him.

Sylvia went into a pet shop in Luton and bought a West Highland terrier. Candy had a short tail and did all the right things: slept on the landing, guarded the house and made sure to drink out of the lovely new dish.

A Gentleman's Agreement

'I've persuaded the boss's son to start up his own factory,' Paddy said, washing his hands one night. 'He needs me to help him get it up an' runnin'.'

I swung around from the cooker. 'You're leavin' his father, Awl Stein? I t'ought you liked him?'

'It's a great opportunity, Lily. His son's makin' me a partner.'

The boys shouted down. He ran up the stairs to kiss them goodnight. I could hear him laughing and joking with them. 'Not another word now,' he called back up to them, as he trotted down the stairs.

'I can't believe the boss's son would make you a partner,' I said, taking up his dinner. 'Have you got it in writin'?'

Paddy sat down and plastered his bread with butter. 'It's a gentleman's agreement. We shook hands on it. He can't do it wit'out me.'

I put down his plate of sausages and eggs beside him. 'Paddy, the Jews I worked for in Dublin were always a father an' son business. They'd never let anyone else in.'

'Your Irish suspicion again,' he said, making a sausage sandwich. 'Just imagine. It'll be somet'in' to pass on to the boys.'

'Where's the factory goin' to be?'

'Still in Hendon. I'm gettin' me licence. He's givin' me a car. Ya'll have to bear wit' me, love. I'll be workin' every hour God gives me till the factory gets on its feet.'

And work Paddy did. Day and night for the next few months, even Saturdays. A big grey Morris Oxford car was now parked in our driveway.

'It can do ninety miles an hour down the M1,' Paddy said, throwing the keys on the table. 'I'm in Hendon in no time.'

The weekends changed. Saturday jobs came to a standstill. And so did the long walks to Bluebell Woods with the boys of a Sunday. Now, after roast pork, Yorkshire pudding, mushy peas and potatoes, it was into the Morris Oxford and off to the Dunstable Downs to see the gliders. But Sunday afternoons hadn't changed for me.

I was happy to stay back with Carol and make their tea: two apple pies, one with cloves and one without, and a tray of scones, some with fruit and some without. I'd be only finished when the back door would burst open and in they'd come, starving.

'Upstairs an' wash your hands,' I'd say, taking their coats.

But the car gave Paddy the freedom for other ventures. Fed up waiting for him one Friday night, I went to bed and fell asleep. He woke me up coming into our room early Saturday morning.

'Sorry I'm late, love,' he said, stripping off.

'What time is it? Where were you?'

'I dropped in to a blue movie on my way home. I've always wanted to see a blue movie.'

'A blue movie? What's that?'

'Nuttin' much.' He rolled into bed, pulled up the covers and fell fast asleep.

I leapt out of bed and dressed, then picked up Paddy's shirt and trousers to be washed.

Down in the kitchen, I dragged out my twin-tub, emptied Paddy's trouser pockets and found a hanky smeared with bright red lipstick. I stood pondering over it. It certainly wasn't my lipstick.

The boys barged in for their breakfast. *Thunderbirds* had finished and they were dying to try out the new swimming pool in Bath Road. I stuffed the hanky into my apron pocket. They gobbled down their dishes of hot porridge, smothered with brown sugar and Lyle's syrup.

'What's wrong, Mum? You're very quiet,' Paul said, shoving his shoes on.

'Nuttin.'

The letter box tapped. Steven let David in.

Wherever the boys went, David went. He took after Chris with his black curly hair, and the boys took after Paddy with their straight brown. But they all had one thing in common – the O'Connor nose.

I counted out a shilling each for pool money and sixpence for a glass of hot Ribena after their swim. 'Hurry straight home, won't' youse?' I said.

The four of them headed down Meyrick Avenue, duffel bags

swinging off their shoulders. I closed the door, stomped up the stairs and into our bedroom. Paddy was snoring away. I shook him hard.

'I'm tired,' he murmured.

'I found this in your pocket,' I said, throwing the hanky on his face.

He opened his eyes and squinted at the red lipstick.

Five-year-old Carol walked in, carrying her clothes. 'Can I get dressed?' she said.

I brought her downstairs and dressed her in the lounge. The door opened. Paddy appeared in his working clothes. 'Show me those jobs ya've been askin' me to do,' he said.

I ignored him.

'Dat lipstick ya found on me hanky was from a girl at the door. She kissed all the men walkin' in an' out. I won't stop off dere again.'

Every single job got done that Saturday – the gate screwed back on its hinges, the fence banged back together, the clothesline tightened and the dripping taps fixed. And when the jobs were done, he drove to the shops and came back with sweets for them all and a huge box of Bassets Liquorice Allsorts for me. By the end of the day, I'd forgiven him.

The following Saturday morning, he jumped out of bed. 'I have to go to work today, love. Dere's new stock arrivin'. Stein won't be in today.'

He was up to London and back in a flash. I was up to my eyes with the washing when I heard the car pull in. The door opened. He whipped off his jacket and slung it on a chair.

'I t'ought you said you had to work all day?'

'The bugger's cheated me, Lily. He's lied to me.'

'What do you mean?'

'The stock was delivered this morning. The orders were made out in his name only. I searched the office for the deeds of the business and found them. Me name was nowhere to be seen on dem. I rang him. He admitted it. He's the sole owner. I've worked all those feckin' weekends for nuttin'.'

'The bugger. I knew it,' I said, emptying the basin into the sink with a vengeance. 'You should've got it in writin', Paddy.'

He stabbed his butt out hard in the ashtray. 'I'll stay wit' him till somet'in' better comes along,' he said, picking up the paper.

And something better did come along.

How in the Name a' God Could I Take Them There?

'How would ya like to go to South Africa?' Paddy said, throwing me his paper.

'South Africa? What do you mean South Africa?'

'Dere's a job in the paper. Dey're looking for someone to run a textile factory. I rang dem an' told dem I'm the manager of a factory here. The boss is comin' to London to interview me. I know I'll get it.'

I could see he was serious and had to sit down. 'South Africa? Jesus, Paddy, could you not get somet'in' a bit closer?'

'Well, what about yer Annie an' Paddy? Dey've gone to Australia.'

'At least there's no trouble there.'

I couldn't talk him out of it. He was up the next morning, singing his head off; he couldn't wait to tell Stein he was leaving. But he wasn't singing that night when he jumped off the bus in the lashing rain.

'God, you're soakin' wet,' I said, taking his coat.

'He took the car back.'

'He took the car back? The mean bugger. After all the work you did for nuttin'.'

A piece of paper was flung on the table.

'An' look at the lousy reference he gave me. He didn't kill himself writin' it.'

I picked it up.

> To whom it may concern
> Patrick O'Connor was employed by me from March
> 1969 to October 1969. During this time he carried out
> his duties conscientiously.
> Jacob Stein

I threw it down. 'My God, you ran that place.'

He handed me two blank sheets of paper from his coat pocket with the factory's heading on top.

'What good are these?' I said staring at them. 'They're blank.'
'You're not goin' to write your own reference, I hope?'

'No, but you are. Yer a better speller dan me. I'll tell ya what to say.'

'Oh, Paddy, I don't know.'

'Dey'll never know. I need a good reference for the South African job. The money is three times the amount I'd get in England. Lily, I'll never get this chance again.'

'I don't want to go. I'm not taking them out of their good schools. Bryan's just started at Cardinal Newman this year, that lovely new school on New Bedford Road. An' they said they'll take Steven next year when he's eleven.'

'Dere's good schools in South Africa as well. The firm is payin' all expenses.'

I told myself not to worry. Nothing would come of it. He wouldn't get the job. But before I knew where I was, he had us all booked on the *Northern Star* liner to South Africa.

'Dere's the ship youse are going on,' Paddy said, walking in one night, waving a brochure.

Thirteen-year-old Paul snatched it. 'Look at the size of it, Bryan. It's like a holiday camp. There's even a pool on board.'

Debbie kicked up hell for weeks. A determined fifteen-year-old, she was head girl in Rotheram and was worried she'd fall behind in South Africa. She was told she'd have to speak Afrikaans if she was to do well.

'I'm not going,' she'd scream every night, running up to her bedroom.

'Yer goin, dat's it,' Paddy would shout up the stairs after her.

The medicals were strict. A spot showed up on my X-ray.

'I've never had TB,' I told the nurse.

But she insisted I have more X-rays.

After numerous flashes from every angle, I was finally cleared.

We found a buyer for our house.

'Don't sign the final contract till I tell ya,' Paddy said, packing his case.

He flew ahead to South Africa to start work and find a suitable house for us.

Over the next three weeks, I was flat out sorting out what to take. The boys talked non-stop in bed every night about the huge ship they were going on. Debbie was learning Afrikaans from a teacher at her school. Sylvia and Chris were all excited. They were going too. Paddy promised Chris a job in his factory.

Everything was going well until one morning, when they were all at school, I heard the gate go. I looked out the window. It was Paddy, walking up the path with his case.

'What's wrong? Why have you come home?'

'Just let me in an' I'll tell ya.' He walked ahead of me into the kitchen, dropped his case, dragged out a chair and sat down. 'I had to come home. I couldn't let ya go to South Africa wit'out tellin' ya everyt'in'. It's no place to bring up yer family.'

'Jesus, Paddy, you've talked us all into it, even Sylvia an' Chris. We're all ready to go.'

'Sit down. Just let me explain. Den if ya still want to go, we'll go.'

I took down two cups and saucers and flicked on the kettle.

'I love the job,' he said. 'The factory's brand new, wit' the latest machines. The boss is delighted wit' me. We'd be well off. Durban is a beautiful city, Lily. The sea is level wit' the land an' the water is blue an' warm. But I couldn't stand the way dey treated the blacks.' He pulled off his watch and threw it on the table.

'Paddy, I've notified the schools, the solicitor, the bank an' all.'

'Just listen, will ya? The boss met me at the airport. He couldn't wait to show me the factory. As we were drivin' along the highway, the blacks were runnin' along the side of the road. "It's a wonder dey don't get knocked down," I said. D'ya know what he said? "If you hit one, Patrick, you must keep going. If you stop, the rest would kill you." Dat's what he said, Lily. Can ya believe it?'

I watched him light up. I reached under the sink for his ashtray. If it hadn't been for the familiar smell of his smoke, I wouldn't have believed he was sitting here in front of me, telling me all this.

'An' here's somet'in' else I hated. The boss saw me offer a cigarette to a black. He took me aside. "We don't do that here, Patrick," he said. I told him I've worked wit' blacks in London an' I got on well wit' dem. Lily, dey're treated like dirt in their own country. Dey sit outside at lunchtime in the heat, eatin' lumps of chicken, while we sit in an air-conditioned canteen.'

I sat gripping my cup of tea, not knowing what to think.

'Now, we'll go if ya want to,' he said. 'Ya'd have a maid an' yer own swimming pool. The houses are lovely. Dey're built outside the city near the sugar canes, up off the ground because of the snakes.'

'The snakes?'

'Dat's another t'ing. If we go, I'd have to buy a gun.'

'To shoot the snakes!'

'An' the blacks.'

'Jesus, the blacks as well?'

'Ya have to shoot dem if dey break into yer house.'

'God, that's terrible.'

'It's up to you now. I'll go back if ya want me to. But we'll need huge bolts on the windows an' doors. An' two Alsatians tied up out the back.'

'Alsatians! Jesus, I hate Alsatians.'

'We'll need dem to keep the blacks away,' he said, stubbing his cigarette out. 'But it's up to you. The boss is expectin' me back. He t'inks I've come home to help ya.'

I sat biting my nails, thinking of Sylvia and Chris. They'd be furious. And what about the young couple who couldn't wait to move into our house? They wouldn't be happy. And the millions of X-rays they made me have. I could have done without them.

'The boys will be so disappointed.'

'It's better for the boys to be disappointed dan grow up wit' hate in dem for the blacks. But I'll go if ya want to. It's yer decision.'

'After all you've told me, Paddy, how in the name a' God could I take them there?'

I'VE ALWAYS WANTED TO SEE AMERICA

'I CALLED IN to see Young Stein today. He's sellin' out,' Paddy said, closing the kitchen door. 'He can't run the factory wit'out me. He wants me to help him sell the machines.'

'You called in to see him? After what he did to you.'

'Lily, it was me dat persuaded him to open the factory,' he said, drying his hands. 'I chose those machines. I know what dey're worth.'

'I t'ought you said you were lookin' for another job?'

'Don't worry, love. I'll walk into a job after Christmas.'

Thump! Thump! Thump!

'That's the boys bangin' down. They're waiting for you to go up an' kiss them goodnight.'

The weeks went by. Paddy stripped and cleaned the machines to be sold. Over dinner one night, he talked about an American who had come into the factory.

'He was delighted wit' the condition of the machines,' he said, pouring me out a cup of tea. 'He bought t'ree an' took me to the Ritz for lunch.'

'The Ritz? For lunch? That was good of him.'

'He wants me to erect the machines in the States. All expenses paid.'

'He expects you to go all the way to America to put up his machines? God!'

'I tell ya what, Lily,' he said, buttering his bread. 'It's a wonderful opportunity for a single man.'

'That's right. A single man,' I said, feeling relieved. 'Listen, Paddy, *Steptoe* is on in a minute. Hurry up. I don't know want to miss him again.'

Christmas came. Our Woolworth's tree was dragged down from the attic with its box of decorations. Debbie set it up in the front room and decorated it. Carol sat gazing at the coloured lights flicking on and off.

Paddy rolled up his sleeves in the kitchen and scrubbed his nails hard. Out came his mother's five-pound pot and the makings of

the pudding. No weighing out ingredients for Paddy. In went the
lot, stirred up with Guinness. Soon the puddings, one cloth and
one bowl, were simmering away.

I lay in bed Christmas morning, listening to shouts of excitement from the boys, strumming their new guitars. Carol rushed in
to show me her new doll's pram, and Debbie peeped around the
door to say thanks for her new French horn. She was now in the
school band.

After mass, the turkey was devoured and the washing-up done.
Then we all gathered round the tree and handed each other little
red net-bags of chocolate gold coins. Paddy drew the curtains and
stoked the fire. I cut up the Christmas cake and the rest of the
pudding. The boys sat reading their annuals – *The Beano*, *The
Dandy*, *The Beezer* – while Debbie read her *Boyfriend* and Carol
laughed at the *Bimbo*. Out came the guitars that night. With glasses
of creamy soda and dishes of crisps, the O'Connor Christmas sing-
song began. Sylvia and Chris came in with their two, and we all did
our party pieces.

The New Year saw Paddy having more and more lunches at the
Ritz.

The American was back.

One night, he was late. I put his dinner on a plate in the oven
to keep warm. It was one of those days when a heavy mist hung
over Luton all day and never lifted. The newscaster said the trains
were delayed and there were pile-ups on the M1. I was in the front
room giving the fire a good raking when the back door opened
and closed. In skipped Paddy.

'I've taken dat job in the States,' he blurted out, throwing his
coat on the couch.

I sat down, the hot poker still in my hand. 'You've taken that
job? You said it was for a single man.'

'I've always wanted to see America. I'm goin'.'

I stared at him. 'Paddy, you're startin' again. You dragged me
from Dublin to Luton then down to Torquay and back again. A
month ago, you had us all on the boat to South Africa. Now you're
talkin' about America. Your mother was right. You should've
bought a caravan.'

'It won't be for long, love. I'll make a bit a' money an' pay off dat bloody interest on the mortgage. We won't know ourselves.'

By the end of the week, Paddy was tearing up and down the stairs, stuffing his shirts and shaving kit into his case. He kissed them all goodbye. 'Now be good for yer mammy, won't youse? I'll bring youse back a present.'

'I'll be dyin' to hear from you,' I said, still not believing he was going.

A car beeped.

'Dere's me taxi. I'll ring when I get dere, love.' He hugged me goodbye and then he was gone.

Our new green phone rang every week. It was Paddy with the same questions. 'Is me wages goin' into the bank? How are the kids? Are dey helpin' ya? I'll ring again when I can, love. Bye, mind yerself for me.'

It was a month before he was back. No sign of the old battered case. A big brand-new one was unlocked on our kitchen table. The boys crowded round as he handed out Levi's, flannelette shirts and piles of white socks. A bottle of Chanel No 5 for me.

'C'mere to me, chicken,' he said, bending down to Carol and strapping a Mickey Mouse watch on her wrist.

'What's that?' I said, pointing to a yellow airport bag on the table.

'Dat's me duty-free.' He took out a bottle of Johnnie Walker.

'Do you want a cup a' tea?' I said, filling the kettle.

'No, love, I'll have a drink. Where's dat box of brandy glasses Stein gave me last Christmas? Dey're goin' to come in handy now.'

Paddy was still asleep the following morning when they all trailed out to school. I packed the Ready Brek away, pressed the sticky lid down hard on the syrup tin and went upstairs to dress.

'Are dey all gone?' he whispered.

'Debbie takes Carol to school now, t'ank God,' I said, fastening my bra. 'I don't have to bring her any more.'

He stretched his arms up. 'C'mon back to bed for a few minutes, love.'

'Sylvia might knock,' I said, sorting out my clothes on the chair.

'When are dey goin' to Australia?'

'End of the year. She's talkin' about it all the time. She's dyin' for a bit a' heat.'

'Come back to bed. I'll soon warm ya up,' he said, fumbling through his wallet.

I glanced out the window. Neighbours on my left and right were hanging out their washing, chatting to each other across my garden. *That's what I should be doing. I've a whole heap of washing downstairs to do.*

'C'mon, love. I've missed ya.'

I'd missed him too, but I wasn't the type to say it. And it didn't seem right getting into bed during the day. Not right at all.

But I needn't have worried. It was all over in a minute.

Paddy rolled back. 'Sorry for comin' too soon, love. It's because I haven't had ya for a month.'

He lay there in his white T-shirt, his hands linked behind his head, talking non-stop about North Carolina, the big posh hotels he'd stayed in, the big steaks he'd eaten. All at the company's expense. 'Dey even said I can have a woman sent up to me room,' he said, grinning.

'My God, is that what they do in America? What did you say?'

'What d'ya t'ink I said?' He laughed and jumped out of bed. 'C'mon, love. I'm goin' to take ya to lunch.'

He danced into the bathroom, singing, then was back in a minute, clean-shaven. He slipped on his good navy-blue suit.

'I'll call a cab,' he said, trotting down the stairs.

After he'd bought the latest Bush stereo record player, it was off to the Red Lion Hotel for lunch. The bill was brought to our table. Paddy handed the girl a tip.

'You gave her a pound,' I whispered. 'Go easy on the money. You haven't a proper job yet.'

'I've somet'in' to tell ya, love,' he said, knocking back his Scotch. 'I'm goin' back to the States. Dey want me to do another job.'

Thank God for Stockwood Park

I T WAS THE last week of the summer school holidays. Debbie had gone away with Pauline, her school friend. Paddy was gone five months, and I was gone mad with them.

'When's Dad coming home from that stupid America?' Steven said, shooting his hot-rod cars across the kitchen floor.

'Yeah, we've had no holiday,' Bryan complained.

I looked over at Paul. He was stretched across the sink, his dirty thumb pressed over the tap, squirting water into a glass of baby-orange juice.

'What are you doin'?' I shouted.

'Making a fizzy drink.'

'Hurry up. Look at the mess you're makin' on the floor.'

Carol trotted in, bumping her pram into everything.

'Why don't you tell Daddy I'm dead?' she said, tucking her dolls in.

'He's ringin' tonight. You can tell him yourself.'

Bryan shot one of Steven's cars into the wall. It went flying, falling apart. The next thing I knew, the pair of them were on the floor, fighting, thumping each other.

'Right, where's that wooden spoon?' I said, running to the cutlery drawer.

A few whacks on their bottoms and they were up and out the back door fast, Paul and Carol slipping out behind them.

Bolting the door, I hurried upstairs to make the beds. The sound of a bus screeching and beeping outside sent me flying to the front bedroom window. Bryan was in the middle of the road on Debbie's skates.

'Jesus, Mary an' Joseph, I'll murder him,' I said, galloping down the stairs.

I ordered him into the driveway then banged the front gates closed. Around the back I marched, wondering what the others were up to. They were over the fence in the allotments. Carol was hanging upside down on the huge elm tree, her little pink dress over her face. Steven was firing stones into my neighbour's water tank. Thick smoke sailed around Paul, who was holding his magnifying glass over a pile of newspapers, setting the allotments on fire.

'Right,' I shouted. 'Get back over here, the lot of youse. We're goin' to Stockwood Park.'

'Not Stockwood again,' they all moaned. 'We've been there every single day of our holidays.'

'I'll buy youse ice creams on the way.'

I grabbed my handbag, combed my hair and put a bit of lipstick on. Up Bolingbroke Road we hiked, the boys wheeling their bikes. Straight down Wilsden Avenue and into the Cross Way shops for Zoom and Fab ice creams.

We stopped at the busy Farley Hill Road. Stockwood Park was on the opposite side. Buses, vans and cars thundered by. I warned them not to cross till there was a gap in the traffic. Gripping their bikes, they were all ready to run.

'Right, go now, quick, quick,' I shouted, grabbing Carol's hand and running with them over the road.

Inside the safety of Stockwood, I could relax and let them go wild on their bikes, speeding all over its grounds, up and down hollows and in between trees. No swings or slides in this park. Only wide open spaces where they could cycle for hours and hours and tire themselves out.

Carrying my cardigan, I sauntered with Carol down a long driveway shaded by huge chestnut trees. *T'ank God for Stockwood Park*, I thought to myself. *I can't understand why no one ever comes here except us.* I reared them in this park. We went all seasons. Spring saw them with jam jars catching sticklebacks in its pond. Autumn, they ran around kicking mounds of golden leaves, searching for shiny brown conkers. When the sun showed its watery face in winter, they'd tramp through thick snow and fire snowballs at each other.

Carol and I approached the spot where Stockwood House, a stately home, once stood. According to Debbie, it had been the home of John Crawley. All that remained of it now were its stables and steps leading up to where its main entrance had been.

'Sit here, Mum. I want to make a daisy chain,' Carol said, running up its steps.

I spread my cardigan out and sat down. It was warm and peace-ful, with not a soul or a sinner to be seen. Closing my eyes, I thought about John Crawley. I could just see him in his brown rid-ing breeches, galloping around his estate on his horse. Was he married? Did he have any children? Did he leave them for months at a time?

I opened my eyes. Carol was in her own world, talking to her daisy chain. A well-dressed man had appeared behind her. His fly was open and his thing was hanging out. And it wasn't Lord Crawley either.

I was up like a shot. 'Carol, come away,' I screamed.

She jumped, picked up her daisy chain and ran towards me. The man slunk off into the nearby bushes.

I grabbed her hand. 'C'mon, let's go an' find the boys. T'ank God Dad's ringin' tonight. You can talk to him on the phone.'

DOWN THE SINK WITH JOHNNIE WALKER

'W E'LL GO UP to Heathrow an' meet Dad,' I said over break-fast.

Porridge was devoured and there was a mad dash upstairs. Carol and the boys were ready in seconds and begging me to hurry.

It was Saturday morning. Paddy was on his way home. It couldn't have been a better time for me. Sylvia and Chris and their two children had left for Australia the week before. I was missing them. No more cosy chats over morning tea with delicious marzipan cake in Sylvia's.

We caught the Greenline Coach to Heathrow and waited excitedly at Arrivals. Crowds of tired people pushing their cases on trolleys poured out of a door in front of us. A man in a red flannelette shirt and white pants swaggered out, wheeling a trolley with a grey zipped-up suit bag on top of his case.

Paul grabbed my arm. 'Is that Dad?'

Paddy heard him, stopped, removed his dark sunglasses and looked in our direction. A smile spread across his face. It grew wider and wider as he ran with his trolley towards us. He grabbed Carol up, kissed the face off her, then turned to me. 'Wadda wonderful surprise, honey,' he said, hugging me. 'I missed ya all.'

'You sound real American, Dad,' Bryan said, laughing.

'You look real American, Dad,' Paul said.

'I've got yer Levi's,' he said, patting their heads and looking around. 'Where's Debbie?'

'She has a Saturday job now in the British Home Stores,' I said.

Paddy sat beside me on the bus back to Luton. Feeling his body close to mine was like old times. We were a couple again.

'Haven't dey all grown?' he said, squeezing my arm.

'Well, you have been away for five months.'

'I'm home now.' He let go of my hand and pulled a small card out of his shirt pocket. 'Pat O'Connor, Textile Consultant' was printed on it. 'I'll be goin' around Europe, buyin' an' sellin' machines for the company,' he said, delighted with himself. 'Don't worry, honey. Dey'll only be short trips.'

'What about Australia? You said we'd go.'

'Whatever ya want. We'll plan for next year.' He pulled another card out of his wallet. 'D'ya see dat, Lily? Dey've given me an expense card. I can fly anywhere in the world on dat an' stay in the best hotels.'

Paddy loved his new job, travelling all over Europe, staying in top hotels and having big business lunches. Each time he arrived home, the yellow duty-free bag came too. Cigarettes and whisky for himself and Chanel for me.

One of his short business trips took him to Dublin. He stayed in Jury's Hotel.

'Jury's Hotel?' I said. 'You stayed in Jury's? God, Paddy, I was always too terrified to put my foot inside that place.'

'I bumped into yer friend, Hazel. She's workin' dere,' he said, pouring himself a Scotch.

'You saw Hazel, did you? What did she say?'

'She was askin' after ya.'

'God, I would have loved to have seen her.'

He saw the envy in my eyes and reached into his pocket. 'Here,' he said, handing me a gold cross and chain. 'I bought ya this in the Ring House in O'Connell Street.'

Christmas night, 1970, wasn't the same without Sylvia and Chris. The boys missed doing their party piece with David. And Paddy and I missed Chris singing, 'Are ya dere, Mor-ee-arr-ritee?'

Soon the children were back at school and Paddy was flying around Europe again. In between trips, he'd sleep in, then jump up, have a shave and pat his face with Old Spice. He'd slip on his new American cream suit and stride down Meyrick Avenue to the Luton Labour Club to play snooker.

'I'll be home for dinner, honey,' he said one morning, giving me a quick kiss.

'Don't be late again, will you? I'm makin' a meat pie with the puff pastry you love.'

One by one, they trailed in from school, kicked their shoes off under the stairs and went into the front room to watch *Skippy*. Debbie was late as usual. Band practice night.

'When's Dad comin' home? We're hungry,' Bryan said, when the six o'clock news came on.

'He'll be home soon,' I said, praying to God he'd hurry.

Seven o'clock came, and everything was ready to be taken up. Paul peeped into the kitchen. 'Mum, there's a taxi outside.'

Drying my hands, I walked down the hall and opened the door.

'Keep the change,' Paddy called back to the driver.

He swayed from side to side, stumbling up the path. 'I'm goin' up to lie down,' he said, pushing by me.

'What about your dinner? They're all waitin' on you.'

'I don't want it,' he said. 'I want a lie down.' He clutched the banisters and climbed the stairs, one by one.

Carol and the boys ducked into the hall and glanced upstairs. 'We're starving,' they said.

I pushed them back into the kitchen. 'I'm takin' it up now.'

The potatoes were mashed hard with a lump of butter and an egg. The pie was whipped out of the oven, got a good stab with the knife and was cut into six pieces.

'How come Dad never eats with us any more?' Bryan said, emptying the sauce bottle over his dinner.

Paul grinned. 'He's drunk again.'

I banged down my plate, ran upstairs, burst through the door and glared at him in bed. His trousers and shirt were lying on the floor, loose change scattered beside them.

'Are you goin' to continue like this? Are you?'

'Go away.'

In a fit of temper, I picked up one of his shoes and sent it flying towards his head.

'Leave me alone,' he mumbled, pulling up the covers.

Another shoe was sent speeding towards him, bouncing off his head. Shocked at what I was doing, I hurried out of the room and into the bathroom, holding onto the cold sink.

A few deep breaths and I was back downstairs. The boys had washed up; they were eager to watch telly.

My dinner went into the oven to keep warm with Debbie's. The hunger was gone off me. All I wanted was a cup of tea. My hands curled round the hot cup for comfort. The door opened. I jumped. It was Paddy in his white T-shirt and trousers. He marched to the sideboard and took out his bottle of whisky and a brandy glass. Without looking at me, he headed into the front room. A loud shout boomed through the wall. 'Shut up, I'm watchin' the goddamn news.'

I tore in. 'What's goin' on?'

'Dey can't stay quiet for a minute. Dey're jumpin' on top of each other.'

Carol and the boys were on the floor in front of the television. 'Go an' get ready for bed,' I said, picking up the cushions. I looked over at Paddy. 'You've forgotten what it's like to be a father; that's what's wrong with you.'

I followed them up, making sure they brushed their teeth.

'Why is Dad so cranky, Mum?' Steven asked, climbing into bed. 'He never comes up to kiss us goodnight any more.'

'He's too tired,' I said, tucking him in. 'You can read for a while.'

After a speedy read of 'Bizzy Lizzy' to Carol, it was back down to the front room to see what was happening. There was Paddy, eyes closed, belt undone, lying on the couch, smoking, a glass of whisky on a stool beside him. The stereo was turned up. Lee Marvin was droning out 'I was boorrnnn under a waannndering star'.

'I'm sick of that eejit an' his moanin' voice,' I said, whipping the record off.

Paddy jumped, knocking his drink over. He stubbed his cigarette out, picked up his bottle, refilled his glass and drained it.

'You never used to drink at home. It's only since you went to that feckin' America.'

He glared at me, his eyes glazed, his mouth twisted. It didn't look like him at all.

I grabbed the bottle off his stool. 'Right, I'm gettin' rid of that bloody Johnnie Walker.'

He staggered after me into the kitchen with his empty glass and stood staring. I couldn't stop myself. I held the bottle upside down over the sink, watching the amber liquid disappear down the plug hole.

'What are ya doin'?'

'No more whisky comes into this house. D'ya hear me? No more.'

He picked up the empty bottle. 'Shit, ya've emptied the lot.'

'That's another thing. I'm sick of you saying: "shit this" and "shit that". Somet'in' else you picked up in that America. You have the boys all sayin' it.'

'Bullshit.'

'I'm certainly not goin' there, I can tell you.'

'I'm not workin' here for shit money.'

'You can't handle the money, Paddy. That expense card is a curse. A bloody curse.'

He picked up his cigarettes. 'I'm not leavin' ya short, am I?' he said. 'Ya'll be rid of me tomorra'. I'm goin' back to the States.'

The back door opened. Debbie walked in, carrying her satchel and French horn.

'How was band practice?' I said, forcing a smile.

'What's wrong?'

'Nuttin'. Your dinner's in the oven, keepin' warm.'

'Mum,' Carol shouted from the top of the stairs. 'Will you come up?'

Paddy stormed from the kitchen and into the front room, banging the door behind him. I ran upstairs to turn out their lights and kiss them goodnight.

'When is Daddy going back to America?' Carol said, as I tucked her in tightly.

'I don't know.'

He slept on the couch in the front room that night. I woke early to see him packing his case in our bedroom. He left without a word. No hugs or goodbyes.

I struggled out of bed and saw them off to school. While I was dressing, three hard knocks banged on the hall door. I raced down the stairs. A courier handed me a green glass container full of fresh flowers. A small card was stuck on top.

> Sorry, Love.
> I couldn't leave without saying goodbye.
> It won't happen again.
> Always yours,
> Paddy.

From Land's End to God Knows Where

No one ran to the door when Paddy walked in with his case. No one asked if he was home for good any more. The boys thanked him for their presents, new transistor radios, then packed their duffel bags and off they went to the pool.

Paddy held up a pair of cream pants. 'D'ya like these?' he said. 'I had to get a bigger size.'

It wasn't the pants that I was watching. It was the duty-free bag on the floor. This was the moment to empty the bottle. *He's pleased to be home and won't get upset with me.* I picked up the bag and pulled out a carton of cigarettes. Now for the whisky. Over to the sink I went and pulled out that familiar bottle. I couldn't believe it. It wasn't Johnnie Walker inside the bottle but a bandy-legged ballerina dancing to the tune of 'The Blue Danube'.

Paddy looked up from his case and roared with laughter. 'I couldn't resist it. I knew you'd t'ink it was whisky.'

'God, I'm glad it wasn't. I couldn't go through that again.'

He took out two red Indian shawls. 'These are for Debbie an' Carol. Where are dey?' he said, sitting down.

'Carol's watchin' the telly an' Debbie's gone on holidays with Pauline an' her parents.'

'Why don't we go away?'

'It's the last week of their school holidays, Paddy. We've nowhere booked.'

'Lily, will ya forget this bookin' business. We don't have to live like dat any more. In the States, dey jump in the car an' go.'

'We've no car.'

'We'll hire one.'

'Where would we stay?'

'We'll just keep goin' an' stop off at motels.'

The very next morning, Paddy raced into Luton to hire a car while I dashed around, packing cases.

'Are ya ready, honey?' he said, swinging the car keys. 'We'll head down Cornwall way.'

Soon we were speeding down the M1, Paddy singing his head off, me gripping the seat, praying he wouldn't overtake.

'Dere's the Circular Road,' he said. 'We'll be in Exeter for lunch.'

But we weren't. We hit a traffic jam. Cars inched along for miles and miles. Every time they moved, Paddy put his foot down and shot up to the next. 'These goddamn traffic jams,' he said. 'Ya don't get dem on the highways in the States. Are ya sure ya won't come to the States, honey? Dey'd all love to meet ya.'

'I don't fancy America. I'm waitin' to hear from Australia House for our interview.'

'So ya've made up yer mind? Ya're determined to go to Australia?'

'Well, I'm not stayin' here on me own any longer. You're in America all the time. Helen's moved back to Bray, an' Johnny's t'inkin' of goin' back to Dublin to live.'

'Write to Sylvia. Find out the prices of houses in Australia. I'll only take dem from home to home.'

The car in front pulled up sharp and we smashed into its boot. Our bonnet sprang up.

'Shit.'

The driver in front gave out hell, pointing to a dent on his highly polished car. Paddy climbed out to inspect the damage, handed him a small card and banged down our bonnet.

'Was his car badly damaged?' I whispered, as he climbed back in beside me.

'Nah,' he said, lighting up a cigarette. 'Luton Car Hire will pay for it.'

The traffic began to flow. Paddy put his foot down. Up flew the bonnet.

'Shit.' He screeched to a halt. We were all flung forward.

'Jesus,' I said. 'What are you goin' to do?'

'I'll tie the son of a bitch down,' he said, slipping the belt off his pants.

'Will that hold it?' I said.

'Sure, honey. It's leather.'

We drove off along the narrow winding roads. I sat back and relaxed, admiring the low stonewalls. They reminded me of Bray. 'This is lovely,' I said.

Snap. Up went the bonnet again. He had to break hard and skidded up onto an embankment.

'Jesus, me nerves are all gone.'

'Don't worry, honey. We'll crawl along to the next phone box. I'll ring the RAC.'

The RAC wired the bonnet down. 'Get it fixed properly at the next garage,' they warned us.

We all piled back in.

'I want to go to the toilet, Dad,' Carol moaned from the back.

'We'll stop at the next motel, princess,' he said.

'What about the garage?' I said. 'The car has to be fixed.'

'Stop yer worryin'. It's fine.'

A flashing motel sign appeared. He slowed up. 'Wait till I check in,' he said, climbing out and hitching up his trousers.

We had burgers and chips then fell into bed, exhausted. After our breakfast of bacon and eggs, we were on our way to God knows where.

'Here we are again. Happy as can be. All my kids are jolly good company,' Paddy sang, as he steered the car around corners.

'What are those people looking at?' I said, pointing to big ugly-looking stone slabs in an open field.

'It's Stonehenge,' Steven called out, leaning forward. 'Can we stop and have a look, please? We learnt about it at school.'

'Is that Stonehenge?' I said. 'It's very bleak looking.'

Paddy glanced over but wasn't bothered. He kept going. We travelled for hours, speeding by one hotel after another.

'When are we stopping?' they all complained. 'When are we stopping?'

At last, Paddy screeched to a halt and laughed. 'I can't go an inch further unless I hit the water.'

The Land's End Hotel welcomed us, with its white double doors wide open. The manager hurried out to meet us, took our cases and showed us up to our rooms.

'We're off to explore, Mum,' Steven said, running out with Carol.

I opened the windows and gazed out at the shimmering blue sea. Carol and the boys were below, trotting off on well-worn paths along the cliff tops.

'We'll stay here for the week,' Paddy said, trying out the bed.

'We'd better go down after them, see what they're up to.'

'Dey'll be fine. Stop worryin'.' He reached over for the hotel's brochure. 'Dey've a bar here. Let's check it out.'

The bar was quiet and cool. I sipped my bitter lemon. Paddy lit up and smiled over at me. 'Just sit back an' enjoy yerself,' he said. 'Ya're on yer holidays.'

A few minutes later, Paul burst through the door. 'Mum, quick! Carol's fallen over the cliff.'

'Jesus, Mary an' Joseph! Where?'

I raced after him towards the cliff. Bryan and Steven were pointing over the edge.

'Where is she?'

Carol jumped out from behind a rock, her arms wide like a magician. The boys burst out laughing.

'Don't ever do that to me again, do you hear me?' I said, trembling.

Paddy strolled up. 'See, I told ya dey'd be okay.'

'It's not a holiday camp. We have to keep an eye on them.'

For the rest of the week, we strolled around Sennen Cove, enjoying the sun and sea air. Every evening, I poured calamine lotion onto sunburnt arms and legs.

I had nothing to do but sit back and relax, and look forward to dining out every night. No more cafés for Paddy. We dined in top restaurants and hotels now. He'd sit back, like a real American, and order Scotch on the rocks while waiting for his steak.

On the last day, we strolled right to the tip of Land's End. A blank white signpost was pointing out to sea. A photographer stood nearby with a box of black letters at his feet. He was waiting for a tourist.

Paddy threw down his cigarette and stood on it. 'C'mon, I know what's it like to be a photographer,' he said. 'Let's give him a go.'

The photographer's eyes lit up. He picked up his box of letters. 'From Land's End to where? What country?' he asked.

'North Carolina, USA?' Paddy said, smiling.

'Geelong, Australia,' I said firmly.

COME TO SUNNY AUSTRALIA

'LOOK, MUM, THAT'S where we're going, isn't it?' Steven said, pointing to a poster across the tracks.

The picture showed a happy family in bathers, playing ball on a sandy beach. Its clear blue sky brightened this dark, draughty tube station under St Pancras. 'Come to Sunny Australia' it beckoned in big, bold, white letters.

Commuters in overcoats glanced up at the poster, then at Paddy and me. Carol skipped up and down the platform. I was glad I'd made her wear her red duffel coat and tights. The boys tricked around in their best corduroy jackets, fancying themselves with their Beatle haircuts, happy to have a day off school. Debbie stood apart. A book peeped out of the pocket of her long maroon coat. She pushed her glasses back up on her nose and pouted. A sixth-form student she was now, so no more school uniforms for her. She hated missing a day, even when she had her bad sinus. Her long brown hair blew up as the tube train whooshed in.

'Quick, all on,' Paddy said, as the sliding doors opened.

Australia House was busy. Families hurried in and out of this huge building. We were ushered into a room for our interview. A well-dressed man shook our hands and introduced himself as the immigration officer. He pointed to a row of chairs in front of a table. 'Take a seat,' he said, sitting down. He opened our application file. 'Can I see your medical certificates, please?'

I passed him a large envelope.

'So, your vaccinations against smallpox are in order. Good. You're all in sound health. No disabilities or history of mental illness. Good. No criminal records. Good.'

He studied the doctor's note from the X-ray clinic. 'I see you have a scar on your lung, Mrs O'Connor,' he said, looking up at me.

'I caught it from my mother, but I've never had TB.'

'Australia does not permit entry to people who have a history of TB.'

'The scar has never been active.'

He slipped out of the room. A few minutes later, he was back with another form. 'If we accept you, you must agree to have an X-ray every year in Australia. Sign here, please.'

He turned to Paddy. 'What are your prospects of employment in Australia?'

'I'm in the textile industry, knitwear. I've written to factories in Melbourne,' he said, taking out a bundle of letters. 'Dey want to see me when I arrive.'

'What about Darwin? We need people there.'

'I don't t'ink dey'd be needin' woollens in Darwin,' Paddy laughed.

The immigration officer moved on to the next question. 'Now, accommodation.'

'I'm havin' a house built before we go.'

'Good, no need for a hostel.' He folded up his file, looked up and smiled. 'I don't think there will be a problem in admitting you into Australia. Are there any questions?'

'I want to go to university,' Debbie said. 'I've left school. I'm at sixth-form college.'

'You'll have to go back to school. You must matriculate in Australia before you can enter university. You'll need to complete Higher School Certificate at year twelve in one of our schools.'

Debbie's face dropped.

'What are the seasides like?' Carol said, giggling.

'We have the best beaches in the world.'

'What about spiders and snakes?' Steven asked.

Paddy glanced at his watch. 'What about the costs?'

'The Australian government assists passengers. You and your wife pay ten pounds each,' he said. 'But you can't leave the country for two years. You have to give it a fair go. If you do leave Australia within the two years, you pay the government back the full fare.'

The immigration officer stood up and shook our hands. 'You will be notified when we have a date for your departure,' he said, seeing us to the door.

'I've got to have X-rays every year in Australia,' I said outside on the steps.

'I have to go back to school,' Debbie snapped.

'I've got to get back to the States or we'll have no bloody money.'

I ran up and down the stairs after Paddy the following morning. 'What about the house?'

'Advertise it in the paper.'

'How much?'

'The same price we were askin' when we were goin' to South Africa.'

'An' what about the furniture?'

'If ya want to go to Australia, Lily, ya have to leave t'ings behind.' He picked up his case. 'Take only what ya need. The bare essentials. We'll buy new furniture.'

'What about all me bed linen an' blankets?'

'Take dat blue chest of drawers an' stuff as much as ya can into it. I'll be back as soon as I can.'

The taxi beeped. A quick kiss goodbye and he was gone.

The Guesthouse

I SOLD THE house overnight with all my Dublin furniture thrown in – my solid dining-room suite with its lovely cocktail sideboard and all. A young couple didn't know themselves getting such a bargain. Agents rang, abusing me for underpricing. I ended up leaving the phone off the hook. Australia House sent a telegram with our date of departure, 1 November 1971. The removalist came and went with our few things.

Paddy flew home a week before we were to leave.

'I'd like to go back to Dublin for a few days,' I said, as soon as he got in the door.

'Sure, honey. I'll book yer ticket.'

This was my first time to fly. On went the gold cross and chain. In no time at all, I was off the plane and on the bus into Dublin.

'Dey're all comin' back, Lily,' Nora said. 'The work here has picked up.'

'An' here am I goin' in the opposite direction,' I said, biting my lower lip.

Next it was out to Bray to see my friend, Helen.

'Coming back is the best thing Seamus and I ever did, Lily,' she said. 'All my family are here. I'm glad I've come home.'

I twisted my cross and chain around and around. 'God, I hope I'm makin' the right decision.'

'You've broken your chain,' she said, looking at me holding the cross in my hand.

I hugged her goodbye. 'I'll be back.'

The plane tore down the runway, leaving Dublin. I glanced around. Everyone was blessing themselves. I did the same, just in case.

Paddy was delighted to see me when I walked in the door. 'T'ank God, yer home,' he said. 'Australia House has postponed our date for a week.'

'But we have to move out of the house tomorrow. The couple are movin' in.'

'Don't worry. I've booked a hotel for us till we leave.'

'Where are they all?' I said, looking around. 'They should be home from school by now?'

'I sent dem up to Stockwood Park on dere bikes wit' Carol.'

'You let Carol go with them? You shouldn't have. It's gettin' dark.'

'She'll be fine. The boys will look after her.'

'Where's Debbie?'

'She's stayin' wit' Pauline till we fly out.'

The following morning, the boys were marched off to school, uniforms and all. Paddy walked into town to hire a car. Carol played outside while I ran around the house giving it a good cleaning.

A low red Ford Capri zoomed up Meyrick Avenue with Paddy at the wheel. We had a terrible job fitting all our cases in.

The hotel on New Bedford Road was nothing but a glorified guesthouse. It was deathly quiet, full of elderly people sitting around on old armchairs. A tall thin lady, fixing a clip in her short grey hair, met us at reception.

'Mr O'Connor,' she said, looking in her book. 'Your rooms are ready. Follow me.'

We traipsed behind her up a narrow stairway to two tiny rooms leading off each other. Each room had only one double bed, one for the three boys, and the other for Paddy, Carol and me. No sign of a television or radio. No nothing.

'Let's make the most of these last few days in England,' Paddy said, combing his hair. 'We'll pick the boys up from school an' have dinner in Luton.'

After chicken and chips, Carol and the boys scraped their ice-cream dishes clean. Then it was back to the guesthouse.

Paddy glanced at his watch. 'Let's go to the Labour Club,' he said.

'I can't leave them on their own. They're too excited.'

'Well, I'm goin' whether you are or not,' he said. 'I want to say goodbye to me sisters, Eileen an' Phil.' He opened his case and took out a clean shirt and began to get ready.

'What about Carol?'

'The boys will look after her. C'mon, hurry up.'

No kitty that night in the Labour Club. All the drinks were on Paddy. In between games of bingo, Eileen and Phil chatted away to us. They were sorry to see us go. 'Well, at least youse'll all be together,' Eileen said, tapping her cigarette into an ashtray.

By the time we drove back to the guesthouse, the children were all fast asleep.

'Dere ya are,' Paddy said, falling into bed. 'I told ya dey'd be all right.'

The boys were up early for their last day at school. We dawdled down for breakfast and waited patiently at our table. The landlady ignored us, darting in and out of the kitchen with plates of bacon and eggs, serving other guests first. Couples came and went.

'Excuse me. We haven't had our breakfast yet,' I said, pointing to the boys. 'They'll be late for school.'

A plate of cold hard toast was put in front of us, followed by small plates of bacon and eggs. The boys ran off to school. Paddy finished his coffee and jumped up. He was off to London to buy more machines. Carol and I wandered into the hall. The landlady collared me. 'Mrs O'Connor, Mrs O'Connor,' she said. 'I want to talk to you.'

'Yes,' I said, smiling.

'Your children behaved disgracefully last night. I will not have my permanent guests disturbed. Will you stay in and control them in future? They are your responsibility.'

Before I could answer, she looked past me. With a wide smile on her face, she rushed towards one of the guests, helping him on with his coat.

I escaped to my room with Carol and slammed the door. 'The cheek of her,' I said, fuming. 'What the hell were they doin' last night, Carol?'

'I think they were having pillow fights.'

'We're gettin' out of here as soon as Daddy gets back. This is no hotel. I'm not puttin' up with the likes of her and her guesthouse.'

I marched Carol down the stairs, out into the fresh air and around Wardown Park. Then it was into the Luton library for the rest of the day. Paddy was back by the time we returned.

'We shouldn't have gone out last night,' I said. 'That landlady let me have it. She gave out hell about the boys. Said they made a terrible noise, upsetting her other guests. You don't leave three boys on their own in a guesthouse, Paddy.'

'We should be able to leave dem on their own.'

The boys burst into our room from school, dying to show me their farewell cards. Paddy pounced on them. 'Can we not leave youse for one night?' he said. 'D'youse have to make a holy show of us every time we go out?'

'I'm leavin' this place,' I said, packing our cases.

'Ya don't know the rules, Lily,' he said. 'I've booked in for five days. Ya're obliged to stay for the full period. If we check out now, she's entitled to claim for the five days.'

'I'm not stayin'.'

'We'll talk about it later. C'mon, let's go an' get somet'in' to eat.'

We tiptoed down the stairs and headed for the door. There she was, fussing over her other guests.

'Paddy, tell her we're leavin',' I said, pulling his sleeve. 'Go on, tell her.'

She raced over. 'Good evening, Mr O'Connor,' she said, holding the hall door open for him.

Paddy smiled and ushered us all out quickly. 'Dere ya're, Lily. What are ya goin' on about? She's all right.'

'If we go out tonight, they come too,' I said, as we all squashed into the Capri.

At breakfast next morning, our table was left last again. In and out of the kitchen the landlady paced, her head in the air. A young Manchester mother sat near us, patting her baby. Her husband, beside her, tapped the table. 'Have you not been served either?' he called over.

'It's the same every morning,' I said. 'She leaves us to the last.'

'She complained about our baby crying last night,' he said. 'We're flying out of Luton for Spain today, and am I glad.'

'She wants our money, but she doesn't want the children.'

A couple walked in. A hot breakfast was put in front of them.

'Right, that's it, Paddy,' I said, springing up. 'We're leavin'. I'm goin'.'

He folded up his paper. 'Okay, Lily. I'll book us into a hotel. You go up an' pack. I'll settle the bill.'

The Glen Eagles Hotel in Harpenden was a godsend. No English landlady there breathing down my neck. The boys had a colour TV to themselves, and Paddy and I could do what we liked for the last two days in England.

PART THREE

Geelong, Australia

What Have We Come To?

'I T'S A JUMBO,' the boys shouted, running over to the window at Heathrow.

Paddy followed them and pointed out parts of the plane. Debbie was not interested. She sat teary-eyed, writing in her diary. Carol skipped around holding Baby Ted.

I stared out the window at the huge blue and white bird that was to take us to the other side of the world. In my mind, I was already gone, but couldn't stop the nagging doubts. Was I doing the right thing, getting around Paddy to go? He'd never go back to Dublin, and I wasn't staying in Luton on my own any longer. *Please God everything will be all right.*

We boarded the plane and were seated in a row together. Carol squeezed into a seat beside me. Debbie claimed the window seat and peered out, looking at no one. Paddy laughed with the boys as the plane roared down the runway and left England. I lay back and closed my eyes. *No use worrying now. Forget Luton, the selling of the house, the packing, the guesthouse. I'm on my way.*

The captain welcomed us aboard and said that Harry Secombe was travelling with us. Debbie looked over at Paddy and smiled; they both loved *The Goons*. Steven unbuckled his belt. 'Can I go up and get his autograph?'

'Ask the air hostess,' Paddy said, glancing down the aisle.

It wasn't long before Steven was back, all smiles.

'Did you see him?' I said, looking at his beaming face.

'The air hostess brought me up a spiral staircase all made of silver. He was sitting on a couch, drinking. He called me over and signed my menu. He looked just like he does on telly, Mum.'

Soon the thrill of being on the plane wore off. Menus had been read over and over. The clouds outside just hung there.

'Are we there yet?' Carol asked every time the plane landed to refuel.

Day turned to night, night turned to day, and then night again. After a few weary hours of snatched sleep, the cabin lights flickered on for yet another breakfast of scrambled eggs and ham. We were only finished when the air hostesses appeared with the trolley, collecting our plastic trays. Then they walked briskly up and down the aisles spraying mist into the air.

'What in the name a' God are dey doin'?' Paddy said. 'Sprayin' us as if we were animals?'

'I'm glad they're particular,' I said, trying to shut him up.

The sky outside blazed a brilliant red. We were nearing Australia. The plane began to drop, and its wheels skidded on to Darwin's runway. We stepped down off it and onto the melting tarmac. It was stinking hot and humid. For a minute, I thought the plane had turned around and spat hot air out of its engines at us. Airport officials, big men, tanned all over, in khaki shorts, looking more like the army than airport staff, ushered us into a stuffy barn-like building. They were so unlike the pale, uniformed officials at Heathrow.

Wanting to freshen up, I made a dive to the Ladies. Sitting down in a steamy-hot toilet, I felt someone watching me from behind. I turned around slowly. Jesus, a monster of a spider was eyeing me. I nearly died. Up went the knickers, down with the skirt and I ran like hell.

'T'ank God, we're not stayin' in Darwin,' I said, as we climbed up the stairway onto the air-conditioned plane.

Four hours later, having flown over miles and miles of desert, we could see lights below, the signs of a city waking up.

'Good morning, ladies and gentlemen,' the captain said. 'This flight will terminate in Sydney. Those of you going on to Melbourne, please report to the BOAC desk on arrival. You'll be transferred to a smaller plane bound for Melbourne. I hope you've had a pleasant flight, and we look forward to seeing you again.'

Was I glad to get off that plane and its choked-up, smelly toilets!

'Why are ya going on to Melbourne?' an official said, stamping our passports. 'It's Pommyland down there. Stay in sunny Sydney.'

I laughed back at him. 'I hope they're all as friendly as you in Melbourne,' I said, sauntering out of customs.

An immigration official was waiting to welcome us. 'Your plane for Melbourne doesn't leave till this arvo,' he said, handing us seven free luncheon vouchers.

After thirty hours of airline-packaged food, it was wonderful to sit down and have a proper meal on a plate. Sausages and chips and freshly made tea never tasted so good.

Refreshed, we boarded another BOAC plane, a cramped VC10. An hour later, we all staggered off in Melbourne.

Annie, my sister, was all smiles when she caught sight of us, drifting out with our millions of cases on two trolleys.

'Hi,' she called over, waving her arms madly.

She was not the worried sister I remembered in England. She was now confident, swinging her car keys. She looked cool and fresh in her blue short-sleeved top, white slacks and sandals, with her black hair back brushed and well lacquered.

'T'anks for comin' to meet us,' Paddy said.

'How long did it take?' Annie asked.

'Thirty hours, a bloody lifetime,' he said, lighting up.

'It took us six weeks by boat. It was one long holiday.'

Annie went searching for her car. We lagged behind, hot and sticky. Paddy pushed one trolley, Paul the other.

'Look at the size of her car,' Bryan said, when she found it.

'It's a Ford Falcon, a family car,' she said, opening the boot. 'We can all squeeze in.'

Paddy packed in several cases. 'Dere's too many of us,' he said. 'Paul an' I will follow behind in a cab.'

Annie drove slowly out of the airport, but took a wrong turn. Fifteen minutes later, still searching for the road to Geelong, she pulled over and took out her road map. Debbie tapped her on the shoulder and pointed to a woman passing by. 'Why don't you ask that lady all in black which way to go?'

'She's a new Australian. She wouldn't know.'

'I thought that's what we were,' Debbie said, laughing.

'She's Italian. She can't speak English.'

We turned right onto the Prince's Highway towards Geelong.

'Wait till you see your house, Lily,' Annie said. 'It's a triple-front brick veneer. They're all the go.'

'I wish it was finished so we could move in.'

'Don't worry. Sylvia's found an old weatherboard house for you to rent. It's near her.'

'A weatherboard? What's that?'

'It's a wooden house. It'll do till yours is ready.'

As she drove down the Prince's Highway, I stared out the window. You could see for miles and miles across flat brown land littered with boulders and the odd spindly silver-bark tree. The deep-blue sky seemed so low, almost ready to drop down in front of you. Cars sped by.

'All the cars are white,' Bryan said. 'In England, they're black.'

'White reflects the sun,' Annie said.

An hour later, we turned off the highway into Plantation Road, then up an unmade road. A few houses scattered here and there appeared lifeless.

Dust blew up around us as Annie pulled into the edge. One by one, we piled out and walked over to a large cream-brick bungalow set on a corner block of land. Its brown-tiled roof overlapped its walls like a sun hat, shading three large windows, all facing the road

'So this is a triple-front brick-veneer bungalow,' I said.

'They don't call them bungalows here, Lily. They're houses.'

The house wasn't at all like I'd pictured it. It reminded me of the old cowboy films with the dirt road and the old house standing on its own. Only this was a new house sprawled over the flat land. No garden, just a heap of huge rocks and rubble in front of it. Not a tree or a footpath to be seen, only tall yellow weeds blowing in the warm wind.

A taxi pulled up. Paddy climbed out with Paul. He didn't look at the house. He gazed around, taking everything in. Holding my arm, he pointed to a tall chimney in the distance. Thick black smoke poured out of it.

'Jesus Christ, Lily, what have we come to? A bloody oil refinery on our doorstep.'

Only Mad Dogs and Immigrants

T HE RENTED WEATHERBOARD in Detroit Crescent looked like no
one had cared about it for years. It stank of mustiness, the furniture was shabby and worn, and the walls were in need of a lick
of paint. But I couldn't have cared less what the house was like, as
long as it had a bed for me to crawl into. I was dying with the
cramps. Whenever I did struggle up, it was a mad dash to the toilet. Paddy rang a doctor.

'Something you caught on the plane,' the doctor said, opening
his bag. 'I'll give you the tablets they give astronauts. That will stop
the diarrhoea.'

I thanked him. Paddy paid him. The tablets did their trick. I was
up in an hour, putting on the kettle.

'Would ya like somet'in' to eat?' Paddy said, opening the bread.

I sat down. 'I'd love a cup a' tea an' a bit a' toast. That's all I
want.'

He poured me out a cup of tea, put the jam away, washed up
and handed me a letter. It was from his boss in America, a note
with only one word written on it – *Help!*

'How did he know where we were?'

'I gave him Sylvia's address. I rang him to see what was wrong.
He needs me back in the States to fix rusty machines. Dey arrived
from Europe. Dey weren't packed properly. Water got in.'

'God, Paddy, we've just arrived. You're not goin' back already.'

'I promise ya, I won't stay away long this time. I'll finish the job
an' leave. The money will help us get back on our feet.'

'What about those jobs in Melbourne? The ones you applied
for?'

'Dey'll be dere when I get back.'

'You'll have to pay the full fare back to the Australian government.'

'The job will pay. Don't worry. I won't go till I see ya settled.'

I sat there fuming, my fingers gripping the cup. 'Where are the
boys?'

'Dey've gone to the pool wit' David.'

'Where's Carol?'

'Out in the porch playin' wit' thousands of ants. Debbie's in her room writin' a million bloody letters.'

I heard the flyscreen door spring back on the hall door. 'I'll get it,' I said, struggling up.

It was Sylvia, hair brushed back like Annie's, looking slim as ever in her white cotton slacks.

'There's a huntsman on your flyscreen, Lily,' she said, darting back down the path.

A spider, the size of your hand, was crawling up the mesh, making his way in.

'Jesus, Mary an' Joseph, Paddy, get him!' I said, leaping away.

Paddy stared over my shoulder. 'Give me a rope an' I'll lead it to the gate,' he said, laughing.

The huntsman heard him. He galloped up the door and onto the wall, through a large crack and into the roof. Sylvia skipped in and sat down. 'Are you any better?'

'I have to be. I need furniture for our new house. Paddy has to get back to the States.'

'I'll go with you an' show you the shops in Geelong, if you like.'

Paddy grabbed up his cigarettes and wallet. 'Call Carol. We'll get a cab. It's stinkin' hot outside.'

'Save your money, Paddy,' Sylvia said. 'The bus stop's not far away.'

The air was thick and heavy with the heat. We rambled past old weatherboard houses. Big black and white birds with powerful-looking beaks warbled above on telegraph poles. The bus pulled in. Carol jumped on ahead of us. The red-faced driver wasn't happy when Paddy handed him a five-dollar note.

'Gimme the right change next time, eh,' he snapped, wiping his forehead with the back of his hand.

'They get cranky when it's hot,' Sylvia whispered, as we plonked down on green vinyl seats.

The bus rattled towards Geelong. I stared out its dusty window at the wooden box-like bungalows. As we stopped at lights, a woman in a long dressing gown and curlers sauntered down her path and peeped into a small tin box hanging off her mesh-wire fence. She took out some letters.

'The letter boxes are outside here, Lily,' Sylvia said.

We passed a large modern building with a big Ford sign. 'There's where Chris works,' she said. 'He'd no trouble gettin' in.'

We pulled in to the town centre a half hour later. My polyester dress was stuck to me. I had to peel myself off the seat.

'This is Moorabool Street,' Sylvia said.

It was a wide, bright and clean street. Unlike on Luton's narrow winding streets, no chip papers or coke tins lay on these paths. Rows of colourful canopies shaded shop windows from the sun. I glanced in Woolworth's window and was amazed to see snow-covered Christmas cards of English cottages and red robins. It didn't look right to see snowy cottages among bathing suits, beach balls and summer sandals. It didn't look right at all.

Carol caught hold of my arm. 'Look, Mum,' she shouted, pointing down towards the sea.

'That's Corio Bay,' Sylvia said.

Yachts of all shapes and sizes shimmered in the distance on the calm blue water.

The hot sun burned down on my scalp and seared through my dress. A perfect day for the seaside, but not for shopping.

Sylvia led us into a shop that sold household appliances. Paddy tore around, looking at all the cookers. 'How about dat one?' he said. 'It's three hundred dollars.'

'How much is that in pounds?'

'Will ya forget about pounds, Lily. It's dollars now.'

I stared at the cooker.

'Everyone wants a Whirlpool, Lily,' Sylvia said. 'They're the best.'

The salesman moved forward. 'It has a rotisserie,' he said, opening the oven and taking out a large fork-like contraption. 'Put yer chook on that. It rotates in the oven for an evenly roasted bird.'

The shop started to spin. 'I feel funny,' I said, grabbing Paddy's arm.

He held on to me while the salesman fetched a chair. Another salesman appeared with a glass of cold water.

'T'anks,' I said, draining the glass. 'I'm right now.'

'Yer dehydrated, Lily,' Paddy said. 'Ya need to drink plenty of water.'

We continued to walk around, opening and closing fridge doors, the salesman scurrying behind us. 'A Simpson. A good family fridge,' he said, showing us the ice compartment at the top.

'You'll need a big fridge,' Sylvia said. 'You have to put everythin' in it, even your bread an' butter.'

'I'm thirsty, Mum,' Carol whined.

Out we traipsed and found a little café. A rusty air-conditioner hummed above its door, dripping drops of water onto the path. Paddy pushed the door open. It slammed behind us, keeping the hot air out and the cold air in.

'God, it's lovely an' cool in here, like a fridge,' I said, pulling my dress away from my skin.

After three glasses of icy water, I stared out the window, not wanting to move.

Carol sat chewing on her straw, her eyes half closed.

'Let's go,' Paddy said. He went through his pockets and dropped a pile of change on the table.

Carol collected it all up. 'Dad, you left your money behind.'

'Leave it,' he said, taking it from her.

'They don't expect tips here, Paddy,' Sylvia whispered. 'It's not like America.'

I looked back at the money, not sure how much he was leaving. He inched me out the door. Outside, a hot north wind blew into our faces.

We followed Sylvia across the road and into a big furniture shop, Waltons.

'Upstairs for beds,' the salesman said.

We climbed up a curved stairway, the air getting hotter with each step. A painting of a dark Spanish girl with gold earrings smiled down at us.

'I haven't seen any blacks here,' I whispered to Sylvia.

'I don't t'ink they're allowed in, Lily. Australia has very strict immigration laws.'

A bar with a laminex top, high stools behind it, faced us at the top of the stairs.

'Dat's what I want, Lily,' Paddy said.

'I don't,' I said, walking on.

'What about dat smoker's table?'

I stood back and studied this strange little brass table. An arm welded to its legs curved up over its table-top, holding a thick amber-glass ashtray in its hand.

'You can have that,' I said, laughing.

Now for the kitchen set. We saw a chocolate-brown laminated table with black steel legs and six chairs with orange vinyl seats. A salesman, dabbing his face with a hanky, tore over, smiling.

'Do you have an extra chair? I need seven,' I asked.

He fetched another chair from the storeroom.

'The seat's back to front,' I said, examining it. 'Have you no other?'

'You Poms want everything perfect,' he said, fiddling with the screws.

'Could you leave us for a minute? I want to talk to my husband.' I turned to Paddy. 'Do we have to take it? Can we try somewhere else?'

'D'ya want to walk around in the heat?'

'No.'

'Den we'll take it. Don't worry. I'll fix the seat.'

I looked over at Carol. She was lying down on a couch. Sylvia was sitting beside her, fanning herself with a Waltons' brochure. For the life of me, I can't remember choosing the beds or the rest of the furniture that day, but Paddy said I did.

The midday sun was directly above us when we trailed out of Waltons. The streets were empty. Not a soul or a sinner to be seen, not even a bird.

'Where's everyone?' Carol said.

'Australians don't go out in the heat,' Sylvia said.

'Only mad dogs an' immigrants,' Paddy said. 'C'mon, we'll get somet'in' for dinner, den we'll get a cab home.'

Sitting in the back of the taxi with Carol and Sylvia, I closed my eyes. The smell of the fruit from Nancarrows sailed up to me from my bag. I didn't know myself being able to afford fresh apricots, peaches and strawberries. In England, it was always tinned peaches or pears after Sunday roast. And the meat? That tray of barbecue chops for just a dollar. And that leg of New Zealand lamb for little or nothing. Tesco in Luton never had anything like that.

'Thanks, mate,' the taxi driver said, when Paddy told him to keep the change.

Burnt toast hit me as soon I pulled back the flyscreen door of the weatherboard house. The boys were back. I plonked the shopping down on the kitchen table and nearly died. The whole table was black, alive with ants crawling in and out of the open jam jar.

PADDY SHOULD BE HERE

TED, THE INSPECTOR from Oxford Homes, led Paddy and me up a new cement path to the hall door of our triple-front brick-veneer house. He saw me bend down and peep in the vents at the base of the walls. I could see right under the whole house. I could even see empty beer cans on the bare soil under the floorboards.

'It's built up off the ground to let the air flow under,' Ted said. 'You need the ventilation. Keeps the house cool in the summer.'

'Right,' I said.

We rambled down the hall after him on bare dusty floorboards. Paddy tapped the cream-painted walls. 'Sounds hollow,' he said.

'Plasterboard throughout, mate. The walls have to be ventilated too.'

Ted slid a large glass door across. 'Your lounge,' he said. 'And there's your Vulcan heater.'

'An oil fire?' Paddy said, bending down to look at it.

'A beaut too,' Ted said. 'It blows hot air in every room through a central ducted heating system below the floor.' He walked over to a wide window. 'Aluminium frames,' he said, sliding it open. 'No rot, no need for paint.'

'That's great,' I said. 'I had to paint our windows every spring in England.'

'But ya'll need flyscreens to keep the mozzies out,' he said, slamming the window shut.

We were led from room to room. No need for wardrobes. Fitted robes in the four bedrooms. And I was pleased to see the toilet separate from the bathroom. Save all those terrible rows when one of the boys wanted to go to the toilet while Debbie was in the bath. A small room with a deep stainless-steel sink led off the bathroom. A laundry for my twin-tub.

Ted unlocked the back door and we followed him out.

'There's your galvanised-iron garage for your car,' he said. 'And there's your Hills hoist for your washing.'

He highered and lowered the hoist and spun it around. It was like the skeleton of an umbrella cemented into the ground.

We strolled to the back of the house. A gap between the walls and the roof worried me. I could just see one of those huntsmen spiders sneaking in when my back was turned.

'Is that all right?' I said, pointing up to it.

'Ya have to ventilate the roof; otherwise it'll get too hot in the attic.'

Ted stood chatting to Paddy about the hot-water tank in the roof, while I scurried around examining the outside of the house. I didn't like the look of a soft, black, rubber seam running from the roof to the ground, right down through the middle of the bricks.

'Is that all right?' I said, fetching Ted. 'The house looks like it's glued together in the middle.'

'Has to allow for movement in the heat. Brickies might not be the sharpest tools in the shed, but they know their job.'

We sauntered back to the front of the house.

'Can you tell me where the nearest shops are?' I said, trying to think of everything before he left.

'There's a milk bar up the road,' Ted said. 'They sell everything.'

'Great.'

'What part of Ireland are you from?'

'Dublin.'

'We thought you were Poms coming from England. My mother was Irish. She came from Kerry.'

Paddy was not interested in talking about Ted's mother; he was anxious to get me settled. Ted looked at his watch and handed him a bill.

'Another thousand dollars?' Paddy said. 'What's this for?'

Ted kicked the ground. 'Your block's full of rocks, mate. We had to dynamite your land to lay the sewer.'

'Dynamite?'

'You're close to the You Yangs.' He pointed to several small mountains in the distance. 'One good thing, your house will never shift. It's built on rocks.'

He jumped into his car and drove off, leaving a trail of dust behind him.

Paddy studied the bill, then looked at the You Yangs. 'That's an extra thousand we've to find,' he said, stuffing it into his pocket.

'We'll manage. The house is paid for.'

'Just as well I'm goin' back to the States next week, isn't it?'

Before I had a chance to look over the house again, a furniture van pulled up outside. After the dust settled down, two young chaps opened the back and lugged in our new furniture, the sweat pouring off them. Paddy ran after them with a tip.

'No thanks, mate. We get a week's wages,' one said, banging the van door.

We rushed around, arranging the beds and chairs the way we wanted them.

'Right, I'll pick the kids up an' get some food for dat fridge,' Paddy said.

Soon the house was alive with all their voices. One by one, they grabbed their towels and tried out the new shower.

By half-past eight, our house lights were on, and all our windows were exposed to the roads. Cars slowed up driving past, and strange faces stared in at us.

'Ya'll need to get Venetian blinds as soon as possible,' Paddy said, peering out the window. 'It'll give ya privacy at night an' keep the sun out in the day. Everybody has dem in the States.'

A week later, Paddy was up early, running around and packing his case. 'I'm goin' to Carolina in my mind,' he sang, as he stuffed in his shaving gear.

I trailed behind him. 'When do you think you'll be back?'

'Before Christmas.'

'T'ank God we got the phone in. Make sure you ring me as soon as you arrive, Paddy, won't you?'

His taxi skidded off down the dirt road. I collapsed back into his side of the bed for comfort, missing his warm body already.

A sharp whistle blew outside several times. I slipped on my dress and peeped out the front door. A young man in a pale-blue shirt and navy-blue shorts, his grey knee socks pulled up tight, sat on his bicycle, waving a letter.

'I'm yer postie,' he called out. 'Yeh need a letter box. Can yeh get one as soon as possible?'

Postie cycled off down the road to the next house and blew his whistle again.

I glanced at the brown envelope with the Australian government stamp on it and tore it open. It was a letter welcoming us to Australia and hoping we'd be happy here.

Signed by Al Grassby, the minister for immigration.

God, that's very nice of him, I thought, shoving the kettle on. *Paddy should be here reading this with me.*

She'll Be Right

THE PHONE RANG. It was Paddy. He'd been sent down to Central America to fix those rusty machines. I could barely hear him. A thousand voices jabbered away in another language.

'Is everyt'in' all right?' he shouted. 'How's Debbie? Is she any happier?'

'She's fine, t'ank God. She's in Geelong buyin' her school-books for next year. I've no worries with the boys. They live in Norlane Pool. Carol's delighted with that wild grey kitten Annie gave her.'

'How are you?'

'I'm hot. The heat builds up in the house when we've had a few warm days.'

'Did ya get the blinds up?'

'They're up, but I can't open the windows. The dust blows in from the dirt roads.'

'We can always go back to Luton, ya know. Ya don't have to stay in Australia.'

'No, Paddy. I came here. I'm stayin' here. I just need a fence up to keep the dust out.'

'Den get one. Me wages should have come through by now.'

The phone went dead. He was cut off.

I flicked through the phone book, searching for a fencer. I rang one. A fella in baggy shorts and unlaced boots came out and stomped about, looking this way and that way.

I walked behind him. 'I want a high fence right around the garden, please. A gate for the front an' two gates for the back leadin' into the garage.'

'Yeh can't have a high fence on a corner block. Cars have to be able to see what's coming around the corner.'

'What can I have then?'

'I can fence the back and sides, and build a low wall at the front of the house.'

'How much?'

'Give me a tick. I'll fetch my measuring tape from my ute.' He rummaged around the unroofed back of his car, searching for his tape. He couldn't find it. So he paced up and down the block in his big boots, measuring the distance with his feet.

'Two hundred dollars will do ya for the fence,' he said, rolling a cigarette. 'Extra for the bricks.'

'When can you do it?'

'As soon as your posts and palings are delivered.'

Without another word, he sped off in his ute.

A truck pulled up that very afternoon. A big leather-faced man in shorts and scruffy boots jumped out. He dumped a pile of wood at the side of the house. I watched him, thinking he'd come over to me with something to sign. He didn't. He climbed back up into his truck and left without saying a word.

The days went by. No sign of the fencer. I rang him. 'The wood has arrived for the fence,' I said. 'When are you comin' to put it up? It's lyin' out there in the open.'

'She'll be right,' he said. 'I'll be there tomorrow.'

But he wasn't. Nor the next day. Nor any other day for that matter.

One night, when the children were all fast asleep in bed, I heard the sound of wooden planks being stacked outside. I peeped through the blinds, but could see nothing in the pitch dark.

I ran to the back door. Its handle turned before I reached it. I stood staring as the doorknob kept twisting. 'Paddy, Paddy,' I shouted, letting on my husband was in the house. Footsteps ran away and a car sped off. My hands shook as I dialled the police.

Within minutes, two policemen knocked on my door. Holding torches, they picked their way around in the dark then sauntered back to me.

'It's your palings,' one said calmly. 'Someone's been lifting them. They're all over your block.'

'They've been robbin' me fencin'? Someone's been robbin' me fencin'?'

'Happens all the time around new houses,' he said, turning to leave. 'If you hear anything else, give us a ring.'

I tossed and turned all night, imagining I heard noises outside. I was raging, thinking about that laid-back fencer. First thing next morning, I was on the phone telling him he could come and take the rest of his wood back. I said that I had found someone else to do the job. That did the trick. He was out like a bullet. Up went the new fence, new wall and all.

Now for the Garden

A T LAST I felt the house was mine, safely tucked up behind a high wooden fence at the back and a low brick wall in the front. And postie was pleased with my new mailbox built into the wall. No more would he have to blow his whistle over and over, waiting for me to run out for the letters.

The very next day, our container from Luton arrived, and not a day too soon. We broke it open. Our few things from Meyrick Avenue were dragged out and carried in. My ornaments were arranged on the mantelpiece, the little personal things that make a home. My pots and pans were shoved into kitchen cupboards, and Aunt Rosie's blankets were pushed into the linen press. Carol unfolded her doll's pram. The boys couldn't wait to set up the stereo and play their records. Debbie grabbed her books and ran back to her bedroom.

Now for the garden. On went the cords, up went the sleeves and out came my few garden tools from the container. I looked around, wondering how in the name of God I'd civilise this block of land. A bent-up old man of a tree, a peppercorn, was the only bit of life on it. And all those rocks. *What the hell will I do with them?*

Then I had a great idea and raced back inside. T. Rex blasted out of the stereo from Paul's bedroom.

'Turn that down,' I shouted to the boys. 'Give me a hand, quick.'

They followed me out reluctantly. 'What do you want us to do?' Bryan said.

'Listen, I'm makin' walls out of these rocks. Help me gather them all up.'

Paul brushed his long black hair back from his face, surveyed the garden, gave the rocks a few kicks, then drifted back into the house and the stereo.

'Why do you want walls?' Steven said, shoving on his denim cap.

'When I was little, I used to go to Roseville, a big old house in Bray. It was for the poor mothers of our parish to give them a rest away from their husbands. I loved its grey stone walls, all covered in creepers. It was like living in the country. Do you remember I told you I met a boy in Bray? He cycled all the way into Dublin to meet me. I walked by him because he was talkin' to another girl.'

'Not those Irish stories again,' Bryan said. 'I'm sick of them.' He dumped my tin wheelbarrow and disappeared indoors.

Over the week, Steven and I worked hard, making my walls take shape. We had a nice little rhythm going. He gathered the rocks, and threw them into the bockety wheelbarrow; I stacked them and built the walls. Carol was out of the way, up the old man of a tree with Smokey, the wild kitten. She loved that tree – it was her ship, her lookout. She kept an eye on us.

Friday morning, I inched the last couple of rocks in. *T'ank God the walls are finished*, I said to myself. The weatherman had forecast a scorcher. I stood back and admired my Roseville Garden. Steven took his cap off and stared at the neatly stacked rocks, one on top of the other. 'Is that it?' he said, wiping his face with his hanky. 'Is that how the walls looked?'

'They will as soon as I get a bit a' creeper growin' in between the rocks.'

'Mum, Mum,' Carol shouted down from her tree. 'Look over there. There's a horse.'

'A horse. Who owns it?'

'I saw a girl put it there.'

'What girl?'

'A big girl. She tied it up and went off.'

The three of us opened the back gates and walked over to the vacant block of land. A large brown horse was tangled around a rope pegged to the dry hard ground. He began neighing, his big tongue hanging out.

'God help him,' I said. 'He's thirsty. Let's get him a drink.'

We fetched a bucket of water. The horse's huge frothy tongue lapped it up.

The hall door opened and Paul ducked out. 'Quick, Mum. Dad's on the phone from Central America.'

I ran in, Steven and Carol behind me.

'Will you get me a glass of water, Bryan?' I said, kicking my shoes off.

Debbie had the phone. She looked at me and laughed. 'You should see Mum, Dad. She looks like a real pioneer woman.'

'I feel more like a convict,' I said, grabbing the phone from her.

In between the gulps of water, Paddy heard all about the huge boulders that I couldn't budge.

'Leave the boulders where dey are,' he said. 'Dey'll look more natural, instead of tryin' to make ornaments out of dem. An' don't be killin' yerself diggin' dat garden. Ring a rotary hoer like dey do here in the States. He'll bring his machine an' dig up the lot. Look after yerself. I'll ring again when I can. Bye, love.'

'Mum,' Bryan shouted. 'There's a horse in the garden, galloping around.'

'Jesus,' I said, dropping the phone and running outside. 'Youse have left the back gates open.'

My Irish walls were flattened. The horse had broken free and galloped through my gates. He was in a corner, eating my box of plants.

'Ring the RSPCA,' Debbie said, coming out after me.

They sent a man out immediately. He heard the whole story from Carol.

'This is typical,' he said, nodding his head in anger. 'They buy a horse and have nowhere to keep it. They tie it up on a vacant block and leave it.'

He shook my hand and thanked me for ringing. Leading the horse away, he told me to call him if ever I needed help.

The following morning, there was a loud bang on the hall door. I opened it. A boyish-looking girl stood her ground in front of me, her hands dug deep into the pockets of her tight blue jeans. A packet of cigarettes bulged from her shirt pocket.

'Are you the stickybeak who dobbed me in to the RSPCA?'

'You left your horse with no food or water.'

'What's it to you?' she said, thrusting her face forward. She pointed to a fella leaning on my front gate. 'My mate will fix you.'

'My husband is a policeman, I'll have you know,' I snapped. 'He'll be home any minute.'

I looked up and down the road, letting on to be watching out for Paddy the policeman. Banging my gate, she slithered off with her mate.

Frightened out of my life, I slipped back inside and leant against the hall door, my heart pounding. *Ah, feck her*, I thought. *I've more to be doing than worrying about her. Where's the phone book? I need a rotary hoer.*

The rotary hoer pulled up in his ute, his kelpie dog barking in the back. A wiry little man in loose shorts and singlet jumped out and wheeled his contraption down from the back of his car. Stones flew everywhere as he ran up and down the garden with his noisy machine. I kept inside out of his way, praying to God my windows wouldn't break. After an hour, there was a terrible crunching noise. His machine fell silent.

I went out to him. 'God, that looks great, t'anks,' I said, pointing to the garden all dug up.

'Me blades are buggered,' he said. 'Your land's full of rocks.'

The sweat was pouring off him.

'Would ya like a cup of tea?'

He looked at me as if I was gone stone mad. 'Have ya anything colder? A tinnie or something?'

'I've a jug of cold water in the fridge.'

'I'll be right.'

He turned my garden tap on, grabbed my new hosepipe and squirted water into his mouth then over his head.

He wheeled his machine back up into his ute while I raced in for his money.

'T'anks very much,' I said. 'I'll get some grass seeds tomorrow.'

He lingered and eyed the ploughed-up block. 'Ya'll need to loam it first,' he said, leaning on his car door, rolling a cigarette. 'Rake it over with the loam, put your seeds in, give it a good watering, an' ya'll be laughing.'

He handed me a number to ring for the loam and sped off in his ute. That evening, a truck full of loam was dumped outside my fence.

'Quick, give me a hand,' I shouted in to the boys, watching the big orange sun sinking fast.

'What do you want now?' Paul said.

'We have to get this loam in before someone else does.'

No in-between lights in this country. It would be dark before you knew it.

The boys worked like hell that night, shovelling the loam into the wheelbarrow and upending it over the dug-up garden. I worked like blazes the next day, raking it over, ready for the seeds.

Once the seeds were down, out came the new sprinkler. Thick deep-green grass sprung up over the week and needed cutting. I bought a Rover motor mower with Paddy's bonus. But for the life of me, I couldn't get the damn thing going. Bryan was only too happy to take it off my hands. After petrol had spilt everywhere, the machine roared up and down the garden.

Over the weeks, I planted roses each side of the path leading up to the hall door. With daily watering, they grew like mad, their blooms bursting into a mixture of flaming yellow and orange colours.

A taxi pulled up a few days before Christmas.

'Here's Daddy,' Carol shouted, looking out the window.

I ran to the door. There was Paddy, staring at the garden. He closed the front gate and walked up the path, dodging the sprinkler. 'You've done wonders, honey, wit' dat bit of barren land.'

Do We Have to Do What Everyone Else Does?

CHRISTMAS MORNING WAS hot and glary. Three brand-new bicycles stood sparkling in the hall. The boys needed bikes for school. Unlike in Luton, there were few school buses. Paddy's new clock chimed on the mantelpiece. His Irish Textile clock had died coming over, and its colourful angels no longer spun.

'Where's this church?' Paddy said, putting the turkey in the oven for me.

'It's in Norlane, St Thomas's,' I said. 'It's a big, bright church.'

Wearing our best Sunday clothes, we all piled into the green Valiant Paddy had hired out to see us over Christmas. A Dutch priest said mass that morning. He talked about the differences between Australia and Holland.

'In my country,' he said, 'church bells woke me up Sunday mornings. In Australia, it's the drones of motor mowers that wake me up every Sunday.'

All the men roared laughing.

After mass, Paddy dropped Debbie and me home to take up the turkey. Then he drove off to Chris for his Christmas drink. The boys went with him.

Debbie skipped around the kitchen in her new long cotton skirt. She sang carols as she lit a red candle and arranged seven gold Christmas crackers on a snow-white tablecloth. I emptied the mushy peas out of their muslin bag into a bowl and took up the tray of little Yorkshire puddings.

'They're back,' Carol said, running in from the garden.

I passed around the dinners. Paddy said grace, crackers were pulled, and we all tucked in.

'Who's for seconds?' I said, jumping up for more crispy potatoes.

Paddy whipped out his hanky. 'Jesus Christ, Lily, will ya close dat oven door? Yer tryin' to kill me.'

No hands went out to grab the roast potatoes. No one wanted them.

I looked down at their half-eaten dinners and thought about Christmas in England. How hungry they'd be; not a pick would be left on their plates. I never dreamt I'd miss the cold wintry weather of Luton.

'Where's dat fan I bought?' Paddy said, jumping up. He balanced the fan on the worktop and turned it up full blast. Cracker jokes blew all over the place.

'Your pudding's cuttin' lovely, Paddy,' I said, slicing it up.

Debbie handed the dishes of hot pudding around.

'Can I have ice cream with raspberry topping instead?' Carol said.

'Me too,' Bryan said. 'I don't want pudding. It's too hot.'

I made up ice cream cones for them all, pouring on the red topping. 'Eat them quickly,' I said, licking my fingers. 'They're drippin' everywhere.'

Paddy gazed down at the sticky floor. 'Why are you buyin' dat red syrupy stuff?'

'Everyone buys it here.'

'Do we have to do what everyone else does?'

They were each thrown a tea towel and the washing-up was done like lightning. I carried in a tray of creamy sodas and dishes of crisps to the lounge, just like we always did. We sat around the Christmas tree, waiting for the presents to be opened. Our tree didn't look the same. You couldn't see its bulbs twinkle in the glaring light. I tried to darken the room by closing the blinds and pulling the curtains, but that only made the room stuffier. The phone rang. I jumped up to answer it.

'Hurry up, Mum,' Debbie sang out. 'Dad's giving out the presents.'

I dashed back.

'Who was it?' Paddy asked.

'Annie. They're all goin' to the beach.'

'Goin' to the beach on Christmas Day?'

'She said everyone goes Christmas Day to cool off.'

'Can we go, Mum?' the boys cheered, jumping up.

'Do we have to, Dad?' Debbie pleaded.

I gave Paddy my *what will we do* look. He shrugged his shoulders and glanced at Debbie.

'We won't stay long. We'll have our sing-song when we get back, love.'

Creamy sodas were gulped down, presents ripped open and shoved away.

'Get your bathin' suits on an' bring towels,' I said to them all.

Paddy changed into his American white pants, grabbed a few Fosters from the fridge and packed them between the ice bricks in his new Esky. 'Well, if I have to go, I might as well enjoy it,' he said, carrying it out to the car.

After an hour's drive in the heat, we arrived at Anglesea Beach, our legs sticking to the car's vinyl seats. We struggled out, enjoying the sea breeze. People were few and far between on this stretch of bright dazzling sand and it wasn't hard to spot Annie's colourful sun umbrella. The sea looked cool and inviting. Debbie wandered off on her own, up onto the dunes with her book.

Carrying my sandals, I tiptoed on the red-hot sand towards Annie's umbrella. She and Sylvia were in their bikinis, sunbathing. I pulled up my short cotton dress to brown my legs and lay down on the car rug beside them. The boys threw down their towels, stripped off and ran into the surf, calling out to David. Paddy dropped the Esky, pulled his shoes and socks off, and sat down under the umbrella with the men.

'Hello, brother-in-law,' Annie's Paddy said, shaking his hand.

'Is he home for good?' Annie said, looking at me.

'I wish he was. He's goin' back next week.'

A few minutes later, Paddy sprang up, brushing his feet. 'Shit, I'm been eaten alive.'

'They're sandflies,' Chris laughed, handing him a tin of insect spray. 'Ya need Aerogard, Paddy.'

'Where's Debbie?' Annie asked.

'Up in the dunes, starin' out to England,' Paddy said.

'She misses Pauline an' her friends in Luton,' I said. 'She was always out at band practice or singin' with her folk group.'

'Once school starts, she'll make friends,' Sylvia said.

'I know. Another year an' I'd never have got her here. Never.'

'You have to come when they're young.'

'The boys an' Carol are fine, but I'll be glad when school starts.'

'Catholic schools are private schools here, Lily,' Sylvia said. 'You have to pay fees an' buy all their books, even their writing paper. Not like England where you got everyt'in' free.'

Annie poured out cups of tea and passed around chunks of Christmas pudding. I sat back and relaxed and let the cool sea breeze wash over me.

Annie was right. It's much nicer here than sweating in that hot stuffy kitchen. Carol's having a grand time, running in and out of a warm inlet, playing with her new little surf board. The boys don't know themselves – it's Christmas Day and they're diving in and out of those huge thumping waves. And look at Paddy! He's laughing his head off with Chris. At last we're all together again. But where's Debbie?

I looked up at the dunes. 'Will you keep a eye on Carol, Paddy?' I said. 'I won't be long.'

I slipped on my sandals, climbed up the sandy dunes and sat down beside her. She was gazing out to sea, her eyes red with the tears.

'You'll make friends at school,' I said. 'You'll be able to go out with them.'

She took off her glasses and dabbed her eyes with the hem of her skirt. I sat silent, the warm soft sand filtering through my fingers, trying to think of something else to say. 'You can go back to England next year for a holiday. Dad will pay your fare.'

She wiped her eyes, put her glasses back on and shook the sand out of her book.

'C'mon,' I said. 'They've had long enough in the sea. We'll go home for tea an' Christmas cake.'

They all piled into the car with sandy towels wrapped around them. I let Debbie sit in the front with Paddy. Hardly a car passed us on the deserted roads.

'Where's everybody?' Debbie said.

'At home celebratin' Christmas, where we should be,' Paddy said, speeding along. 'Dat's the last time we go to the sea on Christmas Day.'

'You must admit,' I said, winding down the car window, 'it was nice an' cool at the sea instead of meltin' in that lounge.'

'Next year, we stay home. We'll have an air conditioner like dey have in the States.'

Now for the Schools

IT WAS THE first week in February, the start of the Australian school year. I woke early and lay listening to those big black and white birds up in Carol's tree, warbling, a sure sign of the heat. The weatherman had forecast a hot one with a cool change to come in the evening. I had been here only a short time, but I had soon learnt that it was important to watch the weather forecast. You could go out in the morning in high temperatures, wearing little or nothing, then a cool change would blow in and you'd be freezing.

The milkman's horse trotted by outside. Slipping on my dress, I grabbed in the bottles, shoved them into the fridge and hurried down the hall, knocking on the bedroom doors. 'It's late. C'mon, get up.'

Debbie made a mad dash for the shower, while I busied myself in the kitchen, making up their sandwiches. No cooked dinners in Australian schools like England. You either made them up a lunch or gave them money to spend in the school tuck shop.

One by one, in school uniforms, they wandered into the kitchen, sat down and poured milk onto their cornflakes. No one said a word. Strange schools awaited them.

Debbie was the first to leave. She had chosen Clonard herself, a small Catholic girls' college run by the Brigidine Sisters in Geelong. An old-fashioned grey uniform was compulsory. Clonard sold her a second-hand one.

I saw her to the door. You'd hardly recognise her in this long, grey, pleated tunic with a blazer to match. She bent down, tied her black shoelaces, then pulled up the grey knee socks. I handed her the green hat and gloves. Biting my lip, I tried to keep in the laughing. She glanced down at herself and then up at me. 'I look like one of the Trinians in this tunic, Mum, don't I? Take a picture of me. I'll send it to Pauline. She won't believe it.'

I took the snap and watched her run for the Geelong bus, clutching her green school bag bulging with books. Her two long plaits, tied up with green ribbons, bobbed behind her. She looked like a little girl again. *T'ank God she's like Paddy and can laugh at herself*, I thought, hurrying back in.

Steven was next. I handed him his new red school blazer. He slipped it on over his white shirt and red tie, then plonked the compulsory red cap on his head. He looked like one of the boys out of a *Boys' Own Annual*.

'You look grand,' I said, smiling. 'Now, make sure your trousers don't catch in your bike chain.'

He cycled off to Chanel College, a draughty school building perched on top of Lovely Banks, a hill overlooking Corio. Sylvia sent her David there. She said it was a good school run by the Christian Brothers.

Paul and Bryan peddled off together in their dull-grey pullovers and long trousers, their green school bags clamped to the back of their bikes. They were good with their hands, always fixing things, so I sent them to the local technical school.

The last one out was Carol. No uniform for her, just her little cotton dress and sandals. She was off to the nearest Catholic primary. It was in Norlane, the next suburb towards Geelong, miles away. Carol wasn't keen on the walk, and neither was I.

Down the wide Bacchus Marsh Road we hurried, making sure to keep under gum trees hanging outside gardens of weatherboard houses. The houses were dead quiet, their striped awnings pulled well down over their windows, as if the people inside were still fast asleep.

My heart dropped when I saw the school. It was only one room, raised off the ground – a portable. We stepped up into it. Old bockety twin-seater desks faced a scratchy blackboard. No colourful pictures decorated these walls, so unlike Carol's bright modern school in Luton. I saw her settled and gave her a kiss goodbye.

Then it was off to the shops for my messages and back home to make the beds. I couldn't believe it; the washing dried as I was hanging it on the line. After a bit of lunch and a quick water of the garden, it was time to fetch Carol.

She ran out to me, her face red and sweaty.

'Come on, love,' I said. 'I'll make you a nice ice cream when we get home.'

We struggled up Bacchus Marsh Road, cars and trucks zooming by, throwing up dust. The hot north wind blew into our faces.

'There's millions of hairdryers in the wind,' Carol sobbed.

'How did you go at school?' I said, trying to take her mind off the heat.

'I hate it. We did nothing.'

'What's the teacher like? She looked friendly to me.'

'The sister's really old. The boys throw things at her.'

'The boys t'row t'ings at her? What does she say?'

'Nothing. She lets them. She sits at her desk and cries.'

'She cries?' I stopped walking and stared at her. 'What the hell am I doin' sendin' you to this school when there's a perfectly good state school beside us?'

An old white Holden slowed up. The driver leaned out the window and smiled. 'D'yeh wanna lift?'

'No t'anks, we're nearly home,' I said, pulling Carol on.

I hadn't forgotten the Moors murders in Manchester. They still haunted me. But I needn't have worried. I learnt later that this was something Australians did: they offered lifts to people walking in the heat.

Carol pushed open our gate and rushed up the path. 'Your roses are all frizzled, Mum,' she said, falling through the hall door as I opened it. She flew to the bathroom and held a cold wet flannel on her face. The house was nice and cool. I was glad I'd remembered to close the blinds before I left.

Bryan walked in, his shirt-tail hanging out, his tie stuffed in his pocket. I handed him a large glass of cold water full of ice cubes. 'How did you go?'

'Sir said I have to have my hair cut.'

'Your hair cut? I'll trim it.'

'I'm making you a coffee table in woodwork and Dad a brass ashtray in metalwork.'

'That's grand. What are the kids like?'

'Some call me Pommy bastard because of my English accent.' He headed off to his bedroom.

I tore after him. 'They call you Pommy bastard? That's awful.'

'I feel sorry for the Italians. They're called wogs.'

'Wogs? God. That's terrible.'

He sat on his bed and kicked off his shoes. 'And I'm not wearing Dad's white socks any more. White socks are for poofs.'

Paul strolled into the bedroom, stared in the mirror and brushed his hair.

'How did you go?'

'I'm making an electric guitar in woodwork, starting up a band, and I'm *not* getting my hair cut.'

The back gate banged. I looked out the kitchen window. It was Steven, wheeling his bike into the garage.

'How did you go?' I said, opening the door.

'I'm sweating. I've a rotten headache. Lovely Banks is a horrible steep hill.'

He followed me into the kitchen, pulled off his jacket and sent his cap flying.

'What are the teachers like?' I said, pouring him a cold drink.

'I've a horrible Christian Brother called Brute. He shouts at us to wake up. And I have to get my hair cut.'

The hall door swung open. It was Debbie. Without a word, she flung her bag ahead of her down the hall, stormed into her room, threw herself on the bed and bawled.

'Jesus, what's wrong?' I said, running after her.

'I feel trapped,' she sobbed.

Carol peeped in. I gave her the eye to go away.

'You'll get used to it,' I said, sitting down on her bed. 'What are the girls like?'

'All they do is study. Study, study, study.'

'Do they not go out?'

'Go out?' she said. 'The only time they go out is for their grandmother's birthday.'

'They don't go out? I don't believe that.'

'HSC is the most important year here, Mum.'

'I don't believe they don't go out at all.'

'You don't understand, do you?' she snapped, belting her pillow. 'I'll have to study all the time to keep up with them.'

There was no use arguing with her. She was headstrong, like Paddy.

I headed back into the kitchen and made myself a strong cup of tea. Next, I heard the shower running. I knew it would be

Debbie. In a few minutes, she'd be out, all smiles, wanting to know what was for dinner, as if nothing had happened.

I reached into the cupboard for my big brown bowl. In went the mincemeat, chopped onion, breadcrumbs, salt and egg. Dusting my hands with flour, I patted the mixture into small flat hamburgers and threw the lot on the pan. Watching them frying, I prayed to God for Paddy to ring and the cool change to blow in.

They Wanted Me as Well

I MARCHED CAROL around the corner to Hendy Street primary school the very next morning. It was in the opposite direction to the Bacchus Marsh Road and only five minutes away. Not only were they glad to accept her, but they wanted me as well – to help out once a month in the school canteen. I bounced home, delighted with myself. This was a great way to meet Carol's teacher and the Australian mothers.

But I wasn't so brave a week later; a bundle of nerves I was, walking into that school. A teacher directed me to the canteen. A group of mothers sat on a long bench in front of a table, chatting. Baskets of sesame-seed rolls, crisp lettuces and bowls of big fresh red tomatoes were spread out on the table. Huge jars of peanut butter and Vegemite caught my eye – they were new to me.

The supervisor rushed forward and called out to the mothers. 'This is Lily,' she said, introducing me.

'Sit here, Lily,' Phyllis said, making room.

I squeezed in beside her. 'What do we do?' I said, staring at an urn of boiling water, bubbling away.

'They're the hotdogs. Don't worry about them. We make up two lots of rolls. One for students who ordered their lunches before recess, and the rest are sold at lunchtime.'

The assembly line began. Maisie cut the rolls, Dulcie buttered them, Dawn slipped the ham in, Gladys slipped the cheese in, Phyllis sliced the tomato, and I popped them into brown paper bags.

We finished in no time at all. The paper bags were sorted into two piles. One pile went into red plastic washing baskets to be taken to the classrooms for the students, the rest were to be sold at the counter. I sat back watching the supervisor take a string of red sausages out of the urn. She slit long thin rolls and popped the hotdogs in. A loud bell rang out – *ding, ding, ding, ding.*

The canteen shutters went up. My heart began to thump. Kids were already lined up in a queue, money in their hands, waiting. The supervisor was in charge of the hotdogs, squirting them with sauce. The rest of us served the rolls and the pink-iced doughnuts.

A young woman, a slip of a thing, queued up behind the children, a bundle of books in her arms. Carol dived in close behind her and kept pointing her out to me. It was her teacher.

'I'm Carol's mum,' I said, handing her a salad roll. 'How's Carol goin' in class?'

'Carol is way behind the other students,' she said. 'She'll have to work hard and catch up with my other students if she is to remain in my class this year.'

'Can you give her some extra work? Her big sister will help her.'

The shutters came down. The supervisor was pleased with me. She told me to choose a roll for my lunch. My face lit up, because the smell of those fresh crispy sesame-seed rolls had me starving.

'Have an Anzac,' Phyllis said, handing me a biscuit. 'Have you had them before?'

'No,' I said, crunching it.

Phyllis wrote the recipe out for me on a brown paper bag. 'They're easy, Lily. A real Aussie bickie. Two cups of oats, a half cup of flour, sugar and melted butter. Then stir in a big spoonful of syrup. The kids love them.'

The rest of the mothers chatted about their children. Dulcie told us how good her boys were at playing cricket. Every Saturday morning, they played without fail. Gladys stayed up all night watching the tennis on television. Dawn loved the bowls. And Maisie couldn't wait for the footy season to begin.

I knew nothing about sport. Paddy wasn't the sporty type. He was left-handed and couldn't kick a ball straight, and the boys took after him.

But it didn't matter that I wasn't up with the sports. The mothers still wanted me in their tenpin bowling team. 'We play against other schools once a month,' they said. 'We'll pick you up.'

Washing-up done, it was time to go. Phyllis strolled back with me. She had to pass my house on the way to her home on the Bacchus Marsh Road. As we stopped at my little iron gate, she leaned over and smiled at my withered roses.

'Roses are no trouble in England,' I said. 'I'm fed up watering them here.'

'Don't waste your water, Lily. Go with the land. Stick a few gums and wattles in. Let them fend for themselves.'

Johnnie Walker's Me Only Friend

IT WAS FRIDAY night, chip night. The oil heater glowed in the lounge. The boys and Carol were glued to the television, watching *Lost in Space*. Debbie was in her room, buried in her homework. I was in the kitchen, peeling a pile of potatoes, deep in thought, worrying about a letter I'd had from Paddy.

He was still down in Central America, staying in a dreadful hotel, the only hotel in some little backward town. The cockroaches and bugs were crawling up the walls when he arrived. Before he could settle in his room, he went out and bought every bottle of disinfectant from their only drugstore. Then he scrubbed out his room, the walls and all. But God help him, he still got the runs and was doubled up in pain most of the time. And that awful factory he was working in, trying to show men how to operate the machines when they couldn't even speak English. He had to teach the workers to count to ten before they could hammer the pins into the drums to make up the patterns. They kept getting nine and ten mixed up.

The lounge door slid across. 'When will dinner be ready?' Bryan moaned. 'I'm starving.'

'It won't be long.'

I poured the oil into the greasy chip pan and plonked it onto the hot cooker. The phone rang. No one budged to get it. I dropped the uncooked chips into a bowl of cold water, dried my hands and raced into the hall and grabbed it. It was Paddy.

'You must have heard me t'inkin' about you,' I said. 'You haven't rung for ages.'

'I've tried every night, honey. The operators can't speak English. "*¿Como?, ¿Como?, ¿Como?*" is all dey say. I feel like tellin' dem to go t'hell.'

'Where are you now?' I shouted down the phone. 'Where are you?'

'I'm in a little place called San Miguel. It's two in the mornin', stinkin' hot. I'm sitting here wit' nuttin' on, sweatin' like a pig.'

'Come home. It's autumn in Australia now, lovely and cool.

We'll manage. Ford's have delivered your new car. It's in the garage waitin' on you.'

A heavy smell of hot frying oil drifted into the hall.

'Jesus, I forgot the pan,' I said, dropping the phone.

I tore back into the kitchen to see smoke rising from the chip pan. Bryan was standing over the bubbling oil, his hands full of watery chips.

'Don't put those wet chips in there,' I screamed, moving the pan off the red-hot element. 'Get back inside an' wait.'

'I'm starving,' he said.

'Have some Anzacs.'

I went back to the phone.

'Is everyt'in' all right?' Paddy said.

'It's fine. They were at the chip pan. Listen, Paddy, are you better? Have you still got those terrible cramps?'

'I had to go to the doctor.'

'What did he say?'

'He was more worried about me blood pressure.'

'Your blood pressure? What's wrong with it?'

'It's high. He gave me tablets to keep it down.'

A loud shout boomed from the lounge. I could hear fighting, Carol screaming. Debbie flew out of her room. 'Shut up, I'm doing my homework,' she yelled in at them.

Paddy heard the noise. 'What's dat racket?' he said. 'What's goin' on?'

'They won't let Carol watch her programme.'

'I should be at home wit' dem. I miss dem.'

'Well, why don't you come home?'

There was a silence.

'Are you there, Paddy?'

'Do you miss me?' he said.

'I certainly wish you were here. I feel as if I have no one.'

'I mean, d'ya miss me at night?'

'Miss you at night? Paddy, have you been drinkin'? Hope you're not on that whisky again.'

'Johnnie Walker's me only friend in this godforsaken place. I've no one to talk to. No one speaks English in the factory, except the boss. An' he's always busy.'

'Then come home. You'll easy get a job here.'

'Dey're depending on me to finish this job down in Central America.'

'T'hell with them, Paddy. They've got their families to go home to. Your family's here.'

'Listen, honey. I'll be back up in North Carolina in July. I'm due a couple of weeks off. Will ya come over for a holiday? The job has offered to pay your fare.'

'Oh God, Paddy, I don't know. I can't leave them on their own.'

'Debbie'll look after dem.'

'Carol's only eight. I'm not goin' without her.'

The line crackled and went dead.

'Go during our winter break in July, Mum,' Debbie insisted, when I told her later. 'I can look after them. I'll enjoy cooking something different every night.'

DAT'S WHAT I LOVE ABOUT THE YANKS

THE FLIGHT TO America took forever. Carol fell asleep holding Baby Ted. I pulled out the book Debbie had stuffed in my bag, *Jamaica Inn*, the first book I'd ever read. I sailed through it and was lost in Cornwall when the plane struck turbulence. I held on tight to the seat as it shook violently like Annie's car hitting pot-holes on the dirt roads. I worried about them back home on their own. I hoped the boys would be good for Debbie and eat her meals. *I'm glad I hid that chip pan.* It was in a suitcase in the attic.

Fifteen hours later, the wheels skidded onto a runway in Los Angeles Airport. Carol and I hurried off to the Ladies to freshen up. We had another plane to catch to North Carolina.

The toilets were packed. I took out Carol's brush to do her hair. 'Borrow your brush, Mam,' an American accent said, taking the brush right out of my hand. I stood there like a fool, letting her. She gave her children's hair a good brushing, then handed my brush back and scarpered from the toilet.

'The cheek of her,' I said to Carol, washing the brush under the tap. 'She didn't even ask me. She just took it.'

We wandered out into this city of an airport. It was teeming with people carrying bags, rushing and pushing everywhere. Dying for a decent cup of tea, we squeezed into a café.

'What would ya like, Mam?' the girl said.

'Can I have tea, please, an' a glass of milk for her.'

It wasn't long before the girl put a glass of milk in front of Carol and a glass of tea in front of me. I called her back. 'The tea's freezin' cold.'

'Ya have to ask for hot tea, Mam,' she snapped. 'If ya don't want ice tea, ya ask for hot tea.'

I was glad to be on that plane to North Carolina and out of Los Angeles Airport. Four hours later, still in my warm winter dress, I picked my way down the steps of the 727 onto the tarmac of Charlotte Airport. Tired and jet lagged, I was hit by the humidity. But it wasn't only the heat that hit me – there was Paddy pointing a movie camera at us. People turned back and stared. Gripping

Carol's hand, I hurried in the opposite direction. Paddy rushed after us, laughing. 'I bribed the guy at the gate to let me through so I could film ya comin' off the plane,' he said. 'An' den ya run away from me.'

'Oh, Paddy, you've gone all American. Get rid of that camera.'

He slung it across his shoulder, his face beaming, his blue eyes smiling. He looked well in his white summer pants and brown sandals. A snow-white T-shirt peeped under a pale-blue cotton shirt, his cigarette packet bulging from his top pocket. He hugged me hard, then bent down to grab Carol. 'Hello, chicken. You've grown so big. I've missed ya.'

She pulled away from him, digging into me. I took her hand. 'She hasn't seen you for ages.'

'C'mon, we'll get yer case.' He led us into the airport lounge.

The big black security fella smiled as Paddy thanked him for letting him out to film me.

'There's our case, Mum,' Carol said, seeing it sailing down the carousel.

Paddy grabbed it up and rushed us out into a massive car park.

'What d'ya t'ink of it?' he said, stopping at a monster of a car. 'I hired it for the holidays.'

'My God, could you not have got somet'in' a bit smaller?'

'It's a Cadillac. Yer in America now, Lily. Everyt'in's big.'

He opened the boot. Our case and anoraks disappeared. Glancing around, I saw Paddy was right. The cars were enormous. And so were the men getting in and out of them.

He drove along a busy road, the air conditioning on full blast. I sat back in the deep seat, my legs outstretched. *Glad that plane trip is over. I'm going to enjoy this holiday.*

My eyes caught sight of a huge black and white sign. *Today is Yours. Make it Count.* I smiled at Paddy. He beamed back at me. A car beeped. He swerved quickly to the right side of the road.

'Was he beeping us?'

'I keep drifting to the left. Don't worry.'

I sat up dead straight. 'Just concentrate, then.'

He laughed, leaned over and slipped a hand on my leg. 'I've been dyin' to see ya,' he said. 'I'm like a little boy lookin' forward to Christmas.'

'Just watch the road, Paddy.'

He turned on to a highway and put his foot down, and the Cadillac roared past car after car. Now and again, signs warned drivers to *Think!* I hoped he was reading them. Holiday Inns, Kentucky Fried Chickens and burger joints flew by, one after the other. Big flapping colourful signs advertised the latest car with the best price.

'It's just like Australia,' I said. 'Everyone drives.'

'Are ya happy in Australia, honey?'

'I am. I love how they call me by my first name. In England, it was always "Mrs O'Connor" this and "Mrs O'Connor" that. In Australia, everyone calls me Lily. I really like it.'

'D'ya see yer sisters much?'

'They're both working, but we meet every Sunday at mass. I wish you were at home. We could go out with them to the Irish Club in Geelong.'

Paddy turned on the radio. Patsy Cline was singing 'Back in Baby's Arms'. He knew every word, and he knew the words of every country song that came after.

I leant over and turned the radio down. 'Where are we stayin'?'

'We've been invited to stay wit' the boss.'

'I'd prefer to stay in a hotel.'

'It's up to you, honey,' he said, putting his hand on mine. He turned around and looked at a sleepy Carol.

Another car beeped. Paddy darted to the right.

I breathed a sigh of relief when he pulled in to a Holiday Inn on the highway. Carol's eyes opened up wide when she saw a swimming pool. Its blue water sparkled in front of the hotel.

'My God, the pool is right on the road,' I said. 'There's no fence or anyt'in'.'

'Can I get in, Mum? Can I get in, please?'

'Sure ya can, chicken,' Paddy said.

We checked in and were given a key to our room, with a single bed for Carol and a double for Paddy and me. Before I knew where I was, Carol was in her bathing suit. Down the lift we went and she dived into the pool. Like a little fish, she came back to life. She had a pool all to herself while we stood watching her. Cars and trucks thundered by, kicking up dust and dirt. A long white car drew up right beside us. A man climbed out and slammed his door. In a John Wayne swagger, he made for the hotel, carrying a bag of bottles.

'He's on a binge,' Paddy said, seeing me looking after him.

'A binge? What's that?'

'Ah, when the job gets too much for dem, dey book into a hotel an' get blotto.'

'Go 'way? That's awful.'

'Dey work damn hard, Lily,' he said. 'Dey only do it now an' again.'

I stared up at the hotel windows and wondered, *Why the hell do these men work so hard then drink themselves to death? I'll be glad when Paddy comes home.*

'We'll go inside,' he said, glancing at his watch. 'The bar is open. Carol'll be fine.'

'I'm not leavin' her here on her own,' I said, watching her little red bathing suit bobbing around in the pool. Head down, bum up, she was diving under the water. 'An' listen, I want to have a shower an' change before I go anywhere.'

Paddy was so agreeable, couldn't do enough for me. He had me in America at last, and we were going out. With Carol dried and dressed, I changed into my red mini-skirt and black sandals. Paddy pulled on his new American beige pants, a much bigger size.

Walking into the restaurant, I felt eyes on me. 'Do I look all right?' I said, sitting down at the table.

'Sure ya do, honey,' Paddy said. 'It's yer skirt. It's very short. Yer givin' the men a treat. Dey're way behind wit' the fashion here.'

The waitress scurried over, put a jug of coffee in front of us and took our orders. Carol and I shared a hamburger with chips, and I made sure to tell the girl I wanted my tea *hot*. I nearly fell off the chair when I saw the steak Paddy was eating. Half a cow lay on his plate with a mountain of chips. Two Johnnie Walkers later, he undid his belt, sat back and lit up a cigarette with a big smile on his face.

The following morning, he ordered waffles with syrup for Carol and me. He then tucked into his bacon and eggs with endless cups of coffee, leaving a big tip.

'Y'all come back now, hear,' the waitress said, gathering up our plates.

Then it was out into the humidity again, looking for the car. It wasn't hard to find, with its huge white bonnet peeping out of its parking bay.

'Where are we going?' Carol asked, as we sped along the highway.

'We're off to see the Wizard, the wonderful Wizard of Oz,' Paddy sang.

He swerved into a fun park. A young fella in jeans stood at the gate, selling colourful balloons.

Carol skipped down the Yellow Brick Road, waving her big red balloon. Paddy trotted behind, filming her, all the while pointing out the wrinkly faces carved into the trunks of trees. The road ended. We grabbed three wooden seats in front of a stage and sat down to watch the show. The spotlight drifted between the Scarecrow, the Tin Man and the Cowardly Lion, all doing their party pieces. Finally the light landed on Dorothy singing 'Somewhere Over the Rainbow'. Paddy joined in and helped her along. Families turned and smiled at him.

It was the Tweetsie Railroad for Carol and me the next day, another fun park. The guards clipped our tickets as we climbed aboard an old western train full of grown men, not a kid to be seen. The train chugged its way around rugged mountains.

'Dey're the Blue Ridge Mountains, Lily,' Paddy said, pointing out through the open window. 'The boss has a holiday home in dem. We've got it for a couple of days. We'll head off this afternoon.'

Leaning out, I gazed up at the brilliant blue-toned mountains. Patches of rusty-coloured trees glowed in the shimmering sun.

Bang! Bang! Bang!

'Jesus, what's that?' I said, my head darting back in from the window.

Bandits, hankies tied over mouths, rode up on horses to the carriages, all the while shooting. Horses kicked and reared into the air, dust going everywhere as they galloped beside the train. Carol moved closer to me. The train guards jumped up, drew their pistols, ran to the windows and fired back. Two giant-sized men, sitting opposite, hung out of the window and joined in with the action. The train screeched to a halt.

'We're being ambushed,' Paddy laughed, whipping out his camera. 'The Yanks are big kids, Lily. Dat's what I love about dem.'

I sat back and thought of the boys, who would have loved this.

More shooting and the bandits dashed off with a doctor's old leather bag, bursting with money, paper notes fluttering to the ground.

'C'mon, we'd better hurry,' Paddy said, when the train returned to Tweetsie Station. 'I don't want to be drivin' up the mountains in the dark.'

I Bought Ya Dat Lovely White Cat, Didn't I?

THE CADILLAC CLIMBED and wound around sharp bends as we drove up the mountains. Paddy was in a great mood. 'In the Blue Ridge Mountains of Virginia,' he sang, as he zig-zagged around the corners. 'D'ya remember dat song, Lily? Laurel an' Hardy sang it?'

'I know,' I said, clinging to the seat and praying. 'But for God's sake, mind the road. You're not used to drivin' in America.'

Carol felt sick. He pulled up outside an Indian gift shop and ran in. 'Dere's a present for ya,' he said, coming out and handing her a fluffy white kitten on a cushion. 'We'll soon be there.'

We continued the winding climb with the window wide open, the air getting cooler. Carol sat back happily, hugging her cat. He steered the car into a narrow track leading up to a two-storey mountain lodge. 'Here we are.'

I crawled out and nearly had a fit. 'God, the house is hangin' off the cliff.'

'It's safe, Lily,' he laughed. 'Look at the big chains anchorin' it to the ground.'

We walked around the top balcony of the house, enjoying the view. Paddy leaned over the rail and gazed at the mountains. Lighting up, he took a deep drag, marvelling at the misty-blue sea of the tree tops below. 'I prefer the mountains to the sea any day,' he said, tapping his ash over the balcony. 'C'mon, let's go inside.'

I felt uneasy inside someone else's home. Personal things lay around, a book left open, a page about to be read, a fridge full of food – someone else's food. Beds made up with fresh covers and sheets – someone else's beds. Paddy had no trouble making himself at home. He kicked off his shoes, lay back on the couch and lit up again. 'Enjoy yerself, honey. I'll fry ya up somet'in' in a minute.'

Tea over, I settled Carol in a spare bedroom. She climbed into bed, clutching her white kitten on a cushion. I tucked her in. Back in the lounge, Paddy emptied the ashtrays and washed up. 'Let's go to bed,' he said, switching off the lights.

He warmed up the bed as I undressed. I slipped off my dress and slid in beside him.

'God, I t'ought I'd never get ya here,' he said, unfastening my bra and slinging it away. 'T'ank God she's in her own room at last.'

Just as we were getting started, the door handle turned and in peeped a little head.

'What are you doing, Mum?' Carol said. 'I can hear you laughing. Can I get in beside you?'

Paddy sat up straight. 'Go back to bed,' he snapped. 'I bought ya dat lovely white cat to keep ya company, didn't I?'

She burst into tears.

'She's used to sleeping with me,' I said, climbing out of bed and hurrying her back to her room.

The Tweetsie Railroad's shrill whistle woke us up the following morning as it puffed around the mountains below.

Breakfast over, Carol begged us to go. 'There's nothing to do here,' she said. 'Let's go back to the hotel with the pool.'

'C'mere to me, chicken,' Paddy said, making up with her. 'We'll go if ya want to.'

DEY'RE BOLD LITTLE BOYS AGAIN

PADDY DROVE ME all around Hickory, meeting his friends. It was the same every time we left them. 'Pat never meets a stranger,' they'd say, shaking my hand. 'He talks to everyone.'

I'd smile, say nothing and climb back into the car. Driving back, I'd think about him having all these friends over here in North Carolina. Would he ever settle in Australia?

'The boss has invited us to dinner tonight,' he said one evening, combing his hair. 'All the workers will be dere. I want ya to meet dem.'

We drove up a long tree-lined driveway to a large English-looking house. The boss and his wife welcomed us at their door. Carol's eyes lit up at their big outdoor pool. We sat down at a long table inside, and I was introduced to the other workers, mostly men, all dressed up and in good form. Paddy laughed away with them. I could now put a face to the people he mentioned in his letters. Dinner finished, the men all sat back, smoked and drank spirits.

'Give us "Piddling Pete", Pat,' one said, tapping his cigar into an ashtray.

'Yeah, Pat,' they cheered, clapping him on.

But Paddy needed no encouragement. He stubbed his cigarette out and began.

> A famous dog once came to town
> Whose middle name was Pete.
> His pedigree was ten yards long,
> His looks were hard to beat.
> He watered every gateway,
> He never missed a post.
> For piddling was his masterpiece
> And piddling was his boast.
>
> The city dogs stood looking on
> With deep and jealous rage.
> To see this simple country dog,
> The piddler of his age.

Paddy paused for a drink. The men laughed and urged him on.

> Behind him all the city dogs
> Debated what to do.
> They'd hold a piddling carnival
> To show this stranger through.
>
> But Pete was with their every trick
> With vigour and with vim.
> A thousand piddles more or less
> Were all the same to him.
>
> Then Pete an exhibition gave
> Of all the ways to piddle,
> Like, double drips and fancy flips,
> And now and then a dribble.
>
> The City Dogs said, 'Pete,
> Your piddling did defeat us!'
> But no one ever put them wise
> That Pete had diabetes.

I was surprised to hear him recite this ballad. The last time I'd heard 'Piddling Pete' was way back in Dublin when we had our little Christmas parties in Mrs O'Connor's. At the end of the night, when the men were well-on and the women were making the tea, Paddy would put down his cigarette, take the floor and have them all in stitches with it. 'Dey're bold little boys again,' Mrs O'Connor would say, filling her kettle.

I could see why Paddy loved working with these men: they made a fuss of him. He was in his element; he was the life and soul of the party.

He took centre stage again. 'Lily, hates me bringin' home pin-up books in case the boys get dem.'

The men burst out laughing, glancing at my red face as I forced a smile.

Paddy took out his hanky, wiped his eyes and went on. 'I brought a pile of books home an' hid dem behind our wardrobe.'

I nudged him to stop. But there was no shutting him up. 'While I was away, Lily decided to rearrange the bedroom furniture. She moved the bloody wardrobe an' found the books. She had murder wit' me when I came home. Ya never guess what she did. She gave dem to the dustmen. Dey dived on dem, didn't know themselves gettin' these expensive pin-up books from the States.'

Another chorus of laughter.

I made a move to go and looked around for Carol. Just in time, too. The boss's wife handed me a pair of my knickers, washed and pressed. I nearly died. They were the ones I had kicked off in bed in their mountain lodge. I quickly stuffed them into my handbag before Paddy caught sight of them.

Love from Your Dream Boat

'We're goin' to Annette's for dinner tonight,' Paddy said, patting his face with Old Spice. 'Ya'll like her. She's Irish.'

'It's our last night. Carol's very tired.'

'We won't stay long.'

Annette opened her door and welcomed us. 'I've got yer favourite drink, Pat,' she said, giving him a hug. 'I've heard all about ya, Lily. Come in.'

I liked her immediately. Her Irish accent took me back home. She reminded me of Debbie with her shiny brown hair sweeping down her back and her long cotton skirts, colourful and light, swirling around her. We followed her up the stairs to her lounge to meet Giacomo, her dark-haired, friendly husband. Drinks were poured out, and Annette served the dinner.

Paddy fell into deep conversation with Giacomo. I lost all sense of time, chatting to Annette about Dublin. It was only when I spotted Carol curled up in a cosy armchair fast asleep that I realised it was late. I sprang up. 'We'd better go,' I said, glancing at a bleary-eyed Paddy. He tried to lift Carol up, but stumbled and lost his balance. He reached for her again.

'You'll drop her; leave her,' I snapped.

'I can carry her.'

Giacomo called a taxi. Paddy and I were silent all the way back to the hotel, Carol fast asleep between us.

And I was silent all the way to the airport next morning. We stood at the departure gates, waiting.

'Sorry about last night,' he said, giving me a tight hug. 'I'll miss ya so much.'

'I wish you wouldn't drink so much.'

'I wish I was goin' back wit' ya.'

Our flight was called. I picked up my bag.

'Wait a minute,' he said, dashing into a newsagent. Out he ran with a card in his hand. 'Yer birthday's tomorra', honey. Here's yer card. I didn't have time to write in it, but the words on the front says it all.'

I sat back on the plane and thought about the three weeks I'd had with him in North Carolina. I enjoyed being with him, his carefree ways. I missed him telling me not to worry, that everything would be all right.

Smiling, I took the card out of my bag and read the words on the front cover. *To My Darling Wife and Sweetheart. I Will Love You Always.*

I ripped the cellophane off, expecting to read a lovely romantic verse inside. But it was a fun card with a picture of a big lump of a man slouched in an armchair with a wide boozy smile. His hand, holding a glass of whisky, sprung out of the card at me.

With Love from Your Dreamboat, the words underneath said.

I was home only an hour when the phone rang.

'Happy Birthday, honey.'

'God, Paddy. It was lucky I came home when I did. Steven's been in the Geelong Hospital with suspected scabies.'

'Scabies!'

'Debbie made spicy curries an' big red spots came out all over his body.'

'How are the others?'

'Bryan's effin' out of him an' havin' punch-ups with Debbie over the shower. Out of that tech school for him, I can tell you. An' the police have been here warning Paul to keep the stereo down. He had it up full blast; a neighbour miles away complained.'

'I'll be home at Christmas, an' this time I'll stay.'

But he didn't. Christmas came and Christmas went. Paddy came and Paddy went. Back to the States to finish yet another job.

THE MAGGIES

THE YEAR 1973 was a lonely one. Paddy was back down in Central America. His calls could no longer get through, so I had to rely on his letters.

Debbie was accepted in Melbourne University over fifty miles away. She chose to live on campus in St Mary's College. She came home every Friday night with her blue cotton bag, full of dirty washing, on her shoulder. I lived to see her and devoured her every word about university life. Sunday night, with her bag of clean washing and a tin full of Anzacs, she'd be keen to get back. She now had an Australian boyfriend, Greg. He sang in the choir with her.

Paul, following Paddy's footsteps, began an apprenticeship in textiles. The job was in Melbourne. He preferred to live at home and didn't mind the hour and a half train and tram trip, there and back. He'd cycle to Corio Station, chain up his bike and jump on the train to the city. He'd be up in the dark and home in the dark. At night and the weekends, he'd be off with Tina, his girlfriend from Sri Lanka.

I marched Bryan off to St Joseph's, a Christian Brothers college in Geelong. No more effin' out of him, and no girls in that school for him to show off to. And no more brass ashtrays for Paddy; Bryan had homework to do every night.

Steven got on with Brute now, the Christian Brother he had dreaded. I met Brute at a parent–teacher night. This nice Christian Brother was anything but a brute. He loved my Dublin accent. He wrote 'Dun Laoghaire' down on a piece of paper and asked me how to pronounce it. 'Dunleary,' I said, smiling. He was delighted. 'I've been waiting for years to ask an Irish person that,' he said. From then on, he called Steven 'Irish'.

Carol had her own special friend, Jennifer, whose parents were Dutch. Jennifer was top of the class. Carol strived to be like her and never refused an invitation to play in her house on the Bacchus Marsh Road.

As for me? No more long bus trips to Geelong for the messages.

Corio Village, a large modern shopping centre, had opened fifteen minutes' walk away. With my shopping over and done with in
the mornings, I spent the afternoons writing long letters to Paddy.
But letters weren't enough. I needed company, someone to talk
to. Debbie stopped coming home weekends, and the school
canteen once a month wasn't enough for me.

Browsing through the *Geelong News* one day, I read that a
Citizen's Advice Bureau was opening up in Corio Village and
needed volunteers. You had to pass an exam to be accepted. I tore
out the phone number, tucked it under Paddy's clock and tried to
forget it.

Over the weekend, I talked myself into it. I wanted to learn
more about this country, and joining the CAB was one way I could
do it. Giving advice to people would help me too, and I'd enjoy
meeting and chatting to the other members.

I passed the exam by the skin of my teeth and began training
with the CAB one Monday morning.

Carrying my cardigan and bag, I strolled under several shady
gum trees on the Bacchus Marsh Road. Those big black and white
birds swooped up and down. 'G'way, g'way,' they seemed to be saying down to me. But I wasn't listening. I was wondering what the
other volunteers would be like. Would they be as friendly as Phyllis
from the school canteen?

Then something heavy crashed down onto my head, nearly
knocking me over. I thought the whole tree was falling down on
top of me.

'Jesus,' I screamed, putting my hand up to protect myself.

I felt a big bird flapping on my head, its huge claws tangled up
in my hair. A powerful beak pecked wildly at my scalp. 'Get off,
Get off,' I yelled, shaking my head frantically.

The bird finally freed itself and streaked away. Holding my
head, I hurried towards Corio Village with a splitting headache.

I was last in for the meeting. The volunteers sat on rows of seats
chatting, waiting on the speaker to begin. They looked like retired
teachers, smartly dressed and wearing glasses. Pinning my name
tag on, I squeezed in beside them. I was still shaking and couldn't
stop talking. 'Wait till I tell you,' I said. 'This huge bird dived on
my head. I got such a fright.'

One of the men smiled at me. 'That would have been a mag-gie,' he said. 'It's spring. They're nesting, protecting their young. Lucky they didn't peck your eyes out.'

The woman next to him glanced at my name. 'You should wear a hat, Lily,' she said in an English accent. 'That's what we do here in spring.'

Here I was, only in the door of the CAB, and I'd learnt something already.

The speaker, a youth worker, began. We all turned to face the front. He talked about the growing problem of teenagers in Corio. 'They need somewhere to go at night,' he said. 'We've opened up youth clubs with trained leaders.'

Right, I thought, my headache forgotten. *I'll ring them tomorrow. The boys are always complaining there's nowhere to go Friday nights. They'll have somewhere to go now.*

The meeting finished with a cup of tea and a chat. Then, after a quick bit of shopping, I made my way home, making sure not to walk under the trees. Passing the big gum, where I'd been attacked, I put my cardigan over my head and watched the branch-es for those diving birds. It was deathly quiet. Not a sign of a bird, only a lady standing under the tree. She beckoned me over and pointed to dead magpies scattered around her feet.

'Look! Isn't that disgraceful?' she said.

'What happened to them?'

'They attacked a little girl up the road. Her father, a new Australian, came out and shot them out of the trees.' She stared up at the branches. 'Who's going to look after their young now?'

I studied the birds on the ground. They looked sad and pathetic lying on their backs. *But the father was protecting his child*, I thought, walking on. *I must remember to buy Carol a hat.*

Hard to Kill a Bad Thing

I HEARD THE gate go and looked out the window. It was Paddy. He was struggling in with his case. I wasn't expecting him home till Christmas. I was about to go shopping.

'I had to get home quick,' he said, when I opened the hall door. 'I hadn't time to ring ya.'

He dragged his case into the lounge, collapsed on the couch and kicked off his shoes. Slipping his heavy gold watchband off, he threw it onto his smoker's table along with his cigarettes and matches. 'If I hadn't come home now, ya'd be takin' me home in a box.'

'What's happened?' I said, trying to take it all in.

'I quit, Lily. I felt so bad I booked my ticket, t'rew everyt'in' in me case an' left.'

'Have you *really* finished with that job?'

'Dey've had every drop of blood out a' me.' He closed his eyes. 'I owe dem nuttin'.'

I didn't know what to think. For four years, Paddy had been coming and going to America. He'd grown to love the life of a single man. And we had grown used to being without him.

I sat down and had a good look at him. I was shocked at what I saw: a man overweight, his face pale and drawn. His hair was untidy, over his ears in need of a cut. The skin under his eyes sagged like a cocker spaniel's. He looked so much older that I hardly knew him.

'C'mon,' I said, springing up. 'I'll make you a cup a' tea. Have you had anyt'in' to eat?'

'Will ya sit down for a minute, Lily.'

He opened his case, and something fell out. I picked it up. It was an ornament of a grey, grumpy-faced man sitting under a tree, with a tiny blue bird perched in the tree above him. The bird was about to do his business on the man's head. '*Go ahead . . . Everyone else does*', the man said, looking up at him.

I didn't like it. *Is this how he's feeling?*

'Why did you buy that?' I said, putting it down.

'I couldn't resist his miserable face with those big droopy eyes.'
And there was more to come.

Digging around inside his case, he pulled out an ugly black ashtray made of clay, bigger than his hand. He passed it to me. Cigarette ash was still embedded in its hollow. 'Moteles–San Miguel'
was printed on it.

I didn't like that either. I put it down. 'Why did you bring that
home?'

'Dere was nuttin' in dat godforsaken hole. It was just me an dat
ashtray. So when I was leavin', I t'rew the bugger in me case.'

'Were you smokin' that much?'

'A hundred a day.'

'A hundred? My God, Paddy, a hundred a day! No wonder your
breath stinks.'

'When yer on yer own in a motel room, ya smoke more an'
drink more.'

I hurried into the kitchen. 'You should have come home
sooner. I kept tellin' you.'

'I didn't want to let the company down,' he said, following me.
'Dey were dependin' on me.'

I flicked the kettle on and took out two cups and saucers. He sat
down and chatted about his friends in North Carolina, how good
they were to him, inviting him into their homes. He pulled out his
wallet and showed me a snap of one of their families.

'You can write to him,' I said. 'He'll understand why you left.'

Paddy shook his head. 'Lily, the company invested in a project
in Central America. I was their man down dere. I let dem down.
But if I'd stayed another day in dat place, it would've killed me.'

'You did the right t'ing. I'm glad you came home.'

He struggled up, walked to the window, dropped the blinds and
closed them. For a moment, he lost his balance and stumbled.

'What's the matter?'

'Nuttin'. Just a bit dizzy. It's me blood pressure.'

'Right,' I said, jumping up. 'You're goin' to a doctor.'

'I'll be right when I have a good sleep.'

'No, you're goin'. I heard a doctor speak at the CAB meeting
last night. They say he's a health fanatic. No one goes near him.
I'll ring him.'

'I've no presents for the kids,' he said, walking back into the lounge.

'For God's sake, Paddy, that doesn't matter. They'll be that delighted to see you.'

I picked up his case, carried it into our bedroom and hung up his jackets. Soon, snoring thundered in from the lounge. I slid the door open. Paddy was conked out on the couch in a deep sleep. A smouldering cigarette lay in that horrible San Miguel ashtray. I stabbed it out hard. Snatching up the ugly black thing, I took it into the kitchen. Into the sink it went. 'You're gettin' a good scrubbin',' I said, squirting the Fairy Liquid on. No matter how much I scrubbed, I couldn't get the ash out of its crevices.

Carol was the first in from school. She threw her spelling book at me. 'Ten new words to be learned for tomorrow,' she said, opening the fridge.

'Quiet. Daddy's home. He's asleep in the lounge.'

Bryan walked in with a bundle of bills. 'How come you didn't check the mailbox, Mum? The letters were all sticking out.'

'Dad's home,' I whispered.

'I can smell his cigarettes,' he said, staring into the empty fridge. 'When's tea?'

I opened my purse. 'Go round to the milk bar for fish fingers, an' see if you can get a packet of sausages for Dad.'

Steven dragged his bag of books in and glanced in the lounge. 'How come Dad's asleep?'

'He's dead tired. Don't wake him.'

I rooted in the cutlery drawer for my crinkly-chip cutter, then pulled out a million potatoes.

Soon the chips were drained and scattered on their plates.

'He's got more than I have,' Bryan shouted, pointing to Steven's plate.

Paddy woke with the noise. He slid the lounge door across, came out and kissed them all.

'I started the Falcon up every day, Dad,' Bryan said. 'Like you told me to.'

'We'll take it for a spin later, see what it can do.'

'I've made an appointment for you at seven, Paddy. Are you okay to drive?'

'I've had a good sleep.'

An hour later, Paul, dressed in his new denim outfit, flew in the back door. 'Mum, the car's gone!'

'Dad's home,' Steven shouted in from the lounge.

'He's not well,' I said. 'He's gone to the doctor's with Bryan.'

The back gates banged open. I ran outside. The Falcon sped into the garage. 'What did the doctor say?' I said, opening the car door.

'I'm fit as a fiddle,' Paddy said. 'As long as I take me blood pressure tablets, cut back on the fags an' lose weight, I'll be right.'

'There you are. What did I tell you? It's hard to kill a bad thing.'

Paddy laughed and packed his Fosters into the fridge. 'Here,' he said, handing me a booklet from his jacket pocket. 'The doctor gave me this.'

I flipped through it. 'It's full of recipes. Everyt'in' is to be grilled from now on. No more sausages or fries.'

'If I have to give up me bangers, I might as well be dead.'

THAT'S IT, PADDY O'CONNOR

PADDY FOUND IT hard adjusting to family life again. Living in a new country didn't help either. We had already gone through the stages of settling in Australia, but he was just beginning.

Each day was the same. Breakfast over, he'd walk to the milk bar for *The Herald* and cigarettes. He'd scour the paper for textile jobs. There were none. It was too near Christmas, and factories were winding down for the summer holidays. He began to worry about the bills. 'Get off dat bloody phone,' he'd shout, every time he heard Steven on the phone to David.

One morning, after they'd left for school, Paddy stood staring out the kitchen window. I glanced out to see what he was looking at. The tall ugly weeds on the vacant block opposite waved over and clouds of dust on the unmade roads whirled up into the air.

'When are dey makin' those roads?' he said.

'Next year. That's what Corio Shire said anyway.'

'An' we have to pay double because we're on a corner block?'

I said nothing, brushing crumbs from the table onto my hands. He sat down and lit up. 'Are you really happy here?' he said. 'Why don't we go back? I'd have no trouble gettin' a good job in England.'

I went off to make their beds. Paddy followed me from room to room, reminding me of the good things about England: the cosy Christmases around the fire, the great times we'd had in holiday camps, the National Health, the free doctors and dentists. 'Surely ya miss somet'in',' he said.

I knew what I missed. I missed the little things like my letter box in the hall door: that lovely sound of letters and cards being squeezed through and the soft thud as they hit the mat. I hated walking to the gate to see if I had any letters, then slinking back inside with none. But I didn't tell him this. Instead I reminded him of those long, dark days in Luton, the days when the mist never lifted.

'Steven doesn't suffer with sinus any more,' I said. 'Neither does Debbie. Here they pray for rain. In England, I prayed for it to stop.'

'The weather's not everyt'in'.'

'I know that, but I feel at home here. The Aussies are real easy-goin', like the Irish.'

Back in the kitchen, I turned on the radio and wished I hadn't. The newsreader warned people to stay off vacant blocks of land. A sudden hot spell had woken the snakes up early and they were cranky. I switched it off.

'Did ya hear dat, Lily? Not only have the snakes woken up, but dere bloody cranky.'

I couldn't stop the laughing, but he didn't give up.

'An' what kind of a country is it dat sells Durex in a milk bar?' he said. 'The kids can buy rubbers here wit' dere sweets.'

'Durex? For God's sake, Paddy, Durex is the name of a cellotape here.'

He peered out the window in the direction of the Shell refinery. I flicked the kettle on, praying to God the smoke wouldn't start drifting out of its chimneys.

Smokey, the wild cat, flew by the window with another mouse in her mouth.

'Dat cat woke me up last night whoring on the roof,' Paddy said, staring after it.

'That wasn't Smokey. They were possums.'

'Possums? What are dey?'

'They're like squirrels. They come out at night for food.'

'Pity we couldn't go out at night,' he said. 'The pubs here are like cafés. Have ya seen dem? Dey're full of cold, hard tables an' chairs.'

'You just miss the Luton Labour Club. That's what's wrong with you.'

'We won't go back to Luton, Lily. We'll go anywhere ya like in England. Anywhere.'

'Paddy, Debbie has finally settled here. How in the name a' God could I ask her to go back now? She loves university. No way would she have got into university in England. Even if she did, we couldn't have afforded the fees. An' do you t'ink Paul would have got an apprenticeship in England? I don't t'ink so.'

'England's been good to me. We'd have nuttin' if wasn't for England.'

'I dragged them here, Paddy. I'm not draggin' them back again.'

He snatched up his car keys.

'Where are you goin'?'

'I need cigarettes.'

A couple of hours later, the back gates banged open. I hurried out. Paddy shot into the garage, taking one of the gates with him.

'Oh my God,' I said, putting my hand to my mouth. 'Look at the big dent in the door of the car. Why weren't you more careful?'

'The gap's too narrow,' he said, slamming the car door.

I stormed back into the kitchen, fuming. He followed me in with a brown paper bag. Out came the bad influence – Johnnie Walker. He stood the bottle on the table then reached into a cupboard for a glass. I snatched the bottle and reefed it open. 'I'm not goin' through this again,' I said, pouring it down the sink.

He sent me flying against the wall.

'That's it, Paddy O'Connor. You've gone too far. Life was easier without you.'

I ran into the bathroom and gripped the cold wash-hand basin, trembling. It didn't look like me in the mirror. This pale face with the angry eyes and tight lips was a stranger. The sound of crying brought me down the hall to our bedroom. Paddy was lying face down on the bed, sobbing. I'd never seen him cry before. I could do nothing but stare.

'What's wrong with you?' I said, not knowing what to say.

'Leave me alone. Go away. Leave me alone.'

Drifting back into the lounge, I sat down and picked up his watch where he'd thrown it. I sat there, stretching its expanding metal band to its limits, watching it slowly fall back into place. The lounge door slid back.

'I'm sorry,' Paddy said, sitting down.

I said nothing and continued stretching the band.

'D'ya want me to go? I'll check into a hotel. You have the house. I'll send ya money when I can.'

'No, stay. Don't do that.' I put his watch down.

'It won't happen again, I promise ya. No more whisky. Just two bottles of beer a night. Is dat all right?'

THE FULL CIRCLE

I COULD HAVE hugged Paul when he said his boss wanted to meet
Paddy as soon as possible.

'That's great,' I said, taking up his dinner.

'Where's the factory?' Paddy said.

'Abbotsford, Melbourne. Catch the train with me tomorrow.'

That night, Paddy laid his clean shirt out on the back of the
couch. He pressed his trousers and polished his shoes, ready for
the morning. Then, after tricking around with the boys, it was off
to bed early for him.

I woke next morning to hear the back door close, the gates
bang and the Falcon skid off down the dirt road towards
Plantation Road and the station. Paul was delighted with himself
not having to cycle there and back.

The familiar trot of the milkman's horse and cart got me up.
I'd better get the milk in and these three off to school, I thought, throwing the covers back.

Breakfast over, Bryan stuffed his peanut-butter sandwich in his
school bag and flew out the door for his bus to St Joseph's. Steven
packed his jam sandwich and cycled off to Chanel College, calling
for David on his way. Carol met Jennifer at our front gate, and the
pair skipped off down the road to school.

All day long, I thought about Paddy. *Please God, Paul's boss will
give him a job. And please God, Paddy will take it.*

The gate went. In walked Carol. I poured out her milk.

'I have to learn the seven times table tonight,' she said, between
gulps.

Then the boys arrived, one after the other.

'What's for dinner?' Bryan said.

'Mashed potatoes, baked beans an' grilled barbecue chops.'

'I hate barbecue chops,' Steven moaned. 'Why can't we have
shepherd's pie any more?'

'I'll make you gravy. You can pour it all over your dinner.'

With those three fed and packed off to the lounge, it was time
to get Paddy and Paul's dinner. The back gates banged. I jumped.

The pair of them walked in from work, laughing.

'How was it?' I said, turning on the grill.

Paddy threw his *Herald* down on the table. 'His knittin' machines are old crocks. The very same as the ones I worked on back home in Dublin. He wants me to fix dem up. Work miracles.'

'Well, it's a start.'

'A start all right. I've come the bloody full circle,' he said, washing his hands. 'I'm back to where I started in Irish Textiles.'

'Well, give it a go.'

'Don't worry, I'll stay wit' him till I get somet'in' better.'

'An' you will after Christmas. You'll see.'

He plonked down at the table and off came the watch. 'Have ya been on the trains here, Lily? Dey're old Victorian carriages, little mirrors an' pictures on the walls. England t'rew dem out last century. Boneshakers, the lot of dem.'

'They call them Red Rattlers here, Dad,' Paul said, taking his denim jacket and cap off.

'An' have ya seen Coreeo Station?' Paddy laughed. 'I t'ought I was in an old cowboy movie out on the prairie. It's just a platform in the middle of nowhere.'

Bryan slid the lounge door across. 'It's *Corio*, Dad,' he said, laughing, 'not *Coreeo*.'

Paul looked up and grinned at Bryan. 'Guess what, Bryan? Dad thought the foot-warmer on the train was a bomb.'

'An' would ya blame me?' Paddy said. 'You would too if a bloody big metal t'ing rolled out from under yer seat.'

For the rest of the week, it was up with the maggies for Paddy and home with the possums.

Friday night, he came in and threw his pay packet on the table. 'Look at dat money. It's a fraction of what I was gettin' in the States.'

'You can't expect to get the same money as you did in America,' I said, draining his chips on butcher paper. 'We have no debts an' the house is paid for.'

'The house is paid for,' he said, with a dreamy look in his eyes. 'I could take out a mortgage on it. Open up me own textile factory. It'd be a great opportunity for the boys.'

I nearly dropped his plate. 'Paddy, don't start. You're no good with the money. You'd drink an' smoke more.'

'Not if I was running me own business. I know now where to buy good machines cheap. Just t'ink, Lily, it'd be a great opportunity for us.'

'You're too soft. You'd let the workers away with murder. I don't want you takin' on that kind of a job again.'

The phone rang. It was Debbie, telling Paddy that her train didn't stop at Corio. Could he pick her up at North Geelong Station? She was home for Christmas.

GOOD ON YA, DAD

CHRISTMAS DAY, 1973, we sat in shorts and T-shirts and enjoyed our roast dinner of turkey and Paddy's pudding. No one complained about the heat any more. They were looking forward to going away the next day. We were getting used to having our summer holidays on top of Christmas. I'd made sure to book a holiday house in Lorne, a popular seaside resort only a couple of hours' drive away.

'C'mon, Lily,' Paddy said Boxing Day, slipping on his white T-shirt and light pants. 'I don't want to be drivin' in the heat.'

The sun was up and belting down on our roof. It was going to be a scorcher, so the weatherman said. I shut the blinds tight to keep the heat out, then hung Paddy's shirt and socks on the line to keep the robbers out. Worried about our mail being left outside, I found a lock and clicked it on the mailbox's little door – and it wasn't to keep the spiders out either. The boys packed their duffel bags into the boot of the car. I crammed the Esky with all our food and Paddy's beer, placing the ice-bricks on top. The seven of us then squeezed into the Falcon, three in the front, four in the back.

We dropped Debbie off at Corio Station, her bag full of pudding and cake. She was meeting Greg in Melbourne. Smokey was next. The Cat's Home for her; she wasn't coming. Then we picked David up. He wanted to be with the boys in Lorne. He climbed in the back beside Steven.

'Did you enjoy Christmas, David?' I said, turning around.

'Great, thanks, Aunty Lily. Mum said thanks for the mince tarts.'

Paddy put his foot down on the Geelong Road. We sped by cars tugging caravans and boats, all on holidays, heading to the beaches.

'How come we're leaving everyone behind?' Paul said, looking out the window.

The next thing we knew, a blue light flashed behind us. A police car overtook and pulled us in.

'Jesus, the police. What do they want?'

'Stay quiet. Leave this to me,' Paddy said, winding down his window.

'Any reason for speeding?' the policeman said.

'Sorry, officer. I'm new to this country,' he said, handing him his International Driver's Licence. 'I'm just over from the States.'

The policeman flicked through it, passed it back and waved us on.

'We're not in any hurry, Paddy. Just take your time.'

'Let me do the drivin',' he said, pulling off.

'Don't keep overtaking. As long as we get there safe. We've a whole crowd of kids in the back. T'ink of them.'

Not one word was said until we reached the cool sea air of Torquay. Paddy pulled up at a milk bar. 'Anyone for ice lollies?' he said, jumping out.

'They're called *icy poles* here, Dad, not *ice lollies*,' Steven joked from behind.

Leaning against the car bonnet, I thought about Torquay in England, with its high cliffs and pebbly beach. How old and hilly England's Torquay was compared to this Torquay, with its long, sandy beach and crashing waves.

Back in the car, we cruised along the Great Ocean Road past sandy beach after sandy beach: Anglesea, Airey's Inlet and Fairhaven. The road narrowed as we entered a forest, the Otway Ranges. The blue sea shimmered on the left and jagged rocks jutted from the cliffs on the right. We weaved around tight bends, the air growing cooler. Paddy wound down his window. 'In the Blue Ridge Mountains of Virginia,' he sang. 'D'ya remember dat song, Lily?'

'I know. I do, but watch the road,' I said. 'Are you keepin' an eye on the signs? No overtaking. No U-turns. Falling Rocks for the Next Ten Miles.'

'I can *read*, ya know.'

'Are you watchin' that caravan in front?'

'No, I'm not watchin' it,' he said, shooting up behind it. 'Course I'm watchin' it.'

'Stop worrying, Mum,' Paul shouted behind me. 'Dad's a good driver.'

At long last, the road levelled and the township of Lorne

appeared. The Falcon crawled down the main street, Mountjoy Parade. The ocean waves rolled in on the left. Cafés, pizza parlours and chemists were doing a roaring trade on the right. Groups of tanned girls in colourful bikinis picked their way across the hot tarmac road to the cafés.

'Can you let us out here, Dad?' Bryan said, winding down his window.

'Let's find this house first,' he said. 'Den ya can do what ya like.'

We turned right, up a dirt road, and skidded to a stop. A small white weatherboard house welcomed us. A rusty tin mailbox dangled from its mesh-wire fence. The key to the house was in it. A musty holiday-home smell hit us as we opened the door. Six wooden chairs and a well-scrubbed table sat in the middle of a large kitchen. A battered cream fridge, stickers all over it, hummed on one side of a new stainless-steel sink. An old chipped cooker, scrubbed clean, stood the other side. The boys dashed to their room and claimed their bunk beds. Carol christened the toilet. Paddy carried the case and the Esky in with a look on his face.

'How much did ya pay for this place?' he said.

I pushed the windows open. 'It's just a holiday house, Paddy. It has everyt'in' in it we need.'

Before I could stick the kettle on, they were all changed for the beach. The boys, heads in the air, filed out the flyscreen door, towels swinging off their shoulders, thongs flapping on their feet.

'Make sure you swim between the flags,' I shouted after them.

Paddy made himself at home. Finding a glass, he poured himself a cold beer, then sat back and kicked off his shoes. Carol sat beside him, arms folded on the table, waiting patiently in her bathers.

'Let me finish me drink first, chicken,' he said. 'Den we'll go down to the sea.'

Carol had her paddle, then the three of us strolled around Lorne. I dragged Paddy in and out of gift shops, buying cards to send back to my pals in Dublin. I checked my list of Irish addresses, making sure I had May and Hughie's, my friends from Finglas, and Johnny's new Irish one.

Carol claimed a table on the path outside a busy open-air café. 'Can we sit here?' she begged. 'Can I have an ice cream?'

Paddy read the menu. 'Sure ya can, chicken.'

We sat down at the table under a big umbrella. I ordered a pot of tea, lamingtons and ice cream. 'Isn't this lovely all the same,' I said, tucking my dress under me.

Paddy lit up. 'Yer easily pleased, Lily,' he said, smiling.

The boys were waiting for us when we arrived back, faces and backs red with the sun. 'There was a shark in the sea,' Steven said. 'The Life Savers ordered us out.'

'Sharks?' Paddy said. 'Pity dey didn't get the lot of youse. Youse are costin' me a fortune.'

Paul gave him a dig then went to the fridge. 'What's for tea, Mum?'

'Fish an' chips,' I said, going for my purse. 'Will you go an' get them? There's a nice little chipper at the end of the road. See if you can get a piece of cod for Dad.'

I had just finished buttering a mountain of bread when they were back. Paul opened up a parcel of hot chips, potato cakes and fish onto the table. 'We could only get flake,' he said, helping himself to a chip.

'Flake, what's dat?' Paddy said.

'Shark,' Steven laughed, making a big fat chip sandwich.

'Do we eat the t'ings now?'

'It's lovely, like cod in England,' I said, buttering more bread. 'Everyone here eats it.'

The boys showered, brushed their hair and straightened their dark sunglasses. They were off to Theo's, a youth club, where they hoped to meet girls. They'd seen it advertised in the chipper.

Carol set out her Monopoly game on the table. 'You be banker, Dad,' she said, handing him the paper money. 'Sit down, Mum.'

I did what I was told, sat down and was given the little iron to move on the board. Paddy was given the little car and she kept the little silver dog for herself.

The dice was thrown and the dog tore along the board, buying up London. Carol fell all over the place, laughing. Paddy was never out of jail, letting her away with blue murder. At the first chance, I leapt up to put the kettle on and slice up the last bit of the pudding.

The weather held out for the week in Lorne. We never saw the boys, except for meals. Paddy, Carol and I strolled around the town, relaxing, chatting and eating. At night, it was off to Theo's for the boys to eat all the club's toasted raisin bread and meet girls. For Paddy and me, it was Monopoly or Scrabble organised by Carol.

Friday morning, our last day, the boys were back from the beach in an hour, lying on their beds, reading *Mad* comics.

'Why are ya not swimmin'?' Paddy said, peeping into their room. 'Don't tell me dere's more sharks in the sea?'

'Sharks, me eye,' I called out from the kitchen. 'The girls have gone back to Melbourne; that's why they're back early. Just as well we're goin' home tomorrow.'

One by one, they strutted into the kitchen, searching for something to eat. Steven and David were tricking around, pushing each other, Paul and Bryan opening and closing the fridge, fed up.

Paddy threw down the paper. 'Get yer shoes on,' he said. 'We'll walk to Erskine Falls.'

'Erskine Falls?' Bryan moaned. 'That's miles away. Let's take the car.'

'The sign at the end of the road says it's an easy walk. It'll do youse good.'

I banged the door shut, and the flyscreen door slammed behind it. Off we all trailed, stinking with Areogard. The boys rambled ahead in their T-shirts, jeans and runners. They laughed back at Paddy, striding in his good leather shoes, his movie camera swinging off his shoulder, his top pocket bulging with cigarettes and matches. Carol and I trotted along with him, cool in our short cotton dresses and sandals.

Around bends we walked. Up and down hills we struggled, and not a car passed us. The Otway trees grew taller, the undergrowth thicker and darker. Carol skipped and chased the blue-tongued lizards off the dirt road.

'Watch out for the snakes,' I warned.

'When are we going to be there, Dad?' she whined, swinging out of him.

Paddy kept her amused by telling her stories about a little man the size of his thumb.

I was surprised to hear his makey-up stories again. He had told them to Debbie and the boys when they were little, but Carol had missed out. He was in America for most of her years.

The Otways were silent, except for the high-pitched buzzing of the cicadas in the heat and the chirping of the green and red lorikeets in the trees. Still no sign of the falls. Dead to the world, we traipsed down a long steep hill and stopped. The sound of rushing water whispered through the trees. We stepped down a muddy track to the bottom of a gorge. A big cheer went up when we spotted Erskine Falls at last. Its clear crystal water streamed down from a high cliff into a shady valley of huge rocks and lush ferns. Shoes kicked off, jeans rolled up, the boys stumbled over slippery rocks to the cool sparkling falls. Slipping off my sandals, I paddled beside Carol in a shallow pool. She bent down and collected pebbles. Paddy sat on a large smooth rock, enjoying a cigarette in the cool damp air. It wasn't long before he looked at his watch. 'C'mon,' he said. 'Get yer shoes on. We'd better make a start back.'

We staggered up the gorge and that unmerciful steep hill. Carol and the boys collapsed. 'We're too tired,' they complained, sitting down on the edge of the dirt road. They dreaded the long walk back to Lorne.

'C'mon, get up, we have to keep goin',' Paddy said. 'It gets dark early.'

No one made a move.

'Stay wit' dem, Lily. I'll be back wit' the car.'

I watched Paddy stride off, his straight back fading into the distance. Carol sat playing with her pebbles. The orange sun began to sink, and the birds grew noisier. The trees creaked as a cool wind blew up. A loud crack. A heavy branch fell to the undergrowth.

'Jesus, what's that?' I said. 'C'mon, get up. We'd better start movin'.'

Taking Carol's hand, I began hurrying down this long road. The boys were up quick smart and marched behind me. A cloud of dust blew up ahead. I thought I was seeing things. The bronze Falcon was tearing towards us. It skidded to a halt, the dust swirling around it. Paddy opened the front door, smiling from ear to ear.

'Good on ya, Dad,' Paul said, as we all climbed in.

THE BIRTHDAY DINNER

'WHAT D'YA WANT to go back to school for?' Paddy said over dinner one night.

'I never wanted to leave school, an' trainin' for the CAB has givin' me confidence.'

'So where d'ya go?'

'Geelong High School. It's at night. I'm doin' fifth-form English. Can you give me a lift?'

'When d'ya start?'

'February. Just after the kids go back.'

I spent the next few weeks reading Debbie's old school books, trying to make sense of them. I was good at spelling, but critical essay writing was beyond me.

Soon it was March, and I was nervous. I prayed to God this teacher wouldn't tell me I was too old to learn. Paddy dropped me off Wednesday night and fetched me three hours later.

'How was it?' he asked.

'It's very hard. We're doin' *Macbeth*. I've made a friend, Isabel. We sit together.'

'What's yer teacher like?'

'Max. He's nice. Very patient. He's given me extra work to do because I'm behind the others.'

I gave Paddy a little pat on his arm. 'I learnt a new word tonight, "onomatopoeia". I bet you don't know what that means.'

He smiled. 'God, I learnt dat when I was a kid, Lily. Let me t'ink now. It's the sound of somet'in'. The sound of me sausages sizzlin' on the pan. Those were the days, when I had me bangers, God bless dem.'

The house was quiet when we arrived home. They were all in bed. Humming to myself, I filled the kettle and opened the biscuit tin. Paddy sauntered off into the lounge, picked up the *Herald* and switched on the television. He sat down, then jumped up again and switched it off. 'Dere's never anyt'in' on worth watchin'. Might as well go to bed.'

I woke next morning to hear the back door close and the

Falcon speed off down the road. I lay there, thinking of Paddy. It was great having a routine with him again. I knew the time he'd leave in the morning and I knew the time he'd be home at night. *T'ank God, he's finally got the wandering out of his blood.*

It was Thursday morning, my turn on Carol's school roster. I couldn't wait to have a chat with Phyllis and the other mothers. They kept asking me about Paddy; when was he coming home? I was delighted to be able to tell them that he was now home for good. I'm sure they were beginning to think I had invented a husband.

Saturday morning, Paddy was up early. Having dropped the boys off at Lara Pool, he took me shopping. In the afternoon, I got stuck into my homework.

Sunday it was mass, then our usual roast dinner of lamb, potatoes and Yorkshire pudding with lashings of gravy. The boys cycled off on their bikes, calling for David. Carol dressed up in Debbie's old skirt and skipped outside to her tree. Paddy helped me finish the washing-up.

'Let's go for a drive,' he said, throwing down the tea towel.

'Where?'

'We'll head out Stieglitz way.'

I called Carol in, and up Lovely Banks we drove, the steep hill Steven hated.

God knows, I heard enough about that hill. Steven never stopped complaining about cycling up it every day to school. If it wasn't the birds attacking him from the trees, it was the spiders and the big red bull ants attacking his bike on the road.

The car wheels struck pothole after pothole, blowing dust up behind us. There was nothing of interest to see either side, except ghostly gums struggling to survive on the flat dry land and the odd red-roofed weatherboard shack, smoke drifting from its chimney.

'Are we near Stieglitz? Can you see any nice little tearooms, Paddy?'

He laughed. 'Forget it, Lily. You an' yer tearooms. Ya're not in England now. We just went through Stieglitz. It was on yer left.'

Just then, I spotted a small piece of land with high railings all round it, a little cemetery out here in the middle of nowhere. 'Let's stop an' have a look.'

We read the big old gravestones, dug down deep in knee-high weeds.

'God, look, Paddy, most of them are little babies an' young children.'

'A lot of Irish names too,' he said, lighting up. 'It's a tough country, Lily. If the drought doesn't get ya, the bushfires will.'

'Can we go now?' Carol said. 'I'm bored.'

All the way home, I chatted to Paddy about a test I had to do on Aborigines. 'I don't know anyt'in' about them, but Debbie said she'd write an essay out for me. I'll copy it an' learn it off by heart.'

'Yer really enjoyin' dat class, aren't ya?'

'I am, even though I'm not very good. I never know the answers to the questions the teacher asks.'

'What does he ask?'

'All about Captain Cook and where he landed in Australia. I hadn't even heard of the man, let alone where he landed.'

Paddy laughed. 'Lily, ya should have known dat. Dere's even songs written about Botany Bay.'

'You're really good. Why don't you do somet'in' at night school?'

'I will. Once I'm settled in a decent job, I will.'

'You could join the library an' start readin' again. You used to be always readin'.'

'You borrow a book for me.'

'I wouldn't know what to choose.'

'Anyt'in' on European history will do.'

For the next few weeks, Paddy devoured one history book after the other. Borrowing those books for him was the best thing I ever did. He sat in the lounge room every night, content. Feet up on his stool, glasses on, he'd lose himself in a book and not the bottle. Even the ashtray was only half full.

His birthday slipped by. I didn't suggest we go out. I was too frightened he'd break his promise and start on the whisky again. It was always a worry, his birthday being the day after St Patrick's Day. It meant a double celebration for him: he'd have one for St Patrick and one for himself.

But I planned something special for Friday night, a surprise birthday dinner. A big steak done the way he liked it, a bit of butter on top and sealed quickly on a hot grill. He hadn't had one for a while. And Debbie was coming home, especially for him.

Friday morning, I jumped on the bus to Geelong to have my hair tinted. Out of Moorabool Hair Fashions I ran and into Myers for Paddy's Old Spice aftershave. Then it was into the bank to pay the insurance bill. The butcher was next for the meat. I was just in time for the twelve-thirty bus home. I wanted to make a cake, a snow cake. Steven was forever asking me to make it.

When I arrived home, I couldn't believe it. Workmen with big trucks were outside my gate. They were finally making the roads.

'G'day,' one of them called over.

Paddy will be pleased, I thought, opening the gate. He was fed up with the dust getting into everything. I peeped in the mailbox. A late St Patrick's Day card from Johnny was waiting for me. In I hurried, shoved the steaks in the fridge and filled the kettle, dying to read Johnny's card over a cup of tea. A loud knock banged off my door. A young policeman in a navy-blue jacket and pants stood there, holding a notebook. 'Are you Mrs O'Connor?' he said.

'Yes.'

'Does Paul O'Connor live here?'

'Yes.'

'How old is he?

'Seventeen. Why? What's he done?'

The policeman took a step back and looked down at his book. 'Is there another P. O'Connor living here?'

'Yes, my husband.'

'What's his name?'

'Patrick O'Connor.'

'How old is he?'

'Forty-three.'

'Can I come in?'

HE WOULDN'T GO WITHOUT
SAYING GOODBYE

I CLOSED THE door and found myself in the laundry. I filled up the basin with hot sudsy water. The laundry floor needed a good washing. So did the kitchen. I rung out the floorcloth tightly and pegged it on the line. *Better get this ironing done*, I thought, taking out the ironing board. Paddy's clean shirts and trousers were ironed and hung up in the wardrobe.

I wandered into the lounge. Paddy's book lay open on his smoker's table, his reading glasses on top, marking his page. I stood Johnny's St Patrick's Day card up beside the birthday ones on the mantelpiece.

Paul burst through the hall door, panting. 'I tried to get home before the police,' he said, giving me a hug.

Sylvia appeared behind him, sobbing. 'Oh, Lily, poor Paddy. I'm terribly sorry.'

'What happened?'

Paul sat down at the table. 'He collapsed while fixing a machine. I was on the other side. He asked me to pass him his compass. As I picked it up, I heard a crash. I thought it was his toolbox falling.'

'Didn't anybody call the ambulance?'

'The boss was out at lunch. The women in the factory can't speak English. They went hysterical, screaming in their own language.'

'Was he just left lying there?'

'I'll make tea,' Sylvia said, changing the subject. While the kettle was boiling, she set out cups and saucers on the table. She put an extra spoonful of tea in the pot.

'Are they sure he's dead?'

'The ambulance men said it was a massive heart attack,' Paul said, stirring his tea.

'How would they know?'

'He went blue.'

'Where is he now?'

'They took him to a hospital in Melbourne.'

I drifted into the lounge and sat down. *He can't have gone. There's some mistake. He wouldn't go without saying goodbye.*

I wished I hadn't gone to that CAB meeting last night.

Sylvia ran around, fixing the cushions and straightening the rug in front of the mantelpiece. 'I've rung the priest,' she said.

The back door opened. Carol walked into the lounge, humming, carrying Smokey. 'Why is Paul home early?' she said. 'Why are you all so quiet?'

'Daddy's died,' Paul said.

'Why?' she said, dropping the cat. 'Why did he die?'

The gate went.

'It's the priest,' Sylvia said, glancing out the window.

The Dutch priest appeared in the doorway. He looked so much taller in the house than he did in the church saying mass.

'T'anks for comin', Father,' Sylvia said.

He shook hands with me, then sat down in the lounge. He nodded as Paul repeated everything to him. Sylvia handed him a cup of tea.

'I've got to go. Chris will be home,' she said, wiping her eyes. 'I'll be back later.'

The priest sat saying nothing. The only sound came from the road workers shouting to each other outside.

The back door opened. Bryan and Steven were home, chatting and laughing. It was Friday night, and they were looking forward to Paddy's special dinner.

'Do you want me to tell them, Mum?' Paul said.

'No, I will,' I said, moving out to the hall. I didn't want to tell them in front of the priest.

Steven stood stunned. 'He can't be. He was fine last night. He sat reading his book.'

Bryan burst into tears. 'I hate God,' he shouted, flying to his room.

The hours dragged by. The priest didn't make a move to go. The phone rang. It was Debbie at the station waiting for Paddy to pick her up.

'I'll have to tell her,' I said, heading for the hall.

The priest stopped me. 'Don't tell her on the phone,' he said.

'You never tell bad news on the phone. Do you know anyone who could meet her?'

'My friend drives,' Paul said. 'I'll ring her.'

Another fifteen minutes chimed.

'I'll let you go, Father,' I said, standing up. 'I know you're terribly busy.'

'Ring if you need me,' he said, letting himself out.

I went into the kitchen and pulled out the potato rack.

A car drew up outside. Debbie ran in, sobbing. 'What'll you do without him, Mum?' she said, hugging me. She flew into her bedroom, slammed the door and howled.

I went on peeling the potatoes, tears dropping down onto them. Paul wandered in with Debbie's bags. 'I won't be long. We're picking up Dad's car from Corio Station,' he said, rushing off, his friend behind him.

Carol set the table, then sat watching me. 'Are we going to be poor now?'

'We'll be all right,' I said, pouring the oil into the chip pan. I placed the pan on the cooker and turned it on.

Bryan and Steven slipped in and sat at the table.

'I'll get a Saturday job in Coles in Corio Village,' Steven said. 'I can give you some money.'

'I'll leave school and get a job,' Bryan said.

'I'll defer the year,' Debbie said, coming into the kitchen, her eyes red and swollen. 'Did you pay Dad's insurance, Mum? I heard him reminding you weeks ago.'

'I paid it this morning when I was in town havin' my hair done.'

The back gates banged. Paul hurried in. 'We picked up the Falcon. It's back in the garage.'

I drained the chips, lifted the steaks onto the butcher paper and turned off the grill. The phone rang. 'That'll be Paddy,' I said, hurrying into the hall. 'He's managed to get a line from Central America.'

It was Sylvia. 'I can't come around. Chris can't stop vomiting. I'll come when I can.'

Back in the kitchen, I took up the dinners. All eyes were on me. 'Mum,' Debbie said, pointing to Paddy's place. 'You've put a dinner out for Dad.'

WHAT'S FOR DINNER, MUM?

A LL WEEKEND, I sat huddled in front of the oil fire, slumped into myself. I kept the blinds closed, black out with the world.

Monday evening, Phyllis left another large casserole dish at the hall door, knocked quietly and hurried away.

Debbie took the dinner in. 'Mum, I've heated it up. You have to eat.'

Another soft knock on the door. Paul led the priest into the lounge and went back to his dinner. The priest sat down, hands joined in front of him and said nothing. I slid the kitchen door over. I didn't want the others to hear.

'C'mere till I tell ya, Father,' I whispered. 'I woke up last night. Paddy was beside me. I tried to hold on to him, but he slipped through my hands.'

The priest sat up straight and stared over at me. 'Sorry?'

'Paddy was in bed beside me. I held his hand tightly. But he pulled away.'

'You must let Patrick go,' he said, shaking his head. 'Don't hold him back.'

'How do we know for sure whether he's dead or not? The doctors could be wrong.'

Another soft knock. In came two young Christian Brothers, their long black robes sweeping behind them. Steven and Bryan's teachers. They shook hands and offered their sympathies, then stood against the wall, looking solemn, saying nothing. Steven carried in two kitchen chairs. The brothers sat down, hands folded in front of them.

Another knock. More visitors from the Catholic schools. Debbie showed in two Brigidine sisters from her old school, Clonard College. 'We've come to offer our sympathies on behalf of our college,' they said, fixing their black habits around them. 'The girls are praying for his soul.'

They all sat upright on kitchen chairs, hands on laps, staring down, saying nothing.

Paddy's clock chimed every quarter of an hour. The silence was deafening.

'I t'ought my husband was the type who'd never die,' I found myself saying.

The dark suits looked up at me.

The kitchen door slid back. Bryan's head popped in and looked at the sisters. 'Would any of you nuns like a cuppa?' he said, smiling.

I leapt up, went into the kitchen and flicked on the kettle. *It doesn't sound right, Bryan calling them nuns,* I thought, but I knew he was only trying to cheer everyone up. And Paddy would have laughed.

Wednesday morning was the day of the funeral. I dragged myself out of bed to find something to wear. Opening the wardrobe, I buried my face in Paddy's suits.

Bryan barged into my room. 'I don't want to go to the funeral. I don't want to see Dad's coffin.'

'You don't have to go. Dad won't mind.'

I wandered into the bathroom and glanced in the mirror. My blond hair, limp and flat, framed a little faded face with worried eyes.

Chris's grey Cortina pulled up. He was driving us to the church. 'Have ya no black t'wear, Lily?' he said, coming in the door.

What does it matter? I thought, looking down at my pink cotton dress and white sandals.

The car floated down Bacchus Marsh Road. St Thomas's Church appeared. Boys in school uniforms lined up outside, Christian Brothers beside them – Bryan and Steven's classes.

This large Catholic church was cold and empty, except for the little Dublin group huddled together at the front near the coffin. The funeral director came over to me. I handed him Paddy's crucifix and asked him if he could put it in the coffin. Chris, his hands shaking, went up to the altar and stood a few sympathy cards on the coffin beside the flowers.

Kneeling down, I felt a tip on my shoulder. It was Steven. 'Mum, Uncle Christy said I have to carry the coffin. I can't carry it on my own.'

'You won't be carrying it on your own. Sit down.'

The students filed in quietly and sat at the back of the church with the Christian Brothers. The Dutch priest said mass.

No one got up to say anything about Paddy. He was only a few months in the country, not long enough to have made any friends.

But the Christian Brothers did their best. They stood up straight with the students and sang Paddy's favourite hymn, his sodality hymn, at the top of their voices:

> Soul of my Saviour sanctify my breast,
> Body of Christ, be thou my saving guest,
> Blood of my Saviour, bathe me in thy tide,
> Wash me with waters flowing from thy side.
>
> Strength and protection may thy passion be,
> O Blessed, Jesus, hear and answer me
> Deep in thy wounds, Lord, hide and shelter me,
> So shall I never, never part from thee.

The hymn took me back to Luton. My heart lifted. It was Easter. Paddy and Chris were belting it out, their voices soaring above everyone else's in St Margaret of Scotland's church.

> Guard and defend me from the foe malign,
> In death's dread moments make me only thine;
> Call me and bid me come to thee on high
> Where I may praise thee with thy saints for aye.

The mass finished.

I stayed on my knees, not wanting to go to the cemetery.

That was too final.

'Come on, ya have t'go,' Chris said, gripping my arm.

As the hearse moved slowly away, I sat back and felt awful. Here was Paddy being buried in Australia when he didn't even want to come.

The cars pulled up outside Eastern Cemetery. In through the wide gates, our little group drifted down a long narrow path to the well-kept lawn section. I glanced at the sea in the far distance, then at the deep grave in front of me. At the lowering of the coffin, I sank silently to the ground with Paddy.

'Ya'll be all right,' Chris said, helping me up.

The priest looked over, noticed me shivering and finished the prayers abruptly.

It was warm back in the lounge with the oil fire glowing. I sat silent with my two sisters and their husbands. Debbie made a pot of tea. A Scottish neighbour dropped in a plate of ham sandwiches and left. Chris passed them to me. I couldn't eat. Paddy wasn't eating. How could I?

The clock chimed the hour. Sylvia stood up.

'I have to do some shoppin',' she said. 'I've nuttin' in.'

'Mine will be wonderin' where I am,' Annie said, taking out her car keys.

I saw them to the gate. 'T'anks for comin'.'

Annie looked at me. 'The priest said you've aged ten years over the weekend. Mind yerself now.'

Their cars drove off on the newly sealed roads. I pulled the gate over and opened the mailbox. Three letters lay inside. One was a bill for the roads, three thousand dollars. Another was from Paddy's life insurance. They said the cheque for the first instalment was received too late; they refused to pay. I opened the third letter. It was from a parishioner from the church, full of advice on how to go on. 'That's your cross,' she wrote. 'The cross you have to bear.'

That was all I needed to hear. I hated that saying.

The hall door opened and Bryan called out, 'What's for dinner, Mum? We're all starving.'

I walked in and threw the letters on the table. 'C'mon, someone set the table. I'll make youse chips an' egg.'

Are We Not to Go On?

Down to Corio Village I marched the very next morning and up the stairs to a solicitor's office.

'We can fight the insurance company,' he said, pulling out a file.

'How much will it cost? I haven't much money.'

'You can apply for legal aid.'

'Right.'

The solicitor stopped writing and looked up. 'Do you own your own house?'

'Yes.'

'You do realise that you'll have to pay legal aid back if you decide to sell your house.'

'So, if I lost, I could never move? The house is all I have.'

'I'm afraid that's how it is. Do you want to go ahead?'

'I'll go down to the shops an' have a cup a' tea an' t'ink about it,' I said, getting up, drifting out of his office.

Down in the shopping centre, I found myself in the nearest café, trying to work things out. Should I take that risk? The solicitor wasn't very hopeful. Said it was hard to fight insurance companies. I had to pay a hundred dollars just to hear that.

Young mothers sat near me, tapping their cigarettes into tin ashtrays. The familiar smoke sailed over to my table. I leant closer to them and inhaled it deeply. What would Paddy do? Would he fight the insurance and risk losing the house?

I strolled out of the shopping centre, looked over at the CAB building and remembered a meeting some months ago on worker's compensation. A solicitor, an older man, said that if a worker died on the job, the spouse was entitled to make a claim.

A week later, I was sitting in this solicitor's office in Geelong. He heard all about the insurance not paying me.

'Bloody mongrels,' he said, thumping his desk. 'We'll fight it.'

'I can't afford to pay you. I owe three thousand dollars for the roads. An' I don't want to apply for legal aid.'

He scratched his head, bent down and pulled a form out of his drawer. 'Your husband died at work, you say? Okay, we'll go for worker's comp. You won't be up for anything.'

'But he was only three months in the job.'

His pen stopped. 'I didn't hear that,' he said, not looking up.

I could have cut my tongue out.

He scribbled away, stood up and shook my hand. 'I'll be in touch. You've got a good case.'

I hurried out into Moorabool Street. Standing at the bus stop, I kept seeing men in flannelette shirts, the image of Paddy, striding towards me. Couples strolled by. I stared after them. They were holding hands. I hadn't noticed that before. *I'll never hold Paddy's hand again.* And my feet would never touch his in bed any more.

The bus rattled home. A bundle of letters stuck out of my mailbox. I pulled them out and sauntered in. Putting the kettle on, I sat down to read them.

Two were from England, Paddy's sisters, Lizzie and Eileen.

'A mother has to hide a broken heart,' Lizzie wrote.

I threw that one down.

'Paddy was always mad about ya, Lily,' Eileen wrote.

I slipped that one in my handbag. It would be a comfort to carry around and read on the bus when I'd see couples holding hands, chatting away.

The other letters were from America, from men I'd never heard of. One was from a man in North Carolina:

> To the Family of Pat O'Connor,
> I received some bad news about a man that I loved and deeply respected. I was a high school graduate with a wife and two children, trying to make a decent living. Pat, who did not know me from Adam, took time to help me with the fundamentals of patterns and machines. Not only did Pat help me on the job, but many nights in the motel Pat would help me with patterns. Due to his friendship and help, I have a good job making a very profitable living. I'll never forget what he told me, 'Never hold back the learning that you have if it may help someone else.'
> With Love, JR Turner and Family

The other was from a man in Haiti:

Dear Mrs O'Connor,

I was so very shocked and sad to learn of Patrick's death. My wife and I met him in a hotel in Haiti for one week. We enjoyed his company very much and we ate and drank and talked together for the whole week. He spoke often of you and his children and deplored that his job kept you apart so much.

At the end of our stay, Patrick rescued me from an embarrassing situation. I was short of $100 to pay my bill. The hotel my wife and I were staying in would not accept my personal check. Good old Patrick cashed my check for me, saving me much embarrassment. He didn't need to do that since we were relative strangers about to go our separate ways. But he was the kindly type of man that put even a brief friendship above the possible loss of $100.

My best to you and your children.

Don Crist

I made a strong pot of tea and sat down. Here I was learning of his life in America, strangers he'd met, things he'd done without bothering to tell me. How many other things did he do? I'll never know.

As each one strolled in, I'd breathe a sigh of relief that *they* got home safe.

'Mum, the priest just dropped this off in the letter box,' Carol said, handing me a packet of empty mass envelopes.

Inside was a reminder that I was behind with the payments.

Steven sauntered in next. 'It's my birthday next month, Mum,' he said, opening the biscuit tin. 'Don't leave Dad's name off my card, will you?'

I hadn't thought of that. Now Paddy's name doesn't go on any of my cards any more.

Bryan marched in and threw his bag down. 'You know the old lockers Dad bought from my school a few weeks ago?'

'Yes, what about them?'

'They're still waiting to be collected. Brother said you don't have to take them. He'll give you your money back.'

'Is that what he said? You tell *that* brother to hold on to those lockers. We still need them. They're for Dad's tools. Are we not to go on?'

Someone banged off the door. I tramped down the hall and flung it open. Two big countrymen in working trousers and scruffy old boots took off their caps.

'Sorry for yer troubles, Missus,' one said. 'We're from the Irish Club. D'ya want any jobs done? Anyt'in' picked up?'

'That's very good of youse. Come in.'

The phone went. It was Isabel from night school. It was Wednesday. Did I want a lift to the English class?

'T'anks, I'll be ready.'

ACKNOWLEDGEMENTS

Thanks to my two sons, Bryan and Steven, for proofreading my manuscript. My Dublin dialogue nearly drove them mad.

I wrote this both for Paddy and my seven grandchildren: Miranda, Chris, Maeve, Fintan, Declan, Mairead and Bridie. One day they may read it and learn a little about Paddy, the grandad they never knew.

SOME OTHER READING

from

BRANDON

Brandon is a leading publisher of new fiction and non-fiction for an international readership. For a catalogue of new and forthcoming books, please write to
Brandon/Mount Eagle, Unit 3 Olympia Trading Estate, Coburg Road, Wood Green, London N22 6TZ, England; or Brandon/Mount Eagle, Cooleen, Dingle, Co. Kerry, Ireland. For a full listing of all our books in print, please go to

www.brandonbooks.com

LILY O'CONNOR
Can Lily O'Shea Come Out to Play?

A bestseller in Ireland and Australia, a fascinating story of growing up Protestant in Dublin.

This vivid memoir of a childhood in the 1930s and '40s is marked by its narrator's consciousness of her status as an outsider, for Lily is a child of a mixed marriage, baptised a Protestant but living in a Catholic community. The originality of this account of a working-class childhood is its portrait of a spirited girl coming to terms with her difference. At its heart this is a universal story of childhood; of hardship and joy, of violence, poverty, pleasure, humour and, over all, humanity.

"Anyone with half an interest in times gone by will enjoy this well-written anecdotal book." *Irish Criticism*

"A vibrant recollection of childhood, this – honest, warm and often moving." *Examiner*

ISBN 0 86322 267 6; paperback

DESMOND ELLIS
Bockety

Humorous and enchanting, a sparkling memoir,
this is the story of a young boy born in 1944
who grew up on the banks of the Grand Canal
on Dublin's Portobello Road, but it is also
everyone's story of the joys and pitfalls of
growing up, told with a delightful and
infectious humour. Desmond, an awkward boy,
romps through his childhood like a rickety
bicycle that won't quite go where it is steered.

ISBN 086322 364 8; paperback original

MAY O'BRIEN
Clouds on My Windows

May O'Brien was fifteen in 1947 when she
started to work in Liberty Hall, headquarters
if the Irish Transport and General Workers'
Union.

"This is a wonderful book... May O'Brien says
in her afterword that this is an ordinary book
about Dublin life in the '40s. Maybe it is. But
it's a story about an extraordinary woman, in
any time." *Irish Independent*

ISBN 086322 335 4; paperback original

THE BESTSELLING NOVELS
OF ALICE TAYLOR

The Woman of the House

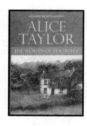

"What shines through in *The Woman of the House* is Alice Taylor's love of the Irish countryside and village life of over 40 years ago, its changing seasons and colours, its rhythm and pace." *Irish Independent*

ISBN 0 86322 249 8; paperback

Across the River

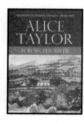

"Alice Taylor is an outstanding storyteller. Like a true seanchaí, she uses detail to signal twists in the plot or trouble ahead. It is tightly plotted fiction, an old-fashioned page-turner." *The Irish Times*

ISBN 0 86322 285 4; paperback

House of Memories

"*House of Memories* shows her in her prime as a novelist." *Irish Independent*

"It is Alice Taylor's strength to make the natural everyday world come alive in clear fresh prose. In this book, as in her memoirs, she does so beautifully." *The Irish Book Review*

ISBN 0 86322 352 4; paperback

THE BESTSELLING MEMOIRS OF ALICE TAYLOR

To School Through the Fields

"One of the most richly evocative and moving portraits of childhood [ever] written…A journey every reader will treasure and will want to read over and over again." *Boston Herald*

ISBN 0 86322 099 1; paperback

Quench the Lamp

"Infused with wit and lyricism, the story centers on the 1950s when the author and her friends were budding teenagers. Taylor describes the past vividly and without complaint." *Publishers Weekly*

ISBN 0 86322 112 2; paperback

The Village

"What makes the story unique is Taylor's disarming style; she... has a knack for finding the universal truth in daily details." *Los Angeles Times*

ISBN 0 86322 142 4; paperback

Country Days

"Like Cupid, the author has an unerring aim for the heartstrings; however, she can also transform the mundane into the magical." *The Irish Times*

ISBN 0 86322 168 8; paperback

ROSEMARY CONRY
Flowers of the Fairest

"Has the ring of authenticity. This is a book to be recommended. . . Surprisingly, the story is told with much humour." *Irish Independent*

"A fascinating first-hand account of one child's experience of TB in the 1940s. It is full of interesting details of the little everyday routines of life on a veranda, with all its pain and its fun. . . A lovely book that gives us a fascinating insight into a world that thankfully we will never know." *Books Ireland*

ISBN 0 86322 303 6; paperback

THERESA LENNON BLUNT
I Sailed the Sky in a Silver Ship

"Much more than a chronicle of life in Ireland, it is the story of a girl desperate to escape the misery and embarrassment . . . The author's descriptive powers vividly evoke her time and place, and she has succeeded in relating her tale of a turbulent childhood and youth with little trace of self-pity." *BookView Ireland*

"From the opening passages of the book the reader is swept back in time and place through the author's descriptive powers, rich narrative, and exquisite use of metaphor." *The Harp*

ISBN 0 86322 304 4; paperback